Don't Help

Recovery Books from Bantam

Here's help, information, and inspiration for alcoholics, addicts, and their families from some of the leading writers and doctors in the field.

LIVING ON THE EDGE: *A Guide to Intervention for Families with Alcohol and Drug Problems* by Katherine Ketcham and Ginny Lyford Gustafson

UNDER THE INFLUENCE: *A Guide to Myths and Realities of Alcoholism* by James R. Milam, Ph.D. and Katherine Ketcham

RECOVERING: *How to Get and Stay Sober* by L. Ann Mueller, M.D. and Katherine Ketcham

A NEW DAY: *365 Meditations for Personal and Spiritual Growth* by Anonymous

ADULT CHILDREN OF ALCOHOLICS SYNDROME by Wayne Kritsberg

LOVING AN ALCOHOLIC: *Help and Hope for Co-Dependents* by Jack Mumey

THE FACTS ABOUT DRUGS AND ALCOHOL by Mark S. Gold, M.D.

800 COCAINE by Mark S. Gold, M.D.

Don't Help

A Positive Guide to
Working with the Alcoholic

Ronald L. Rogers
Chandler Scott McMillin

A
BANTAM
TRADE
PAPERBACK

NEW YORK · TORONTO · LONDON · SYDNEY · AUCKLAND

DON'T HELP

A Bantam Book / June 1989

PRINTING HISTORY

*Originally published by Education & Training Institute
of Maryland, Inc. 1984 and Madrona Publishers 1988*

Library of Congress Cataloging-in-Publication Data

Rogers, Ronald.
    Don't help : a guide to working with the alcoholic / Ronald L.
Rogers, Chandler Scott McMillin.
        p.   cm.
    Bibliography: p.
    ISBN 0-553-34716-0
    1. Alcoholism.   2. Alcoholism—Treatment.   3. Alcoholism
counseling.   I. McMillin, Chandler.   II. Title.
HV5275.R64   1989
362.2′9286—dc19   88-39960
                                                                              CIP

Published simultaneously in the United States and Canada

*Bantam Books are published by Bantam Books, a division of Bantam Doubleday
Dell Publishing Group, Inc. Its trademark, consisting of the words "Bantam
Books" and the portrayal of a rooster, is Registered in U.S. Patent and Trademark
Office and in other countries. Marca Registrada. Bantam Books, 666 Fifth Avenue,
New York, New York 10103.*

PRINTED IN THE UNITED STATES OF AMERICA

OPM   0 9 8 7 6 5 4 3 2 1

Contents

Foreword   vii

Acknowledgements   ix

Authors' Note   xi

1. Alcoholics and "Helpers"   3

2. Old Models and New   25

3. How Alcoholism Works   62

4. How Alcoholics Drink   80

5. Mixing It Up   107

6. Enabling and Provoking   127

7. Getting Started   149

8. Working in Groups   174

9. One on One   192

10. Recovering   211

11. Ways To Fail   221

12. Sobriety Works   244

The Stages of Alcoholism   252

Treatment Plan for the Recovering Alcoholic
    Insufficiently Involved in AA   254

Treatment Plan for the Recovering Alcoholic
    Who Has Used Sedatives   255

Suggested Reading   257

Foreword

THE DISEASE MODEL, AS THE AUTHORS OF THIS BOOK have noted, has experienced phenomenal growth in strength and popularity during recent years. In retrospect, the reasons are now obvious.

First and foremost, the psychological, social and spiritual disasters of alcoholism and other addictions can only be fully understood as distortions and exaggerations of otherwise normal problems.

Second, in spite of its reliance on complex evidence from the biological sciences, the Disease model has the virtue of simplicity. It's much easier for a recovering alcoholic to think of himself as suffering from a disease that affects his ability to drink than it is to root about in his psyche for supposed causes of his present difficulties.

Observe an audience of alcoholics as they hear an enlightened explanation of their disease for the first time. There is an unmistakable ring of authenticity in their responses. You'll witness spontaneous reactions of surprise and relief at the discovery that they are not by nature weak-willed, emotionally inadequate, or morally defective, as they had always been told.

We must realize that even as this new understanding relieves them of guilt for being alcoholic, it bestows on recovering alcoholics an overriding moral imperative, a personal responsibility to do what is required to recover. No longer is it acceptable to blame outside circumstances or other people for relapse. With full understanding, these become mere excuses, not reasons for relapse.

Third, the Disease model inspires the alcoholic to change, to emerge from the quagmire of illness into true selfhood. Instead of passively waiting in ignorance for rescue by a magical therapist, the alcoholic knows with certainty that there will be no remedy other than through continued total abstinence. His motivation comes from within, from the will to survive rather than from external sources. He can learn to see fellowships like Alcoholics Anonymous as resources for recovery instead of humiliation for misbehavior.

Finally, the Disease model provides a practical basis for structured treatment. Like the diabetic or cardiac patient, the alcoholic can now be given practical, understandable directions for recovery, based on the proven experience of hundreds of thousands who have preceded him. If he thoroughly follows these directions, success is virtually assured.

What Ronald Rogers and Scott McMillin have done is to apply this new understanding of the disease to the practical tasks of treatment and recovery. Like so many others, they have found themselves having to first rethink long-held beliefs and redesign traditional approaches. The result? A method and rationale of treatment in which the much-abused phrase "alcoholism is a disease" signifies real understanding.

James R. Milam, Ph.D.
Kirkland, Washington

Acknowledgements

This is a book for anyone closely involved with a drinking alcoholic. This is also a book for practicing clinicians, and as such does not spring from inspiration. The ideas embodied here are the result of hard work and ingenuity on the part of many superb counselors—too many, in fact, to name here.

We can, however, thank those whose support contributed to the existence of this book: Dr. Peter Hackett of the University of Virginia; Kitty Harold, Eileen Barker, and Jean Mercready of Arlington Hospital; Sandi Hill of Baltimore Recovery Center; Lee Hopwood of Suburban Hospital, Bethesda, Maryland; and Dickie Spenser of the Sealift Command.

Acknowledgement is also due Drs. Miriam Siegler, Humphrey Osmonds, and Stephen Newell, who came up with the idea of making models of the various definitions of alcoholism, including the eight basic models we have used in this book. They described their models in a chapter titled "Models of Alcoholism, Models of Treatment," in their book *Models of Medicine, Models of Madness* (New York: MacMillan, 1974).

We offer special thanks to Morris Hill, who introduced us to the idea of treating alcoholism as a chronic disease. It was he who first described the three goals of treatment and used them as the basis for a program at Arlington Hospital in Arlington, Virginia. Since then, Hill has taken this model to a number of other programs, including Suburban Hospital in Bethesda and the Baltimore Recovery Center.

And of course we must thank James R. Milam, Ph.D. His ideas form the core of our treatment approach and the basis for the Chronic Disease model itself. His pioneering insights—and his courage in stating them—have greatly diminished the stigma attached to alcoholism. For that, every alcoholic, everywhere, should be grateful.

Authors' Note

In writing a book in which most of the information applies equally to people of both sexes, we were faced with the dilemma of sex-specific pronouns. We don't like referring to the alcoholic as "he" or "him" throughout the book, because we really do mean "he/she" and "him/her." But just try to write an interesting sentence using "he/she" whenever you need a pronoun.

As a result, we chose to use the male pronoun whenever we needed to refer to a generic alcoholic. We hope readers will understand.

Similarly, despite occasional references to counselors in the text, we are writing for alcoholics who are considering treatment, as well as their families and all sorts of helpers, including clinicians and counselors, those studying to be counselors, and friends and relatives of alcoholics.

This book is not intended to supply all the information a helper needs to work effectively with an alcoholic. Rather, it is designed to serve along with other books that we believe are equally essential to successful treatment of this chronic disease. Accordingly, we have provided a suggested reading list in the back of the book.

Don't Help

1

Alcoholics and "Helpers"

T O E X P L A I N T H I S B O O K ' S A D M I T T E D L Y U N U S U A L TI-
tle, here's a short fable about a counselor who provided
entirely too much "help" to his patient.

Once upon a time, in a land close to the western ocean, there
lived a psychotherapist who was asked to accept an alcoholic
patient into treatment. By some twist of fortune, this therapist
had never come into professional or personal contact with alcoholics, and so had very little knowledge of how to treat them.
Nevertheless, he was confident that he could be of help to any
patient who was in need of it, no matter what the problem.
    Their first interview went smoothly. The patient was ob-
viously not intoxicated, which the therapist thought might be a
good sign, and he even seemed to enjoy discussing his past during the preliminary history-taking. At the end of the session, they
agreed on a schedule of visits.
    The therapist went to his library to learn about various treat-
ment strategies for alcoholics. The first reference he encountered

recommended treating alcoholism from a psychoanalytic point of view. This was attractive to the therapist, since of course he was familiar with such theory from his own training. According to the book, alcoholic drinking was only the superficial manifestation of a complex problem which actually began during infancy, when the patient was weaned too soon from his mother's breast. Thus the alcoholic "nursed" his bottle of liquor as a substitute for more basic gratifications. Treatment involved pointing out the true roots of this behavior to help the alcoholic free himself from his regressive emotional state. Eventually, the alcoholic would be able to drink safely again, but for the same reasons as other people, and not because of an underlying emotional need.

With this in mind, the therapist keyed his discussions with the alcoholic to that period of infant development where the problem supposedly originated. The patient's current life was seldom mentioned. The therapist believed that this was natural, because more important issues were being discussed.

Finally, the therapist completed the interpretation, firmly linking alcoholism with interrupted nursing.

"That's amazing," said the alcoholic. "It's hard to believe that all my problems stem from feelings I don't even remember."

"You repressed them," responded the therapist. "Most people do. Nevertheless, they shaped your life."

"I guess you're right," the alcoholic said. "Anyway, I feel like now that I know what the real cause of my problem is, I can take it or leave it as far as alcohol is concerned. I want to thank you for helping me with this, Doc. You've really opened my eyes." With this, he took his leave.

The next evening, the therapist received a call from the patient's wife.

"Doctor," she shrieked, "my husband has gone insane!"

"Calm down and tell me what he's done," the therapist demanded.

"He's gotten completely smashed again, that's what he's done!" she shouted. "He drank everything we had in the house, and about midnight he decided to clean out the gutters! I pleaded with him not to, but he climbed up on the roof, then knocked the ladder over and couldn't get back down. He ended up clinging to the TV antenna until the fire department rescued him. Then as soon as they left, he drank a whole bottle of cooking sherry and passed out in the middle of the kitchen floor. What am I supposed to do with him?"

"Bring him to my office tomorrow," the therapist replied. Although he managed to sound confident over the phone, he was confused as to the motives for the alcoholic's sudden reversal just as treatment was beginning to work. He decided to explore other strategies that might be more effective.

Returning to his library, he discovered a book on alcoholism and its role within the family. To his considerable surprise, he found this author disagreed with the developmental view and maintained that alcoholic drinking was part of a "game" played by certain families as a sign of larger disturbances within the family structure. An "illness of relationships" had developed, it seemed, which led to the selection of one member as alcoholic, or depressed, or crazy, while the rest of the family covertly supported this behavior. In order for the "sick" member to recover, the entire family had to receive treatment.

Impressed with the persuasiveness of this argument, the therapist insisted that the patient's wife also be included in the session. He then encouraged them to share their feelings about each other and about their own lives in general.

Just as the book predicted, an enormous conflict existed. The alcoholic maintained that his wife's nagging drove him to drink excessively. His wife believed that he was an irresponsible bum who'd never do anything but lie about his drinking or make phony promises to quit.

The therapist patiently interpreted this in the light of his knowledge of family dynamics, and told them that their problems within the relationship were the real issues. When these cleared up, so would the drinking. Though his wife appeared skeptical, the patient eagerly accepted this interpretation.

"You've given me a whole new lease on life, Doctor," he said. "I've been living with this awful guilt for so long, I can't believe that it's somehow all behind me now. I always knew that my drinking really stemmed from my problems with my wife, but I could never get her to go along with that. Now she'll have to pay attention to *me* for a change. We're really getting somewhere now. It's only a matter of time before all this is over, once and for all."

Although he cautioned the man against unreasonable optimism, the therapist was impressed with his obvious sincerity. He was eager to see how quickly the patient responded to therapy now that the real issues had been exposed.

And so he was even more surprised at the second phone call from the alcoholic's wife than he had been at the first.

"You're not going to believe this," she told him when she had calmed down. "We went out to dinner last night, and he insisted on having a glass of wine. I didn't want to nag, so I kept my mouth shut. Next thing I knew, he'd left the table before dinner was even served, and disappeared into the bar to get another drink. Just left me and our guests there at the table. He never did come back, though I went to get him three or four times, and finally the rest of us went home and left him there at the bar. About three o'clock in the morning, I get a call from the police—they've got him locked up for being drunk and disorderly—because he apparently started insulting a couple of nuns in the restaurant."

Needless to say, the therapist was stunned by this almost complete reversal in the alcoholic's behavior, from optimism and commitment to completely irresponsible behavior. He began to wonder if his patient weren't indeed sociopathic—lacking the necessary conscience to inhibit his actions. He determined to find an even more radical treatment for such a disturbed patient.

He returned once again to his library and discovered an article on a confrontation approach for use with drug abusers. In this model—or way of viewing the disease—the abuser was described as a self-centered, manipulative, and basically antisocial individual, who hid these character defects behind a mask of normalcy, and who disguised his lack of motivation with superficial attempts at changing his behavior, which inevitably failed. The only way this patient could be reached, the author maintained, was on a "gut level," achieved through personal confrontation.

So *that's* what's going on, thought the therapist. No wonder it hasn't been working. Radical confrontation was obviously essential.

When the alcoholic arrived for his next appointment, the therapist was prepared. The man indeed looked as though he felt very guilty for his actions, but the doctor resolved not to be fooled by appearances. This time, treatment was going to take place on a gut level, not an intellectual one.

He began, firmly and forcefully, to explain to the patient what was really wrong with him.

He detailed the obvious self-centeredness behind the alcoholic's behavior, and his unconcern for the feelings of others. He pointed out how manipulative these recurrent drinking episodes were, demanding attention both from his family and his counselor. He described the irresponsible waste of valuable therapeutic effort which occurred when the alcoholic stubbornly refused to get better in spite of treatment. He exposed the patient's underlying unwillingness to change, which was sabotaging therapy. This, said the therapist, proved beyond a doubt that the alcoholic didn't really want to get well.

His patient, stunned by this sudden change in his doctor, looked even more miserable than before. Tears rolled down his cheeks. He apologized profusely for having betrayed the trust that had been placed in him, and for being such a burden to his family. He said he now possessed more than enough motivation for treatment. In fact, he went on, he was willing to give up alcohol entirely, to demonstrate his sincerity. From that day on, he claimed, liquor would never pass his lips.

Despite his doubts, the therapist was impressed. He began to believe that his relationship with this patient had turned a corner, and that treatment would be much easier from this point on. Honesty, along with gut-level communication, was clearly the best policy for alcoholics.

For several weeks the patient improved as the doctor had predicted. He looked better, and kept his appointments faithfully.

If he seemed a bit nervous at times, that was probably because of anxiety over the important issues being dealt with in therapy.

One night, though, the therapist received an unpleasant surprise. As he returned home from his office, he discovered his alcoholic patient waiting for him on his doorstep—unconscious, and reeking of alcohol.

Coldly angry, he stepped over the sleeping form without even attempting to rouse him. When he got inside, he called the police, and asked them to remove a drunk from his doorstep.

When the patient's wife called the office the next morning, he informed her that treatment was officially terminated—and that they would receive a rather large bill, which was due immediately.

After this, of course, the therapist lost track of the alcoholic. The bill was never paid, which reinforced the doctor's conclusion that the man had been a sociopath. He made sure he accepted no more alcoholic patients in treatment.

Some two years later, while visiting a patient in a local hospital, the therapist passed by a large meeting in the cafeteria. To his amazement, the speaker was none other than his former patient.

He couldn't resist sneaking into the back of the room and sitting down to listen. The man looked and sounded wonderful. He was talking about how much better his life had been since he'd finally stopped drinking.

The therapist leaned over to whisper to the man in the next seat.

"Do you know that fellow?"

"Sure do," the man responded. "I'm his AA sponsor."

"Well," the therapist said, "I used to know his physician. Apparently at one point he was . . . ahh . . . very hard to work with."

"Oh yeah, he told me about that," the man replied. "Listen, that man up there owes that doctor a lot of thanks."

"For what?" asked the therapist, surprised. "For helping him?"

"No, for giving up on him. If he'd kept on helping him, he'd probably be dead by now."

Well, that is a fairy tale, but not by much; though the particulars are fictitious, the experiences of that helper and that patient are more the rule than the exception.

Obviously, success with alcoholics didn't come naturally for this psychotherapist. That the patient did recover, paradoxically, only *after* he left treatment, is an experience so common that we were encouraged to give this book its strange title.

Don't Help. What kind of message is that, you ask? Are these lunatics saying that alcoholics don't *need* help? With all the crazy problems they have? Insane!

It's not that we're against helping sick alcoholics. We've just seen so much wrong-headed and ineffective counseling administered in the name of "helping" that we thought it best to attack that term directly.

For a variety of reasons, the history of alcoholism treatment is dominated by mistakes of all kinds: false starts, wrong turns, unworkable theories, hollow successes, complete failures.

The problems faced by the therapist in our fable aren't unique. A counselor sets out to help a sick person get well. As a result of his efforts, the patient seems to get sicker. And far from having been hopeless, that same patient turns around and proceeds, usually without professional help, to recover.

What did the therapist do wrong? He insisted on treating the illness as he understood it—the problem being that he didn't really understand it at all. His fault lay not in lack of effort, since he tried hard enough to make his approaches work. He certainly believed that each in its turn *should* work. And yet, when push came to shove, they simply didn't.

Again, this isn't unusual. Because of the peculiar nature of alcoholism, almost any approach seems well suited to certain aspects of the illness, but only a very few approaches actually benefit the typical patient. We've accumulated in the literature a

storehouse full of "treatments." The great majority of them are
of little value in practice.

We realize we're disparaging much of what passes for treatment in America today, but we don't intend to criticize without
offering alternatives. Our purpose is to explore the practical matter of working with alcoholics so that anyone—family, counselor, therapist, doctor, nurse, whoever—can separate the wheat
from the chaff among the various approaches and, also, to offer
the benefit of our own experience, culled from years of facing
everyday problems in treatment.

Our criteria for separating "good" from "less good" and
"just plain bad" among methods is simple. We ask only two
questions. First, does it usually work? Second, can we make use
of it? Anything which satisfies those two standards we'll classify
as good. Anything which is basically sound but which requires
extra training or equipment we'll classify as less good. We rate as
bad any approach which is hard to use and doesn't work anyway.

There are a surprising number in the latter category.

We're concerned with finding techniques which work best
with alcoholics. We're interested, for example, in how alcoholics
get from a point where they don't believe that any alcoholism
problem exists, to a point where they're willing to accept treatment for it, to a point where they're actively working to recover,
to a point where they are demonstrably a lot better, know it and
want to hold on to it. We call that recovery. That, as far as we're
concerned, is what should result from treatment, and *does* if
treatment is done properly.

We think that over the past years we've gotten a pretty good
idea of what it means to work with alcoholics properly. That's
what we want to share.

Origins of AA

For most of history, very few clinicians wanted any part of
alcoholism. We say "most of history" because our guess is that
alcoholism has been around for about as long as alcohol itself—some ten thousand years. We assume that for most of that

time alcoholics behaved as badly as some of them do now, because the terms "no-good" and "drunk" became cemented together in the popular consciousness until they were inseparable.

The twentieth century produced substantial changes in the way Americans regarded alcoholism. After the collapse of Prohibition demonstrated that legal sanctions didn't stop people from making or drinking liquor, even if they *weren't* addicted to it, the problem of alcoholism was returned to the medical profession, something like a package that had been incorrectly addressed. Most medical practitioners wanted no part of it, so alcoholics were passed around within medical ranks like a hot potato. The new breed of psychoanalysts showed brief interest, but quickly tired of numerous failed treatments. As a result, psychoanalysis achieved little more for the problem drinker than a slight elevation in status, from no-good drunk to hopeless alcoholic.

Then, in 1935, an organization was born under the unlikely leadership of a band of these same "hopeless" drunkards. It gave itself an equally unlikely name: Alcoholics Anonymous. The most startling thing about this group wasn't its name or membership, however. It was simply that it seemed to *work*.

All along, the real problem with treatment had been the lack of a program which was successful more than 20 percent of the time. In fact, there wasn't anything which appeared to work even 10 percent of the time.

No wonder people got discouraged. They expended considerable effort without any noteworthy impact, ending up with a nagging feeling of hopelessness. In such a situation, the harder you try, the more discouraged you'll get.

AA was the first program to reverse this trend. Of course, AA didn't work for everyone, either. It did, however, work for a good many of exactly the kind of people who needed it most. Anyone could see the results. Quite a few of these former no-good drunks went around testifying how much better they were, and attributing this to AA.

Moreover, instead of selecting its customers, or charging high fees for its services, AA made itself available to anyone who wanted its assistance. Meetings sprang up all over, and the organization seemed to welcome, and thrive on, the very people everyone else had abandoned.

And for all of this the group charged: *nothing*.

Increasingly Successful Types of Treatment

To charge nothing while providing help is in itself so antithetical to the trends in modern medicine that it should have caused treatment professionals to stop and take note. They might have asked themselves: As we move towards more sophisticated and expensive techniques, have we, in our endless fascination for the complex, missed a simple solution to the problem?

Of course, in this area as in so many others, human nature predominated. Instead of questioning their own methods, most professionals continued on in exactly the same direction they'd been heading, making the same decisions in treatment, accumulating the same number of failures, and arriving at the same old conclusions about alcoholism and alcoholics.

Attitudes always change slowly, but that's especially true in fields like medicine, psychology, and religion, which pride themselves on being able to explain our experiences to us. Nonetheless, the example was there: every day, drunks began their recovery in the AA community.

And even though we now had something which worked, we had little understanding of *how* it worked. This isn't unusual in medicine; many of the drugs we rely on to save us from the most serious illnesses remain largely a mystery to the scientists who discovered them. They're used because they work and because they don't produce too many harmful side effects. AA was like a new drug which had been discovered to treat a fatal illness. It was "given" because we had nothing else to substitute for it, and alcoholics certainly *needed* it.

In the early 1940s, a researcher named E. M. Jellinek began his pioneering work on alcoholism which played, years later, a significant role in its recognition by the medical profession as a true disease. When that recognition finally came, in the 1950s, treatment agencies began to welcome alcoholism back into the theater of treatable problems, out of the wings and a bit closer to center stage. The ensuing decades saw a phenomenal growth in specialized programs for alcoholics, and these programs further revolutionized treatment.

The principle behind most of them was engagingly simple: combine medical treatment with education and counseling, maximizing the chance that the addict won't return to drug use by convincing him to change his *attitude* towards the drug itself and its role in his current problems. This was an improvement on the revolving door syndrome which had dominated treatment for years. Alcoholics would enter hospitals because they were sick, but would only stay in the hospital long enough to get over the most dramatic phase of withdrawal before returning to the streets. Thus, they resumed drinking as a sort of knee-jerk response to continued withdrawal. So programs began keeping their patients a bit longer, and using whatever therapies they could think of at the time, as much to fill the day as anything else. They discovered that these alcoholics really *liked* learning about their illness, and were quite capable of understanding (if someone bothered to teach them) the nature of alcoholism.

They wanted not only to understand what happened to them when they drank, but quite a few of them wanted to know how to stop it from happening.

Now we had two tools to use. We had the supportive structure of AA, which guided the alcoholic through recovery and taught him how to live without alcohol. And we had the intervention and educational mechanism of the extended program, be it in or out of a hospital. In the 1970s, we saw a growth in our ability to identify and intervene in alcoholism before it actually endangered the victims' lives: employee assistance programs, for example, brought alcoholism into the realm of occupational health. During the same period, we saw a proliferation of schools for drunk drivers, which tackled our most serious alcohol-related social problem.

Of course, now that society was paying attention to alcoholism, we began to learn something about it. Methods improved. We got some idea of what worked and what didn't. We incorporated this knowledge into our approach.

As a result, we now *treat* alcoholics, in the best sense of that term. This is incalculably better than the service they once received. We teach them how to recover, rather than explaining to them why they probably *can't* recover. While not 100 percent effective, our approach is legitimately useful, and it gets results.

The Need for More and Better Training

For all this improvement, however, most people who work in this field still have entirely too many experiences like those of the therapist in the example. This is especially true for those helpers who haven't had much *specific* training in alcoholism. Unfortunately, that group includes most of the doctors, nurses, psychologists, social workers, ministers, hypnotists, rehab counselors, parole and probation officers, school guidance counselors, occupational health staff, personnel directors, teachers and principals, acupuncturists, faith healers, and anyone else who has ever worked with alcoholics, along with all of their families, friends, and neighbors.

In the first place, there just aren't that many education programs available; and even where they exist, the average person doesn't seem to appreciate the need to use them. Most "helpers" appear to believe they know quite enough about alcoholism as it is. Therefore, up until the very recent past, physicians were content to treat alcoholics for all sorts of alcohol-related problems, both physical and mental, despite the fact that they had received only a few *hours'* training in the subject in school. Social workers routinely directed the lives of some of their alcoholic clients without the benefit of any comprehensive instruction in the nature and treatment of alcoholism. Pastoral counselors felt qualified to advise parishioners and their families about alcoholism, often on a lifetime basis, while having no background in the area whatsoever. These people did the best they could with the tools they had.

What they didn't know was that their tools were completely

inadequate and that better approaches were available to anyone who knew where to look.

Sadly, though, lack of training is only part of the difficulty. Many who do receive comprehensive training still have problems in treating alcoholics; in fact, they often have as many problems as those who know very little.

Why? Because, like the therapist in our story, they learned to rely on philosophies and techniques which don't usually work.

As part of the emphasis on alcoholism in recent years, we've created a whole new profession: alcoholism counselor. We've seen the appearance of alcoholism specialists in related fields: medicine, psychiatry, social work. There are a lot more treatment personnel available than there once were. Yet we haven't devised a reliable set of methods by which to train them, nor have we put any method at all (reliable or not) into effect on a wide basis.

Most counselors come from two sources. Some are products of traditional schooling in the helping professions. Others arrive via a new route: they have recovered from alcoholism themselves. Both have problems when they become counselors. We believe those problems arise because of gaps in the *education* of both groups.

In the first place, as we've already pointed out, the helping professions haven't had much success in treating alcoholics. Part of this is due to the fact that most of the approaches they have used in treatment are based on methods and philosophies designed to treat illnesses other than this one.

For example, alcoholism has been regarded for so many years as simply another mental or psychological disorder that few professional training programs bother to instruct their students in the *physiological* aspects of the disease. Instead of learning how to work with patients who experience profound physical disturbances, counselors are trained as though there were no physical component at all. They become psychotherapists. They learn about transference, countertransference, self-esteem, stress reduction, group dynamics. They are taught to establish therapeutic relationships, to facilitate group process, to clarify relationship difficulties, to recognize hidden agendas and manipulative behavior. And, very naturally, they expect to be able to apply these skills to alcoholics as they do to other patients.

Here's where the trouble starts. We've seen innumerable examples where these techniques, applied by well-trained therapists in the therapeutic relationship, simply didn't fit the needs of the alcoholic. It's as though they were improperly designed. The more perceptive the counselor, the sooner he or she will notice this. A really stubborn counselor can continue for years in an attempt to make therapy work, to the detriment of clients.

Another part of this, of course, results from the inevitable gap between education and the everyday world. All counselors have to toss out a considerable portion of what they learn in school simply because it doesn't work in practical situations. Architects, engineers, lawyers, doctors, along with lots of other professionals, have similar experiences in trying to use their training. Many of the formulas, models, and structures which are regarded as "real" in the classroom don't survive the transition to everyday life. Lawyers know that practicing criminal law isn't going to be like reruns of *Perry Mason,* but that knowledge doesn't mean they graduate from law school ready for the wheeling and dealing of sentencing, plea bargaining, and the like. Doctors know that medical practice isn't filled with diagnostic excitement and surgical drama, but that doesn't mean that they come out of medical school understanding what it's really like to be a doctor. Counselors have the same problem. It sometimes seems that the more thorough and correct the counselor's training, the greater the disparity between that training and the real world of the clinician.

We don't think we're exaggerating. Taking a graduate of some training program and putting him to work in an urban clinic or hospital is like taking Tarzan to New York: no matter how much you told him about the traffic and the noise, he'd still be in for an enormous shock. It's no easier to go from the ivied halls of college to the local version of Waterneck County and work with clients who have to climb off a tractor to come to their therapy sessions.

The Training of Alcoholism Counselors

But we're digressing; our point isn't that *all* training is flawed, but that counselor training in particular is based on ineffective models—theories—which predispose the practitioner to failure when he tries to apply them.

Why are these models ineffective? Partially, we suspect, because many of them are directly or indirectly based on the work of Sigmund Freud and the pioneers of psychoanalysis. Though Freud's theories are fascinating to read and form the basis of much of our understanding of human interaction and development, they are *weakest,* we think, in their approach to addictions.

We figured this out while watching counselors "do therapy" with alcoholics, who often simply got worse as a result of their efforts.

Of course there *are* alcoholics who recover in psychotherapy. We're discussing a disease which affects millions of victims, and in a sample that large you'll find any kind of occurrence. Nevertheless, well over half of the alcoholics we've treated in the last ten years reject therapy as ineffective, destructive, or both. In seven years of watching psychiatrists and other therapists treat alcoholics with typical psychotherapeutic approaches, we've seen very few indeed recover. That's in *seven years* of observation.

There's a message there somewhere, don't you agree?

We were reluctant to recognize this at first. We had our own investment in the psychotherapeutic approach. We had learned how to get our clients to see their problems in therapeutic terms; we learned to interpret behavior and provide feedback so that change could occur.

Over the years, however, even this investment couldn't prevent us from recognizing that the approach didn't work. We came to believe, under sheer weight of evidence, that our alcoholic patients either didn't improve in therapy, or improved *in spite of* therapy.

We observed concerned, sensitive, intuitive counselors doing no better than the rawest beginners. We saw intelligent therapists having the same trouble with these patients as did the barely competent. When this kind of situation exists, it leads one to question the nature of the approach itself.

Freud himself never had much luck with addictions. He gave cocaine to several of his patients and was puzzled by the problems they had with it. He used nicotine until cancer of the jaw killed him, and in fact kept right on smoking through the surgical removal of most of his face. Analytic insight obviously was no protection for him.

We believe that these twin handicaps—impractical training and ineffective models—combine to make it nearly impossible for a counselor to treat alcoholics effectively. He or she has to undergo an unlearning and relearning process that takes years, assuming the individual sticks with it. Many don't; they simply, like the therapist in the story, give up. We can't say we blame them.

Recovering Alcoholics As Counselors

Counselors who enter the field through the other door—after recovering from alcoholism themselves—have a few advantages. They of course know that recovery *is* possible, having experienced it. They also know, on the same basis, that recovering is an extended process, which doesn't occur overnight, and which in fact involves quite a bit of two-steps-forward-and-one-step-back flexibility that isn't easy for most people. Instead of dry theories, recovering alcoholics have some practical knowledge to impart to their clients; this is worth more than two or three hundred of your average college courses to someone who's trying to change his behavior.

Unfortunately, there are also some disadvantages to coming from this background. It's a major transition in role and status from fellow sufferer to counselor/therapist, and the experience of AA isn't adequate preparation for this. Here someone is, suddenly being paid real greenbacks to get the job done, wondering how in the world to manage it. Friends in AA now see that person in a different light; they act differently and the counselor sees himself differently. The agreements which were the solid ground under relationships have changed. There are new expectations on both sides. It's another ballpark.

What's behind this transformation? A variety of things. Certainly, the prospect of getting paid for one's knowledge and opinions changes everything. Instead of being a friend to a suffering newcomer in AA, the counselor is now working for a client. Expectations will be based on that fact. Rather than simply taking a newcomer to AA meetings and talking about his own experience, the counselor will have to define roles, set boundaries, decide on problems and goals in treatment, put up with resistance. That's all included in the deal. This is a structured relationship, designed to serve a purpose: the facilitation of change.

And it's not possible to be as selective in one's contacts as may have been possible in AA. That organization is remarkably self-selecting; one may meet a great number of people, but one chooses a circle of associates that is much smaller. Invariably, it will be composed of people with whom one has more than just a history of alcoholism in common. Those who are making it in the program—that is, getting well—will associate primarily with other winners. One can know people who are having a hard time staying sober, but will rarely establish strong relationships with them, unless as a sponsor. And even in that event, one makes sure to limit involvement to the point where it doesn't interfere with one's own program.

When someone steps into the helping role, however, these boundaries change. The counselor is regarded as someone who helps people not because they have something in common, but because they need help, and the counselor is skilled at giving it.

We've known many recovering people who balk at being seen in this light. That's understandable; it adds a number of additional expectations that weren't there before.

Nonetheless, these expectations are part and parcel of why sick people go to a counselor. They don't arrive in an office or hospital or program because they think the counselor has something in common with them. They show up hoping to be helped in any one of a million ways. The fees they pay give them permission to ask for that help, and as far as they're concerned, those same fees obligate counselors to give it.

Just because some patients dance around this expectation, rather than voicing it directly, doesn't mean they don't feel it.

And this turns out to be traumatic for some recovering people, especially if they have trouble with obligations and demands made on their time and energy by other, sicker people. Patients, not unreasonably, expect their counselor always to act, think, and feel better than they do. They don't want anything to do with a helper who's anywhere near as sick as they are.

This, too, is understandable. Anyone might befriend such a character, relax with him, confide in him, empathize with him, feel comfortable when he's around; but no one would pay him money to help with a serious problem.

We know that some training programs, and some counseling philosophies, make a point of being tolerant of the therapist's idiosyncrasies as well as the patient's. It's okay in their view for the clinician to acknowledge his own conflict, confusion, and psychological disarray within the therapeutic relationship.

Don't be fooled by this, though; his patients will expect exactly the same degree of competence that anyone's patients expect. They'll demand to work on *their* problems, and to be able to lean on the counselor as they do. If that counselor becomes too involved with his own goals and difficulties to allow the patient to do this, then the patient will somehow tell the counselor to go sit on it.

Or, perhaps, simply quit showing up for sessions. Or, to use a typical compromise as an example, continue treatment but quit paying. Or even decide to use frustration with therapy as an excuse to get drunk.

Selfishness is something we'll all tolerate in ourselves, but not in our helpers.

Again, the most common basis for relationships within AA is empathy. No counselor, however, can rely on empathy in practice, despite the fact that there are training programs which emphasize this ability to the exclusion of all others. A significant percentage of patients will be people from backgrounds dissimilar to the counselor's; it will be hard to be more than superficially empathetic with many of their concerns.

To be effective, the counselor has to rely on something besides empathy, because when working in a setting where one can't select the patients, there will also be—brace yourself—patients the counselor doesn't much like.

Here is where the professionally trained person has a big advantage. He or she has been instructed in how to develop the counseling relationship into a *work setting,* replacing the patient's no doubt unrealistic expectations of personal transformation with clearly defined issues to work on. Unfortunately, because of profound misinstruction about the nature of alcoholism, the professionally trained person often identifies the *wrong* issues. He simply doesn't understand how alcoholism functions, or how alcoholics recover.

Without a considerable amount of training, a goodly number of recovering alcoholic counselors burn out early in their careers. They may have had unreasonable expectations about emotional rewards resulting from the therapeutic relationship. They may not have figured out that additional training would have helped them. They may have labored under the misconception that being sober was enough.

It isn't. There's a lot more to learn. It doesn't matter through which door one enters; there's still a great deal to be absorbed, dealt with, understood, abandoned.

Counseling education usually doesn't reflect this, even if it was specifically designed for alcoholism. At last count—who counted this we don't know—there were no less than *104 separate definitions* of alcoholism. If someone went to the trouble of coming up with a new definition, you can bet he or she developed a corresponding treatment approach as well. That means, at the least, 104 disparate theories of alcoholism, with techniques and philosophies of treatment to reflect each.

That's all very well for the theorists and librarians of the world, but the counselor and his clients want to know which is the *best* approach. Which one is most likely to lead to success?

The rest of the definitions, approaches, and theories, as far as most sick alcoholics and working counselors are concerned, can be filed in the round file and given ceremonial cremation as soon as possible.

Where This Book Is Heading

In writing a book on counseling, then, we can't help but run into the dilemma of other approaches. We can't claim to be smarter than the inventors of the aforementioned 104, and nothing could be duller than the thought of having to weigh each approach on its individual merits. That would put us to sleep even faster than it would you.

Fortunately, someone came up with the idea of lumping the various theories under the headings of *models* of alcoholism, which gives us a basis for discussing them in the following chapter.

And if there's one thing we'd like to do, before we move on, it's to set forth our goals in writing this book. We recognize that we cannot write the perfect book for all helping situations, so we've tried to compromise by keeping our focus very broad. When there's a need to be specific, we'll get specific, but over all we'll try to maintain a general view of the issues. We will try, hard as it may be at times, to leave the application of our advice to the wisdom of the individual. Rather than telling you what to do in the event of a hangnail, we'll inform you that hangnails do occur, whether that's significant, and what we'd do if we had a patient showing us his big toe. Then we'll let you decide how to handle it. That's our first goal: to remain generalized in approach, discussing a wide range of situations.

Which leads us to our second goal: we want to keep our advice practical. We have between us more than twenty years of hard-won experience with this particular problem. When we started as counselors, at opposite ends of the country, that's what *we* needed most—practical information. However, we found this kind of information so rare that we might well have killed to get it.

In support of our preference for practical information, we recently heard an expert on adult learning explain that adults respond to usable, preferably work-related education, rather than the diet of speculation and abstraction that educators too often like to feed them. In accord with that, our third goal is to remain simple in language and presentation. We aren't trying to impress anyone. We're trying to teach a skill which has suffered, throughout its brief history, from overcomplication and lack of clarity.

We seek last to present in this book information about alcoholism and counseling which is consistent with the state of the art. If we present two options to a given problem, we mean that both should work. We're not interested in things that sound like they'll work but don't. We've spent too many years disposing of that kind of misinformation ourselves.

There, finally, are our goals: to provide *generalized* information which will turn out to be of use when applied in a wide variety of situations; to concentrate on *practical* rather than theoretical matters, where that's possible; to keep our presentation *simple* and our information *understandable;* and to apprise you of the very *best* of alcoholism treatment as we know it in our own not-so-humble estimation.

We think we're taking on a very large task indeed. As a last comment before we set about it, we need to point out that we are trying to assist whoever is out there trying to help alcoholics to recover, laypersons as well as professionals. We're not in the business of helping people pass various certification exams. We think certification is a step in the right direction, which will go a long way towards standardizing education for counselors, but by no means will ensure an abundance of good counselors. That would be a naive expectation. After all, there's a glut of poor lawyers who passed difficult bar exams. An old joke sums up the flaw in relying on certification to ensure professional competence. Question: What do they call the fellow who finishes last in medical school? Answer: Doctor.

So do the alcoholic and yourself a favor: don't think education is simply a matter of certification. You as a helper want to judge yourself and your methods by their *effectiveness.*

As any one of us goes about learning, we need to remember that no one starts out as a blank sheet on which ideas can be printed. We all believe we know what alcoholism is, and what makes an alcoholic. These ideas have been handed down to us within our culture, and they are so ingrained that unless we recognize them for what they are, they'll simply overwhelm any new learning we undertake. Then our experiences will begin to fall into the same patterns as our unsuccessful predecessors', and before you know it, we'll be looking at no-good drunks and hopeless alcoholics again.

To put it simply: we're taught, quietly but effectively, that alcoholism is something that it's not, and that the alcoholic is someone that he isn't. Society—families, friends, counselors, educators, all of us—will have to learn to set these misconceptions aside.

Second, but no less important: alcoholism-treatment professionals may have very unrealistic attitudes, when they enter the field, towards the science of psychology and the art of therapy. They have trouble knowing what is reasonable and what isn't, within the context of the counseling relationship. These attitudes need relearning before they can be replaced by more workable ones.

Out of all this learning and relearning, we who have titled our book *Don't Help* will try to build a model which works.

Relearning begins on the next page.

2

Old Models and New

L ET'S GO BACK, FOR THE MOMENT, TO THOSE 104 definitions of alcoholism. We needn't review them individually, but we do have to recognize that each represents an effort on someone's part—researcher, clinician, or whatever—to differentiate *his* idea of the problem from everyone else's.

Of course, if it's so important to be different, then we have to assume that all these definitions disagree in some essential way about what alcoholism is, or what causes it, or about some other key issue. It should also be obvious that many will actually contradict one another.

Thus, it should be possible for someone to be diagnosed alcoholic under the criteria described in one definition, while failing to meet the criteria for alcoholism under a different definition.

In fact, it may be possible for someone to fit the criteria for alcoholism described by, for example, twelve definitions, while at the same time failing to meet the criteria of twelve others.

And of course we might imagine that a patient who was so

indisputably alcoholic as to meet all the criteria described in all the definitions would still get quite a bit of contradictory advice about what *caused* his alcoholism and what might be done to remedy the situation.

There's just too much room for anyone who doesn't really *want* to receive the label of alcoholic—you can include the entire human race in that group—to slip away from it with plenty of room to spare.

As a result of this confusion, a counselor is left in the unenviable position of having to treat alcoholism without knowing for sure what it is.

Defining "Alcoholic"

Why, you might reasonably ask, does this problem still exist? Why don't the researchers and the clinicians get together and decide what it is they're treating?

That's really a very good question.

Part of the problem stems from a terminal case of disagreement about the relative importance of *physical symptoms* versus *psychological* or *emotional distress* versus *life problems* in diagnosing and treating the alcoholic. Which comes first in the alcoholic's experience? Which is the key to determining who has the illness?

Frequently an individual will have difficulties in one of these areas but not in another. Perhaps he has tremors when waking up in the morning, along with occasional memory loss for events which occurred while drinking; however, the same person may adamantly deny any alcohol-related family problems, remorse over drinking, depression, or emotional outbursts. If the examining counselor believes someone has to have all the other problems to be alcoholic, then he's going to have to discover some to go along with the blackouts and the shakes. He'll find himself having to pull teeth to find symptoms to match his diagnosis.

Some of the most enduring problems in diagnosis come from the group of definitions which emphasize *problems due to drinking*. Many people favor these approaches because they're so inclusive, but, by the same token, they are far and away the most vague. One typical example states that an alcoholic is anyone whose drinking interferes with one or more of the major areas of life: marriage and family, health, work, school or career, social or legal status, and the like.

How then should we categorize someone who drinks a martini, accidentally swallows the olive, and chokes to death? Drinking very definitely interfered with his health, but was he alcoholic? Or what about a college senior who gets drunk on graduation night, punches a fellow in a bar, and is arrested for drunk and disorderly behavior—is that a symptom of alcoholism? If, five or ten years later, he makes a pass at a woman at a party while he's half sloshed, and gets in trouble with his wife, must we add that as another symptom?

What if his employer has a strict rule against drinking during working hours, and he's discovered having a beer at lunch? If he's fired, does that count towards a diagnosis?

Similarly, definitions which rely on descriptions of the alcoholic's craving or compulsion for alcohol run into problems because many nonalcoholics report occasional strong cravings for liquor—the legendary cold beer on a hot day being only one example. And until they develop fairly pronounced withdrawal symptoms, most alcoholics will not experience compulsions to drink—they'll say they simply *choose* to drink when they do, and they'll be correct.

Some experts have tried to reconcile these contradictions by retreating into catch-all definitions which by twists and turns of wording seek to include all the criteria for alcoholism ever described. In the process, they invariably render their work useless, since their definitions are so broad they can't reliably differentiate the alcoholic from anyone else.

Let's take another, harder look at the question: Why is it so hard to define alcoholism?

The first problem is that the illness so often emerges only very slowly. Its symptoms appear and disappear, only to return later. When we discuss alcoholism, we should think of something that occurs over the course of a lifetime, in stages. The earlier the stage, the more difficult it is to differentiate alcoholism from alcohol abuse—the irresponsible use of a powerful mind-altering chemical.

Then there's the universal preoccupation with amount and frequency of drinking. How much do alcoholics drink? What's the difference between the heavy drinker and the alcoholic? Is it important to know whether or not you drink every day, or what kind of alcoholic beverage you drink, or if you can stop once you start, or if you drink only on weekends? What if you just sip your drinks, and never let yourself get drunk? What if you're drinking only twice a month? Where is the dividing line between alcoholic and nonalcoholic?

Additionally, of course, there remains some disagreement over whether or not alcoholism is a disease at all. People who question its inclusion among the ranks of true diseases usually ascribe alcoholic behavior to other causes, such as depression. Then, alcoholic drinking is explained away as attempts to self-medicate the underlying problem.

Also, it seems to us, the problem in definition exists because alcoholism is so *selective*. No matter how you define alcoholism, the simple truth remains that most drinkers do not become alcoholic. So the really baffling question has been: Why not? What is it about the alcoholic which accounts for his contracting the disease while his next-door neighbor doesn't, despite a virtually indistinguishable lifestyle? Your definition has to apply not only to the millions of drinkers who become alcoholic, but also, by excluding them, to the far greater number who don't.

A final difficulty in understanding alcoholism arises from our fondness for separation of mind from body. Much of our philosophy and religion takes great pains to divide human experience into *parts,* such as body, mind, spirit, will, and soul. This separationist outlook has permeated psychology as well, which has been built around an idea that there exists a mind which directs, albeit sometimes poorly, a subordinate body. Freud went so far as to partition this mind into conscious and subconscious, ego and superego and libido, without having the means to demonstrate the existence of any of these. Behaviorists, on the other hand, avoided this unscientific leap by ignoring speculations about the workings of a mind altogether, concentrating instead on the observable behavior of human beings (or, frequently, of laboratory rats). These investigators tend to treat the brain as a sort of "black box" to which they have no key.

The problem which underlies both approaches is essentially the same. We really don't know very much about how the human brain works. Freud could speculate freely about its hidden processes because no one could dispute him with more reliable information. Despite his own mapping of the psyche, Freud believed, quite logically, that many of its serious disorders were entirely chemical in origin; yet he had no idea *how* these disorders came about. By the same token, the behaviorists, who chose to act as though the brain had no moving parts, were able to learn more than any other group in human history about the behavior of laboratory rats, but still could explain little about the workings of their own brains.

It helps to remember that our brain represents the most complicated piece of matter we've yet encountered in the universe. That's why, for example, we know so much more about the stars in the constellation Orion than we do about our own brains. We do assume, however, that all our mental processes, from deciding to brush our teeth in the morning to falling in love to figuring out how to send a man to the moon, result from chemical activity in this very same brain. Therefore, the way we think, feel, act, and react is directly related to the manner in which our brains work, and anything which affects those chemical processes is going to affect just about everything we do, whether we're aware of it or not.

This is especially important to remember when one discusses a disease like alcoholism, because the temptation is great to divide its effects into mental and physical, and this is where we so often get into trouble. Drugs such as alcohol act on biological processes. They somehow unlock the black box in a way we don't fully understand, and thereby influence our thoughts, feelings, and actions. The best way to understand how drug-related diseases work is by *relating* psychological events to biological processes, rather than by trying to *separate* them.

As a species, we've been living with alcohol for approximately ten thousand years—longer than we've had such inventions as the written word. Thus, we've had more than enough time to devise a sufficient number of theories to confuse ourselves thoroughly.

So the place to begin a study of alcoholism is with an examination of the way people view the disease.

Comparing the Models

To make comparison possible, several researchers have divided the literature into *models* which enable us to look at how we analyze and explain alcoholic behavior. These models represent not specific theories about alcoholism, but general trends in thinking and attitude.*

All these models are alive today, and every counselor who works with alcoholics will encounter them, though often when he least expects it. The point is to realize that each influences the way any alcoholic is treated in America today, and also to recognize that each model, even if strange to you, makes sense to someone who believes in it. These someones will be found among counselors, doctors, nurses, friends, neighbors, and, most importantly, among alcoholics.

Because alcoholism is such an ancient illness, you seldom meet someone who has no opinion at all about it. Instead of beginning with a person who, like a clean slate, is open to learning about the problem, we all begin with a set of preconceptions about what it is, what causes it, and what to do about it. Part of the counselor's job will be to help the alcoholic identify his own favorite model, and to decide whether it's possible to recover from alcoholism while operating within it. If the verdict is no, of

---

*Miriam Siegler, Humphrey Osmonds, and Stephen Newell. "Models of Alcoholism, Models of Treatment," *Models of Medicine, Models of Madness*: New York, Macmillan, 1974.

course, then both are going to have to come up with a more workable approach.

Here are what we see as the models of alcoholism.

The Impaired Model: "Alcoholics Can't Change"

In the Impaired model, the definition of alcoholism is along these lines: "Alcoholics are drunks whose primary occupation is the consumption of booze. It's their nature to drink, and they can't change that. If they ever do stop drinking, it's only a matter of time until they start again. It doesn't matter why this happens; it just does."

Does that sound terribly negative to you, or cruel? Perhaps you see it as simply realistic. The Impaired model represents one of the most enduring of all approaches to alcoholism.

Obviously, treatment under this view would be a waste of time and effort. Those who operate in this model generally concede that some kind of custodial care should be offered to alcoholics who can't care for themselves but, certainly, no other kind of treatment would be effective.

On the other hand, drunks, which is what alcoholics "really" are, should be avoided by everyone, prevented from coming into contact with children, and kept out of normal society.

Why? Because they're "disgusting."

Despite education about alcoholism, this model is enormously widespread. Its adherents develop a curious combination of tolerance and avoidance in their attitudes towards the sick alcoholic.

This is the model that resulted in the creation of that American classic, the town drunk. Townspeople shuffle him away from their doors; cops roust him from the park bench; hospitals take him in when he falls down and hurts himself; judges send him to jail when he gets out of hand. Some cities and larger communities have skid rows which really are "town drunk towns." It's only a question of size.

More importantly, this is an extremely common model

among helpers. It's easy to find doctors, nurses, and ministers who operate within it. To give an example: we once worked in a hospital which had a large and successful alcoholism program. This particular program maintained a bed especially for admissions through the Emergency Room. For some reason, however, the bed was almost always empty. One day an Emergency Room nurse was asked why the bed wasn't filled more often, since there had to be a lot of sick alcoholics wandering into every Emergency Room in every hospital in the country. The nurse looked at the questioner as if he was crazy, and informed him that of course, at least five sick alcoholics a day came for help, but the head nurse wouldn't let them see the doctor. She controlled the call list which determined who was brought in for examination, and as soon as the patient mentioned alcohol, she put his name at the bottom. She'd frequently call in patients who arrived *after* the alcoholic. This resulted in a minimum waiting period of about two hours. Of course, no alcoholic can sit that long without going into withdrawal, so very few of them were ever there when their names were called. When the head nurse was asked what she thought she was doing, she made no attempt to disguise her bias at all. "I know they all just want drugs," she explained. "If they're really sincere, they'll be waiting to see the doctor, and frankly, I'm sick and tired of watching people waste money on these alcoholics, who just get drunk again anyway. Unless this patient is willing to prove he's motivated, I'm not going to let him take up a perfectly good hospital bed that a sick person might need."

She said this with such absolute certainty that it was almost possible to believe her. She didn't know that two nurses and a doctor on the ER staff were recovering alcoholics who'd have been disturbed to know they were hopeless drunks.

Where does the Impaired model come from, and why has it survived? The answer to both questions is the same: it springs directly from observation of (and experience with) *late stage* alcoholics who can't think, function, or care for themselves. These alcoholics drink destructively without the capacity (let alone the willingness) to change their behavior. Their livers and brains work poorly, and they often have a kind of profound insensitivity to their surroundings, which leads people to conclude they don't care.

The Impaired model, then, is a natural consequence of giving up on the chronic alcoholic. It also results from *misinterpretation* of the factors involved in alcoholic relapse. If you don't understand much about how alcoholism works, then, when you see an alcoholic who's received some form of treatment and drinks again anyway, you're likely to conclude that treatment is worthless, rather than investigating the type of treatment the alcoholic received, or other factors which might have interfered with recovery.

Hospital staffs, you should remember, see a considerable number of relapsed alcoholics among their patients. The reason for this is simple: alcoholics who *don't* respond to treatment tend to develop more severe problems due to drinking, and those who do get better avoid hospitals with the same vigor as the average person. Thus it's easy for a helper to conclude that all treatment fails; many of them do believe exactly that.

Similarly, there are quite a few Americans who grew up in families where there were one or more alcoholic members who didn't get better, and who progressed into the late stages of alcoholism. These family members will have accepted the concept of the Impaired model almost as a matter of self-preservation. Some family analysts have designated this point as the control stage, where frustrated family members simply give up on the alcoholic, and begin to live their lives as though he weren't really there at all or had already died of the disease. We know one man, for example, who has lived for twenty years with an alcoholic wife who has remained drunk in her room for the majority of that time. She hasn't, he swears, ventured downstairs more than a dozen times in the past five years. Her husband and her children tried to get her to quit drinking for about ten years, and finally just quit trying. Her husband brings her food, watches after her, and sleeps in a *very* separate bedroom. He is only thankful, he says, that she doesn't smoke, or she might have burnt the house to the ground years ago. Curiously, all three of her children, whose attitudes towards alcoholism resemble their father's, have become nurses. It's not hard to imagine their approach toward their alcoholic patients.

People who operate in the Impaired model will invariably, when confronted with a less severely impaired alcoholic, assert that he or she isn't really alcoholic at all. To these folks, the only alcoholism is that which we identify as late-stage alcoholism. We once encountered a policeman who had picked up one notable drunk in his small California town no less than eleven separate times, each behind the wheel of a car, with a blood-alcohol level well over legal intoxication. This officer had driven the offender home without charging him in every single instance. When asked why he did this, the officer replied that the man wasn't really an alcoholic, because he still had his job and was even an honorary deputy sheriff. He knew the man couldn't be an alcoholic because his own father had been alcoholic, and this man was entirely different. Therefore, this fellow was simply a "problem drinker." He thus shouldn't be charged as though he were a common drunk.

When you come across an alcoholic who grew up with an alcoholic parent, you'll often find that he has adopted the Impaired model to deal with that parent's drinking, and is now approaching his own drinking problem from that viewpoint. He'll fail to recognize drinking as a problem until it's nearly too late, and then, when he does recognize it, regard his own situation as hopeless. This makes recovery a little like trying to climb out of a coffin that's already been buried. It is a typical problem in treatment that is based directly on the way the alcoholic views his own illness. Any counselor will have to learn how to remedy this, if prolonged recovery is to occur.

The Dry Moral Model: Denouncing Demon Rum

Morals, of course, have to do with right and wrong, and moral models put blame for alcoholism on the individual's inability or unwillingness to do the "right thing." Thus, moral models often disparage the idea that alcoholism is an illness, while emphasizing the concept that alcoholics need to learn to act rightly rather than wrongly. The definitions of right and wrong depend largely on who happens to be judging the alcoholic at that particular moment.

There are two common variations on the moral model: the Dry and the Wet. In this one, the Dry Moral model, alcoholism is regarded as the natural consequence of the use of a very unsavory and dangerous drug, alcohol, by someone without sufficient moral strength to resist its temptations. The assumption is that alcohol does the same thing to everyone who uses it, and that moral people simply choose to leave it alone entirely, or to drink it so sparingly that it has no effect on them. In the nineteenth century, when the Dry Moral model was extremely popular, this second option was strictly the province of men, whose will was adjudged strong enough to "handle it." Ladies, delicate-tempered, avoided liquor altogether. (Many of them regularly used laudanum, which they did not realize is opium in alcohol, but wouldn't have dreamed of tasting whiskey.)

Alcoholics, in this view, were victims of the insidious drug. They had ranged too far off the road of moral thought and action, and therefore fell into a cesspool of drunken neglect and compulsion.

Could such a person be saved? Yes. What was required was that the alcoholic recognize the sinfulness of his state, sincerely ask for help, accept punishment from the appropriate moral authorities, and then, once forgiven, become one with the moral community, never again to stray from its bosom. Step three, involving punishment by the moral community, was where treatment might fit in another approach.

There was, of course, no treatment in the Dry Moral model, because there was no illness. But some types of discipline were thought to be helpful in encouraging the drunkard to mend his ways. These included pouring the alcoholic's supply of liquor down the drain, or otherwise removing it from the premises; forcing the alcoholic to go to church, where the presence of God would elevate his spirit; finding him a wife who was stronger-willed than he was, who could thenceforth control him better than he controlled himself; and, if he was already married to such a person, advising her to make sure the offender was thoroughly nagged, hounded, and made to feel ashamed.

As far as the law allowed, it was recommended that society as a whole support this brand of familial pressure by ensuring that the alcoholic was properly fined, threatened, or jailed for his transgressions. Some judges and policemen used their authority freely to "make impressions" on any drunks with whom they came into contact.

Religion has always been a dominant force in this model, and its apogee was during the Prohibition and Temperance movements that grew so strong, under the leadership of people like William Jennings Bryan, that alcohol itself was outlawed early in the twentieth century.

The failure of Prohibition was so traumatic to the nation that it's likely the experiment will never be repeated. What America discovered was that alcohol had survived in common use for ten thousand years because of one very good reason: people wanted it. It wasn't only alcoholics who wanted it: nonalcoholics regularly broke the law to obtain it, leading to the appearance of a black market for alcohol such as has never been seen in our history for *any* drug. Since that experience, the Dry Moral model has taken a back seat in American culture.

To explain how alcoholism was dealt with in this model, we need only tell a joke that has made the rounds every so often for the last forty years. Someone who'd been selected as the butt of the joke would receive a letter like this one.

Dear Sir,

Please excuse my forwardness in writing but your name was given to me by a mutual acquaintance as someone who might be interested in helping me in my time of need.

I am a traveling preacher and temperance lecturer who makes the rounds of smaller communities carrying the word of God and declaiming the evils of that insidious beverage, liquor, and of the ruin it brings to those who use it. My usual method is to speak briefly of the proper religious attitudes which one should take in life, and then introducing my traveling companion, Clyde, a poor pathetic drunkard who strayed from righteousness early in life and has never been able to return. After a lifetime of drunkenness, he is quite deformed and piteous to the eye, as his flesh is as yellow as a corpse's, and his gait like unto a cripple's, and he drools and gurgles so appallingly that his language is oft mistaken for a foreign tongue, and he can remember no farther than one moment to the next, so that the proceedings of his own life are like a closed book to him. He is indeed a most disgusting creature, and this illustrates my point exactly.

Indeed, it is because of this I write to you. Clyde recently succumbed to his illnesses, and I no longer have an example, as it were, for my lectures. Your friends suggested that you might be available to take Clyde's place.
Yours,
Rev. Harry Smith, Jr.

Oddly enough, despite its humorous intent, this serves as an excellent illustration of how the Dry Moral model attempts to deal with alcoholism. We know of a man who runs a treatment program and is also a popular lecturer on alcoholism. One of his favorite techniques is to stop in the middle of a lecture and point at a matron somewhere in the front row. Since almost all the people in his audiences are recovering alcoholics, he likes to ask this woman a question such as, "Excuse me, ma'am, but I can't seem to recall—have we ever slept together?" When the startled woman insists that she'd never do such a thing, he can then respond, "Have you ever had an alcoholic blackout? If you have, how do you *know* we haven't slept together?" Most of his listeners say they feel curiously relieved after an hour or so of this kind of harangue, having been reminded that, but for God's grace, they might all have become Clydes. In fact, we call this technique *Clydeing,* in honor of the Reverend Smith's departed example.

Like the Impaired model, the Dry Moral model results from

experience with a drinking alcoholic. Most of its disciplinary "treatments," not coincidentally, are those which are tried by families and friends of alcoholics during the days of active drinking. Pouring booze out, hiding it, threatening divorce, and the like are all par for the course when one is attempting to get someone else to stop drinking. In this stage, the well-meaning family members put the sole blame for alcoholism on alcohol itself. It's a natural thing to do. That's why people pour liquor down the drain—as if there weren't a store around the corner, where the drinker would buy more.

The Dry Moral model, emphasizing the importance of punishing alcoholic behavior, lost favor not only because of the failure of Prohibition, but because so many alcoholics, instead of responding to these punishments, cheerfully sacrificed jobs, marriages, and drivers' licenses in the quest for alcohol. And yet, many of us persist in the belief that alcohol is the sole source of the disease of alcoholism, and that the solution is to scare the alcoholic away from the drug. What usually happens when the family tries to scare him is that *they* learn to hate demon rum but he doesn't.

More importantly, a significant percentage of alcoholics themselves have been raised in the Dry Moral model. Because of their views, these alcoholics inevitably experience a great deal of remorse for any alcohol-related misbehaving, and operate on the assumption that the more remorseful they can make themselves feel, the better their chances of success. Usually, these same alcoholics adopt so much of this guilt that they get drunk again in general disgust with themselves and despair about the future.

The Wet Moral Model: "Social Drinking"

The second moral model is the Wet one. Rather than preaching avoidance of alcohol, it advocates something called *controlled drinking*. Basically, an alcoholic in this model is someone who doesn't drink within the rules set down by society. The alcoholic thus represents an unacceptable form of behavior which must be corrected.

Again, there isn't any indication here that alcoholism might be an illness or that alcoholics are sick people. No particular attention is paid to identifying types or degrees of alcoholic drinking, since these don't affect the basic moral choice: Will the individual decide to do what is wrong or what is right in terms of alcohol use? If he does what's right, he should be rewarded with all the privileges accorded to responsible drinkers in society; if he chooses the wrong path, he must be censured until he again chooses the right one.

In the Dry Moral model, the choice is between drinking and abstinence; in the Wet Moral approach, alcohol itself may be regarded as nothing more than a drug which should be used *responsibly*. The choice to drink responsibly is identical to the choice to obey traffic signals or to respect your neighbor's property or to refrain from making a pass at his wife. All such choices involve two steps: first, one must know the difference between right and wrong, and second, one must choose the right over the wrong. If you know what's right, you're obligated to do it.

Alcoholics, as everyone is aware, violate all sorts of rules of conduct about drinking. Some of them manage to confine their rule-breaking to unwritten laws; they receive mostly social pressure to conform. Others violate the written code; they constitute a significant percentage of the drunk drivers, killers (and victims), suicides, and the like.

The cause of all this rule-breaking, according to the Wet Moral model, must be *irresponsibility*. The alcoholic, it's assumed, simply doesn't take responsibility for his drinking behavior. When faced with a choice between right and wrong, he makes the wrong choice. Therefore, all therapy for alcoholism should be aimed at getting the alcoholic to choose correctly. Rather than drinking too much, the alcoholic should learn—and here's where the underlying assumption shows itself—to drink *less*. Rather than drinking in the wrong places at the wrong times, the alcoholic should learn to drink appropriately. Rather than breaking laws while intoxicated, the alcoholic should learn to obey the laws no matter what his condition.

This, in case you hadn't noticed, is the most common model

in America today, through which most of our countrymen view their own drinking and everyone else's as well.

It's this model, for example, which is used in the DWI schools to which people convicted of driving while intoxicated are sent. These schools were designed to fill both of the model's requirements for moral choice. First, these schools teach the offender something about the toxic or performance-altering effects of alcohol. Concepts such as the relationship between blood-alcohol level and behavior are introduced. Suggestions as to what ultimately will happen to drunk drivers, and what they will do to other people, are made in the form of grisly movies about traffic accidents. Finally, in accordance with Wet Moral thinking, the people attending are advised to use their new understanding to avoid driving while under the influence, to regulate their drinking or their driving so as to remain within the law.

All this makes perfect sense within this model. We observed the workings of such a school for four sessions. The information presented was accurate and the staff seemed well trained. Yet, when we broke into small groups to discuss what we'd learned, we were astonished to hear the stories of the students. They talked rather freely about their own drinking habits and frequently mentioned blackouts, tremors when they awakened in the morning, and the fights they had with their families over drinking. Seven out of ten showed clear signs of alcoholism under any definition. Some of them couldn't imagine going twenty-four hours without a fair amount of alcohol, and yet they all drove cars every day. As we listened, we saw the flaw in the Wet Moral model at its most obvious: the class was predicated on the belief that the students could learn to make responsible choices about drinking, when in fact many of the students couldn't even think rationally about the subject and were well past the point of being able to make any decision to drink less.

We asked the program staff if they were aware they were treating people who couldn't imagine doing what was recommended, and they acknowledged they were. "In our first-offenders group," one said, "we estimate 50 percent of our students are alcoholic, and in the second-offenders program, it's closer to 80 percent. We know they can't make choices about drinking, except to quit altogether, but most of them won't do that, and the law says we have to teach them *something*."

This is an excellent example of the problems that arise when the Wet Moral model is applied to alcoholism. When the disease reaches the stage where it severely impairs an individual's ability to control consumption, then "moral" choices as to when to drink, or to cut down or control consumption, will become meaningless. In a population such as alcoholics, where people regularly experience memory losses due to drinking and withdrawal symptoms when they don't drink, efforts to teach them to drink within society's boundaries will be futile. A model which pretends everyone can control his or her drinking in precisely the same way goes against the experience of millions of drinkers.

There are actually a number of treatment facilities for alcoholics that have tried to instruct people in controlled drinking. All of them, to our knowledge, have claimed some degree of success. Nonetheless, most of these efforts have met, ultimately, with failure. One program in an eastern city decided to reward alcoholics for drinking less with cash. Another used electric shock to discourage excessive drinking. Nevertheless, for most of the patients treated at those institutions, the problems with alcohol returned.

Our interest in the Wet Moral model is more than simply academic. The fact is that, besides being the most popular among Americans in general, it's the one encountered most frequently in any alcoholic caseload.

You see, despite the fact that most alcoholics can't live within the tenets of this model, someone apparently forgot to tell them that, because they all seem to try.

This is the source of the legendary alcoholic emphasis on "will power." Factors such as physiological addiction, alcohol toxicity, progressive loss of control, abnormal tolerance, and liver or brain disease are routinely ignored. Moral models concentrate on the individual's responsibility for choosing right over wrong. In the Wet version, it is assumed that *any* man or woman can, through an effort of will, control his or her use of alcohol.

Abstinence, in these terms, would be a cop-out, an unequivocal statement to the world that the abstainer was weak-willed. Thus, for an alcoholic to decide not to drink at all—and thus, take responsibility for his own behavior—he has to admit he lacks sufficient moral and intellectual strength to beat alcoholism on his own.

Now it should be obvious why, in part, all those alcoholics struggle so valiantly to avoid quitting drinking. We call them *practicing* alcoholics during this phase. "What's a practicing alcoholic?" goes the old joke. "Someone who hasn't got it right yet," comes the response.

And that's exactly what most alcoholics will do—spend a significant portion of their lives trying to get it right. Definition of right: regaining the ability to control, through an effort of will, their use of alcohol.

If you subscribe to the idea that alcoholism is a disease that involves progressive loss of control over drinking, then you'd probably conclude that the faster the disease erodes the individual's control over alcohol, the harder the alcoholic in the Wet Moral model would work to overcome this erosion through will power. You'd be correct, because that's exactly what happens.

This faith in will power is at the center of most alcoholics' approach to their problem. We once took an informal poll of fifty alcoholics newly admitted to treatment. We asked them what they believed to be the most important single asset in recovering from alcoholism, and they replied, almost unanimously, that it was will power. Why?

"Because if you had enough will power you wouldn't have ended up in treatment in the first place," one fellow said. He described to the group his efforts over the past three years to learn to drink socially, and the array of different strategies he'd devised to help him in his struggle. Each time he initiated a new strategy, he'd "be okay for a few months," and then "something would happen," and he'd get in trouble again. Apparently, it had taken almost all his energy on a twenty-four-hour basis just to drink normally, as he called it. He'd even changed jobs twice because he thought his work was too stressful, and he was wondering if he could stay married, because he thought his wife's nagging made him overdrink.

His story reminded us of a cartoon. A fellow is standing in the middle of some apparently Himalayan town, talking to another man. The speaker, though obviously American, is dressed in the robes of the natives, while the listener wears a backpack and hiking gear, and is clearly a tourist. "First, I gave up all my possessions to obtain spiritual enlightenment," the speaker is saying, "then I moved here, leaving my job and my family in my search for truth. Now, if it wasn't for booze, I don't know what I'd do."

We wanted to ask that fellow in the room of alcoholics if he didn't think it would be easier to quit entirely rather than devoting his life to learning to "control" his drinking. At his present rate, he'd likely end up with nothing left *but* his bottle. And who'd be in control then?

Some time later, we asked the same question of a group of alcoholics who had had a year or more of sobriety—most of them in AA. What did they see as the most important single factor in recovery? The most common response was, as one woman put it, "Giving up on the idea that you had to learn to drink like everybody else." "It makes all the difference in the world to admit that you tried your damnedest but it didn't work," added a man in the group. "Then you can get about learning how to live without alcohol, which is the hardest part, anyway."

Truthfully, we've never encountered, in any treatment relationship, an alcoholic who hasn't devoted a considerable amount of time towards conquering drinking through will power. In fact, the alcoholic seeks help because he *hasn't* been successful. Many are firmly entrenched in the Wet Moral model, and rather than wanting to learn to live without alcohol, they expect to be taught how to live with it, in a more peaceful fashion. The counselor needs to uncover this model and this secondary agenda so he can help the client decide whether or not this is a realistic goal. If the patient is an alcoholic, it's not going to be.

The client probably already knows that, but was just hoping that maybe someone would see something else he could try.

To summarize, the Wet Moral model is a very effective way to view the drinking behavior of approximately 90 percent of the drinkers in our society, because they drink in precisely this way, choosing to behave appropriately or inappropriately on the basis of their relative moral development. There's only one group of drinkers to whom we would not recommend the Wet Moral approach, because it doesn't work for them. For *alcoholics,* this model, with its emphasis on will power and controlled drinking, is a one-way ticket to complete failure.

The Psychoanalytic Model: The Addictive Personality

Around the beginning of the twentieth century, Sigmund Freud and his disciples began to devise their theory of human psychology. One fundamental concept was that most abnormal behavior was the result of some underlying psychological conflict, often called a neurosis. Wherever these neuroses existed, they caused behavior that in turn became symptoms by which the presence of the neuroses could be recognized. The correct way to treat abnormal behavior, then, wasn't to deal with the behavior directly, but to uncover the underlying neurosis and treat that. When neurotic conflict was resolved, symptoms would subside. Simply correcting surface behavior, on the other hand, would result in the appearance of yet another symptom.

Alcoholics, who happen to have something of a reputation for abnormal behavior, naturally came under the scrutiny of these new theorists. Psychoanalysts began to speculate about the nature of the neuroses, or combination of neuroses, which ultimately must be responsible for alcoholism.

Gradually, as the popularity of analytic precepts grew, alcoholic drinking began to lose its status as a problem at all. It became instead a *symptom* of a problem. Many analysts objected to the term alcoholism itself, asserting that it was misleading to name a disorder after its symptoms.

This word *symptom* was to dominate the analytic, and therefore the psychiatric, approach to alcoholism for most of the century.

This assumption—that alcoholic drinking represented the presence of a hidden psychological disorder—received very little resistance from the medical community. Perhaps most believed that this adequately explained the prodigious failure rate of most alcoholism treatment of that time. "Now we'll let the psychiatrists and psychologists have a shot at it," the prevailing attitude seemed to say.

And so the alcoholic population of America (at least that small percentage who entered treatment) became involved in psychotherapy. Studies were done, articles published, research initiated, theories advanced about the causes and treatment of alcoholism. Some clinicians began describing an *alcoholic personality,* which accounted for the addictive behavior of the alcoholic. For them, the proper goal of treatment became the healing of this sick personality.

Viewing the addictive personality rather than addictive drinking as the focus of treatment radically changes the entire experience. If the patient is seen by the therapist as improving, in terms of his work on a specific emotional problem, then he may be encouraged to regard himself as being successful in treatment even if he still drinks copiously. If he isn't working on what the therapist thinks he ought to be working on, he may be encouraged to regard himself as failing even if he long ago stopped drinking.

Alcoholism never fit very well into the constraints imposed by this model. In the first place, a certain degree of self-awareness and intellectual acuity is required for the analytic process, and drinking alcoholics had trouble providing it. Additionally, the one most noticeable feature of analytic therapy is its marked slowness, and sick, troubled alcoholics almost never completed treatment. Third, the all-important gut feelings, which much therapy is geared toward exploring, fluctuated not so much as a result of the therapy as with any change in blood-alcohol level. And finally, alcoholics kept forgetting the insights they gained in the previous sessions.

Nevertheless, alcoholics, along with much of the rest of America, began exploring feelings and motives. They began to ask themselves, "Why?"

Unfortunately, where the average American got a little better or experienced no change in therapy, the alcoholic frequently got worse.

When we examine the way alcoholism works, we can imagine how this happens. Most alcoholics enter treatment because they're experiencing symptoms of loss of control over their drinking. They have very likely been working overtime (or double- or triple-overtime) to keep those symptoms from getting even worse. Finally they realize how difficult the whole situation is, and decide to get some professional help. When they enter therapy, however, they're commonly led to believe that the problem isn't really the drinking behavior, but the *personality of the drinker*. Accordingly, they get into the process of analyzing and scrutinizing their every thought, feeling, and memory, and stop paying attention to their drinking—which then proceeds to degenerate at an even faster rate, accompanied by still more flagrant problems.

On the other hand, if the alcoholic enters therapy with a short period of abstinence under his belt, then a few weeks or months of dwelling on his anxieties, inadequacies, resentments, and frustrations are usually enough to put him right back on the bottle.

The problems with the alcoholic personality as a model, however, went far deeper than the difficulties of therapy. It proved surpassingly hard to identify the combination of personality characteristics which composed this alcoholic personality. One group of researchers maintained it was "emotional immaturity;" others insisted that alcoholics were normally over-aggressive, overly shy, narcissistic, masochistic, possessed low self-esteem, had no tolerance for frustration, and on and on ad infinitum. It seemed as though every conceivable personality defect was intimately involved in alcoholism. Yet none of these traits, singly or in combination, seemed to explain adequately the nature of alcoholic drinking.

Even more distressing, the most reliable researchers were unable to find the supposed causes of alcoholism in the individual before the onset of alcoholic drinking.

In other words, though it appeared that alcoholic drinking *led* to a variety of personality problems, it did not seem to *result* from personality disturbances.

What does all this mean?

Simply that there is a very good chance that alcoholism is not caused by an alcoholic or addictive personality, and that the basic assumption of the Psychoanalytic model therefore was incorrect. Then, by simple inference, the basic assumptions which underlie numerous forms of treatment (which grew from the belief in the alcoholic personality) must also be incorrect.

This might contribute to the relatively poor recovery rate resulting from psychotherapy. Not only was insight-oriented psychotherapy difficult for alcoholics to complete, but they might not even need it in the first place.

If this is indeed the case, it will no doubt require an extraordinary amount of effort (and education) to get the mental-health establishment to see it. Most come from personality-oriented training which has become the foundation of their clinical philosophy. For example, one therapist recently delivered a lecture on hypnosis which we happened to attend. In the course of his talk, he mentioned that an alcoholic patient had been referred to him because she wanted to stop drinking. He had advised her that this was impossible unless she was willing to devote herself to long-term therapy for her "chronic depression." Our guess is that eventually this woman, assuming her drinking continues to cause her concern, will decide to stop on her own, probably with the help of AA. If she really does suffer from a chronic depression, then it will improve in the absence of alcohol, and if her depression was related to her drinking, it will largely disappear over the course of the first year or two of abstinence.

If her therapist should happen to encounter her some years later, he will no doubt be amazed at the transformation. He'll most likely assume she experienced a spontaneous remission in her depression, or worked through her emotional problems in some fashion.

We'd bet a week's salary that he *wouldn't* attribute it to sobriety and AA.

Though the past fifteen years have seen a gradual replacement of the Psychoanalytic model by the Disease model, it remains a powerful force in alcoholism treatment for several reasons. First of all, as we mentioned, most of the treatment professionals in all areas of the mental health field were trained in this model. Second, though most forms of alcoholism treatment acknowledge that alcoholism is indeed a real disease, very few of them treat it as such. Many of the techniques used by these programs are holdovers from the days of psychoanalytic dominance, as though no one is quite sure how to replace them.

The Psychoanalytic model still exerts considerable influence over the way any alcoholic is treated in America today.

If only it worked. . . .

The Family Interaction Model: Treating Systems Instead of Individuals

Family-oriented models enjoy considerable popularity within the mental-health community. They vary tremendously among practitioners, but all share a focus on *family interaction* rather than on alcoholic behavior. Family theorists disagree on the cause of alcoholism itself. Some insist that alcoholic drinking is simply a role assigned within the family, and therefore cannot be separated from that system. Others attribute alcoholic drinking to an independent disease process which both *victimizes* and to a certain extent *is nurtured by* the family.

If this confuses you, don't feel bad—it confuses us as well. The Family Interaction model is perhaps the least defined of the so-called professional models, and is therefore most likely to contain internal contradictions. Nonetheless, its invaluable contribution lies in recognizing that the family has been for many years a neglected child of alcoholism treatment.

Anyway, in most variations on this theme, the family unit not only "selects" the alcoholic for his or her role, but then keeps the alcoholic drinking through a complex series of interpersonal transactions. Therefore, therapy must be directed towards the family rather than towards the alcoholic. A common analogy is to a mobile sculpture: if you move one part, all the others move along with it. Family therapists use this to imply the futility of treating the alcoholic without addressing the needs of the entire family, both individually and as a system.

One positive result of the popularity of this model has been a concerted attempt to study the dramatic impact of alcoholism on the lives of people who live with it. In fact, quite a few of these persons are as confused and as miserable as the alcoholic. As might be expected of a disease with a strong genetic component, the pattern of destructive effects can be traced within a family not merely for years but through generations. Family therapists acknowledged what alcoholism clinicians had known for decades: sometimes, significant others become involved in the cycle of destructive drinking in an unhealthy way, negatively influencing recovery and promoting relapse. If these behaviors could be identified and changed, recovery might be a little easier.

Another invaluable contribution was the discovery that an alcoholic in denial, resistant to treatment, can be reached through his family, provided they receive training in intervention (see the last section of Chapter 6).

From a practical standpoint, the Family Interaction model has a few significant flaws. First (and most important), its literature is remarkably bereft of information about the disease itself—perhaps because the initial practitioners didn't believe alcoholism was a disease in the biological sense.

As a result, we find that counselors trained exclusively in this model may know less about alcoholism than their alcoholic patients—a bad position to be in when you're passing yourself off as an expert. Given what science has discovered about alcoholism, this can be a bit like attempting to treat diabetes as a symptom of poor communication. So it seems fair to point out that even if this isn't a psychoanalytic approach, it's emphatically psychological in orientation.

Second, we think there's a real danger in mistaking the *results* of alcoholism for its causes. It's obvious to anyone who works with alcoholics that the pervasive mental and emotional disturbances that accompany drinking affect those around the alcoholic. Yet, once again, those disturbances seem to be the product of the illness, not its source. Even though a family's misguided behavior may encourage continued drinking, that doesn't mean the family caused the disease; in fact, the family is simply one more set of victims.

Last, this can also be a very impractical model for working counselors, because family involvement is sometimes unavailable. AA demonstrates clearly that many alcoholics recover without help from their families, and without the other members of the family receiving therapy for their own problems. Recovering alcoholics don't all move away from their sick spouses, nor do families always change their attitudes towards the alcoholic, even after years of abstinence. In fact, we'd venture to say that if total family recovery were a prerequisite for recovery, most recovering alcoholics would still be drunk.

The simple fact is that an alcoholic must be prepared to maintain sobriety no matter what the circumstances. In the same vein, any counselor who purports to treat alcoholism must be prepared to do so whether or not there is any family involvement, just in case there isn't. Then, if family support does exist, family recovery will be one more plus for the patient.

Clearly, the real strength of this model is in the treatment of family members other than the alcoholic or in cases where there are several alcoholics within a family. That's where the Family Interaction model really shines—when it can identify and strive to remedy the complex dysfunction that the disease can cause.

The Old Medical Model: A Patchwork Quilt

Alcoholism has been with us for such a great portion of human history that we probably have as much experience with it as with any health problem excluding death. Doctors have always been forced to deal with alcoholism because its effects are so numerous and so severe that, no matter what the rest of society thinks of the alcoholic, the physician is obliged to treat him.

The Old Medical model grew out of this experience. Alcoholism was seen as a severely debilitating condition which is potentially fatal and contributes to myriad complications.

How does one contract alcoholism? Through excessive use of alcohol. Therefore—and this is the crucial point—it's a *self-inflicted illness*.

Why do alcoholics lose control? Because alcohol causes the organs of the body to deteriorate. This in turn interferes with the body's ability to tolerate more alcohol.

Thus, the act of drinking too much causes alcoholism, which in turn causes further drinking, which produces more problems, which motivates still greater consumption, and so on. Why do alcoholics drink too much in the first place? Nobody knows. The Old Medical model defers to other models in this area; doctors have attributed drinking to situational stress, failure to resist temptation, underlying psychological problems, or just plain irresponsibility.

The prevalence of the Old Medical model in the medical profession accounts for two phenomena characteristic of treatment.

First, the preoccupation with medical complications of alcoholic drinking (rather than with alcoholism itself) often leads to a profound neglect of treatment after the initial detoxification. Under this model, most hospitals confine their relationship with the alcoholic patient to that two-to-five-day period immediately following a visit to the Emergency Room. The alcoholic (if lucky) is medically assessed, admitted to a hospital bed, given tranquilizers, admonished about his health, and then discharged. The majority of these patients resume drinking, sometimes within *minutes* of leaving the hospital. Their condition quickly deteriorates, and they are forced to once again seek medical help. When a given Emergency Room grows tired of their complaints, they move on to another hospital. Once they are known at most of the local hospitals, they begin "riding the circuit": going from institution to institution, until they find one which will accept them. Circuit riders become so familiar with hospital routine that they offer to fill out their own paperwork and even request medication ("Listen, Doc, I don't mean to tell you your business, but phenobarbital works a lot better for me than

Librium . . ."). This has become known as the Revolving Door Syndrome.

The second phenomenon associated with this model is a preoccupation with efforts to scare the alcoholic sober with tales of death and physical deterioration. We couldn't begin to count the numbers of alcoholics who have been told by physicians and nurses that they'd be dead within six months if they didn't quit.

Of course, after you've heard this for several years, you tend to stop listening.

The Old Medical model is a patchwork quilt of ideas, not all in perfect agreement with one another. It's really a Moral model aided and abetted by a knowledge of medicine. Where prohibitionists threatened the alcoholic with hellfire and brimstone, medical practitioners trot out enormous deformed livers to graphically illustrate the patient's future.

The Old Medical model is the source of many concepts that over the decades have seeped into the popular consciousness. See if any of these are familiar:

- Alcoholics are people who don't care about their health. Otherwise they wouldn't abuse their bodies.
- Alcoholics must be shown the destructive effects of alcohol so they'll be too scared to drink again.
- After the first few days, alcohol withdrawal is over. Any craving the alcoholic has after that is because of some psychological problem.
- You have to drink a lot for a long time to become alcoholic. If you're young, or you don't drink more than your doctor does, you can't be alcoholic.
- Excessive drinking is a form of slow suicide. Alcoholics don't have the guts to kill themselves outright—most are Catholics to boot—so they take the extended route.

It's important to remember that this is not necessarily a *dry* model. If liver impairment and malnutrition lead to loss of control, then when the liver is improved and the diet regulated, the patient should be able to drink "moderately." Imagine the physician's surprise when his patient gets a clean bill of health, returns to social drinking, and develops problems soon afterward.

This is still the model taught in many medical schools. It virtually guarantees failure in treating alcoholism. The patient will receive excellent medical care, of course. But that will be small consolation when he finds himself receiving neither respect nor understanding from the doctors and nurses from whom he seeks help.

Why do medical professionals get so angry at the alcoholic? Because they believe his problems are self-inflicted, and that he's simply too lazy or weak or irresponsible to follow the good advice given by his physicians, instead choosing to abuse medical services that should be devoted to people suffering from "real" diseases.

We have the Old Medical model to thank for this attitude. Fortunately, a New Medical model emerged which began, slowly, to replace it.

The New Medical (or Disease) Model: Alcoholism As a Real Disease

The New Medical model grew directly out of the dramatic increase in knowledge over the past fifty years about alcohol and its effects. Since we're going to discuss this approach in some detail in the next chapter, we'll confine ourselves here to a brief discussion of its evolution.

The spiritual father of the Disease model is E. M. Jellinek, who was the first to begin the process of identifying alcoholic drinking practices and relating them to a disease process rather than to some other cause. His research spurred others to begin thinking of alcoholism as something that could rightfully be studied in and of itself, rather than as part of some personality disorder. It also planted the thought that alcoholism could just as well be treated as an independent disease rather than as a part of other problems. Once this seed took hold, alcoholism treatment began, slowly, to change.

The first tangible evidence of this change was that some hospitals began to take alcoholic patients out of the psychiatric units, and, though they frequently continued to treat them as psychiatric patients, at least put them in separate facilities. Psychiatrists began to treat alcoholics in separate group sessions which kept alcoholism and other mental disorders apart.

Then the professionals began to look around for effective treatment, and noticed that while they were struggling to limit the dramatic recidivism rate, a group called AA was doing quite well treating the same people who weren't responding to professional help. So AA, which already had a foothold in hospitals from its earliest days, was now openly welcomed by many.

Meanwhile, scientists and researchers of all kinds were really studying the illness as an illness, and discovering all sorts of interesting things about it.

One of the most fascinating discoveries was that most alcoholics didn't need psychiatric help to recover. When they were able to stop drinking for an extended period without relapsing, they found that most of their emotional problems simply went away.

It was also apparent that alcoholics as a rule didn't need psychiatric help to *stop* drinking, either. AA was much more likely to be effective than psychotherapy.

Then it occurred to researchers that perhaps this was because alcoholism wasn't a psychiatric problem. If it wasn't, then what were all these psychiatrists and psychologists doing treating it as though it was?

With this in mind, they began to look again at the physical side of alcoholism. They found that such things as tolerance and physical dependence and organ deterioration played a crucial role in alcoholic behavior, and those were most emphatically *physiological,* rather than psychological, processes.

But wait a minute, someone said. What about the addictive personality? Isn't that why alcoholics relapse after treatment? AA answered that one: alcoholics relapsed, basically, because they didn't know how to stay sober. If you taught them how to live with themselves and without alcohol, and if they had enough sense to follow directions, they did just fine. For the ones that did have psychological illnesses, there was a much better chance of treating them sober than while they were drunk.

And what *causes* alcoholism? another group asked. Doesn't excess drinking cause the physical addiction? What makes the alcoholic drink that much in the first place?

Slowly, the Disease model began to provide answers to that. Instead of searching for psychological differences between the alcoholic and the nonalcoholic, researchers began to look for a physiological difference.

What scientists began to believe, in increasing numbers, was that they were looking not at a response to developmental problems, but at an inheritable disease, one of a group of chronic diseases that throughout history has been mistaken for personality disorders. And it began to appear that the alcoholic's problem was not in his mind, but in his body.

Which in turn indicated why attempts to return alcoholics to social drinking had so often failed: there existed a physiological defect which sabotaged the effort. No amount of psychotherapy, obviously, could be expected to remedy such a defect; nor, for that matter, could anyone reasonably expect will power to correct it. Therefore, the simple remedy involved *stopping all alcohol intake*.

The alcoholic wasn't required to believe that he was crazy, weak-willed, immoral, or disgusting; he was only required to give up drinking. Any method through which he chose to accomplish this was perfectly acceptable. If he found he could maintain abstinence by beating himself over the head with palm fronds, then he should get started. The only qualification for a method of recovery was simply that it work, because progressive diseases don't tolerate relapse very well.

Therefore, if you were an alcoholic who had been in psychotherapy for five years and continued getting drunk once every few months, you would be encouraged to re-examine the effectiveness of your recovery program. You might understand your *feelings* better than most people, but your approach wasn't getting the job done as far as alcoholism was concerned.

In our view, the Chronic Disease model has become as significant in terms of alcoholism treatment as AA, because it definitely recommends removing the alcoholic, once and for all, from the realm of the psychologically inadequate and the morally impure. We hope you agree with us that this would advance the cause of effective treatment by at least a century and improve the chances for recovery, self-acceptance, and self-respect for every alcoholic, everywhere.

The AA Model: Living without Alcohol

As far as we're concerned, the AA approach has turned out to be the most important development in alcoholism treatment in the twentieth century. As we've said, there wasn't much in the way of effective treatment for this illness before AA and there is very little effective treatment now that doesn't use AA. It's not an exaggeration to say that AA changed everybody's method of treating alcoholism.

Nonetheless, the organization isn't free of criticism from within the treatment community. Some clinicians, mostly psychotherapists, believe that AA is too dogmatic in its approach; there is very definitely a mutual distrust between many a recovering alcoholic and mental health professionals.

There are solid reasons for this. Not long ago, we came across an impassioned letter in a journal from an "expert" in substance abuse who had been appalled by the angry response he got from AA members when he spoke of his attempts to teach alcoholics how to drink without problems. He clearly regarded himself as a victim of prejudice; in his model, controlled drinking for alcoholics was entirely possible, and he couldn't understand why everyone didn't see it his way.

That this expert should be surprised at the angry response illustrates how little he knows about how most alcoholics recover.

What is AA and why has it been so irritatingly successful where so much sophisticated treatment has failed?

First, foremost, and finally, AA is a *practical self-help group*. It isn't a religion; though God is a constant subject, and spirituality a constant reference, AA members represent all kinds of faiths. It isn't a treatment program, though alcoholics get better through its efforts every day; it includes graduates, and dropouts, from all approaches. It isn't designed to promote itself within the popular consciousness, or to change, in any organized way, America's views towards alcoholism, or to lobby for or against any issue. In fact, it's designed *not* to do this.

AA has a governing body which doesn't really govern, an admissions criteria which includes just about everyone who wants to belong, and its own bible which had to be printed in large type to make it look impressive, since its message was so simple that at first some believed no one would take it seriously.

AA is such a mass of contradictions that it's difficult to explain how it works at all. Frankly, we suspect that it doesn't work the same for everyone. It can't, since its membership is so varied. A program which is direct enough to reach a nearly irrational alcoholic in the midst of a binge, and at the same time provide daily interest and meaning to someone who hasn't touched a drop in forty years, is obviously operating on more than one level.

It became evident to us some time ago that part of the reason AA members have so much trouble explaining AA is that each person sees it so emphatically through the lens of personal experience. We once knew a rock-and-roll singer, a periodic binger for twenty years, who attended her first AA meeting while a patient in a hospital. Her life had been centered around concerts, television, records, and the like. After she returned from the meeting there was a look of amazement on her face.

"My God," she said, "where has that been all my life? But they really ought to work on the lighting, and get a better sound system." She thought the whole meeting was rehearsed for her benefit.

In a sense, she was right. AA *is* geared to the newcomer, "the suffering alcoholic" mentioned in its literature. And despite the emphasis on spirituality and the enigmatic higher power, every bit of AA wisdom is tied in some way to the practical task of living without alcohol.

Which, of course, isn't as easy as it sounds. If it was, all those people wouldn't attend AA.

AA isn't really the offspring of one man, though Bill Wilson wrote much of its early literature and was the impetus behind its early growth. Wilson's great discovery—that two alcoholics could help each other stay sober and succeed, where each on his own would probably have failed—meant that an exchange of ideas was integral to the program from the outset. No one's ideas existed without modification by others, and so AA from its inception relied on the absolutely most inefficient form of government: consensus. Today, with over a million members in AA, you never get a true consensus on any issue. Nevertheless, the organization continues to function.

Since AA is a grass-roots model, which developed independently of professional approaches, it should be compared with the Moral models and the Impaired model to understand its significance. AA has always recommended abstinence, not because alcohol is evil, but because sobriety seemed to be the only *sure* way to avoid drunkenness. Where the Wet Moral model emphasized choosing right over wrong behavior, the AA model said that the choice for alcoholics wasn't the same as it was for nonalcoholics. Alcoholics were allergic, and therefore had different needs and responsibilities as far as drinking went.

And of course, where the Impaired model gave up on the chronic alcoholic, the AA model guaranteed success to those who followed its suggestions.

A grass-roots model doesn't explain the phenomena of alcoholism as thoroughly as the more sophisticated professional models. AA in its early years relied on the term *allergy* to explain the complicated biological anomalies which dictated the course of alcoholism. The Old Medical model, which represented prevailing medical belief at the time of AA's inception, could barely explain alcoholism at all. The Psychoanalytic approach wasn't much older than AA, and already its best practitioners were giving up on the kind of alcoholics who formed the core of AA. It wasn't until the newer Disease model made its appearance that the experience of alcoholics in AA was clearly related to the course of alcoholism itself, and such factors as tolerance, loss of control, and the selective nature of alcoholism were at least partially accounted for.

The only way to really learn about AA is to talk to its members. To be quite honest, even after ten years, we're frequently as amazed at the way it works as any newcomer.

The expert we mentioned earlier who was shocked by the response of AA members should realize that the only reason he encounters such reactions is because he's recommending something that goes against the better judgment of most AA members. Nonetheless, we imagine he'll keep right on advocating controlled drinking, as many experts have done for many years. No one has any right to expect him to behave differently.

Yet neither does he have a right to expect the members of AA to sacrifice their sobriety for more promises from an "expert." As long as AA works, that's all the justification it needs for inclusion as one of our very best treatment models.

The Models: A Brief Comparison

We've said that the history of alcoholism has been marked by arguments and disputes between people who all believed they had the single correct answer, and we've no desire to enter into that any farther than necessary. As far as we're concerned, all the models exist because they reflect some facet of the illness, and therefore describe accurately some form of alcoholic behavior. Nonetheless, any counselor has to make a choice—not necessarily of one model to the exclusion of all others, but of one which will work the best for most patients.

Let's compare the models in terms of how they seem to work, or fail to work, with alcoholic clients.

The Impaired model, of course, isn't a treatment model at all; it's a "nontreatment" model, a defensive position taken in the face of chronic drunkenness and relapse. You don't expect alcoholics to get better in this approach; rather, you wait for them to die.

The Dry Moral model is deeply embedded in the attitudes of

many people who were raised in religious homes. It's found more in rural areas than in urban settings, but it easily crosses racial lines and is nearly as common among blacks and other minorities as among whites. The Dry Moral model does fit the most important approach to alcoholism in that it recommends total abstinence, but it also seems to carry guilt in its back pocket, and only those who can accept a heavy dose of preaching can recover within it. People who can live with this approach make themselves known without inquiry. In fact, they often try to convert everyone they meet. Many alcoholics who were raised in Dry Moral environments, however, would rather die drunk than give in to such precepts; thus it isn't widely effective in treatment.

However, a phenomenally large segment of the population can operate successfully in the Wet Moral model—about nine out of every ten U.S. drinkers. Unfortunately, all of these are non-alcoholics. It simply doesn't work for drinkers who *experience withdrawal symptoms when they don't drink* or *can't control their drinking*. For obvious reasons, these people aren't going to be able to consistently make "right" choices while drinking. The Wet Moral model simply doesn't provide any method by which to restore to the alcoholic his power over drinking, and of course it's one thing to choose to go to the moon, and another thing to actually be able to get there.

This model is endlessly attractive to alcoholics, however, because it doesn't insist you give up alcohol.

The Psychoanalytic model relies on uncovering motives and conflicts as a prerequisite to changing behavior. That's flawed—obviously—by the fact that alcoholics seem to have problems with alcohol no matter what their reason for drinking it. As far as identifiable mental illnesses go, about 7 or 8 percent of patients have them, and insisting that every alcoholic receive psychiatric treatment would be similar to an optometrist insisting that everyone wear glasses just because some people need them.

To be perfectly honest, psychotherapy frequently appears to make recovery more difficult by encouraging "alibiing" and concern with the past at a time when personal responsibility and attention to the present are essential.

The same problem occurs when the counselor relies exclusively on the Family Interaction model. This approach is very useful as a subsidiary to a stronger model, such as the Disease model, but it doesn't stand very well by itself. Studying family interactions can provide insights into how to change behavior patterns, but won't provide understanding of how a disease works, either for the patient or the counselor.

The favorite tactic of the Old Medical model—scaring alcoholics out of their wits with threats of death and cirrhosis—works well with alcoholics who really *are* just a swig away from the coffin. The rest simply don't believe it. They may politely look impressed by the threats while secretly thinking the therapist is just doing this to justify a salary.

We use a combination of the AA and the Disease models for one reason and one reason only: it works for the greatest number of our patients. We like the Disease model for:

• Explaining to our patients what alcoholism is and how it works;
• Helping them to decide rationally whether or not they've got it, and
• Showing them how to treat it *successfully*.

We use the AA model to do the treatment, on a long-term basis, because it's the only really workable one we've found.

We think the two models fit together very well. We'll try to show you, in the rest of this book, how they can be used successfully. We already know they work for most patients and most counselors who use them; it's simply a question of showing *how*. Then the individual can cut and paste as the situation demands.

Our idea is to help get as many alcoholics better as is humanly possible. With the help of your ingenuity, we think we can succeed.

Now, having discussed a range of views about alcoholism, we'll zero in on one—the Disease model—and show how that can be used to treat sick alcoholics.

3

How Alcoholism Works

ALCOHOLISM IS A DISEASE.
To understand this, you need only ask yourself two simple questions: What is the definition of "disease"? and Does alcoholism fit within it?

"A disease," reads our handy medical dictionary, "is a morbid process with characteristic identifying symptoms . . ."

In other words, it's an ongoing process which is bad for you, and which can be identified by certain symptoms that routinely occur during its course. Alcoholism, obviously, isn't good for you; nobody's health and welfare improves because of alcoholic drinking, and in fact it kills quite a few people every year. The symptoms of alcoholism are taught to every medical student in the world. So far, it clearly qualifies as a disease.

". . . regardless," our dictionary continues, "of whether the etiology or prognosis is known or unknown."

The etiology is the *cause,* and the prognosis is the likely *outcome* of the illness. As the definition makes plain, you can argue about causes and outcomes until kingdom come, without changing the fact that alcoholism is legitimately a disease.

The amazing thing is that it took so long to recognize this. People were taught that alcoholism was the result of some other problem, and spent untold years speculating about the real culprit behind alcoholic drinking.

Now let's take a closer look at the Disease model, which we've chosen to use in treating alcoholics. The ultimate test for any model lies in how well it explains, or fails to explain, the various phenomena associated with alcoholism. There are five basic questions that any good professional model should answer. First, it should provide in its definition of the problem a clear general description of the features of alcoholism, so that it can be classified with similar diseases while at the same time differentiated from other kinds of illnesses. Second, it should state specifically the identifying symptoms of the disease, so that it can be recognized. Third, it should set forth some explanation of the causes of alcoholism, because that's the first question everyone asks, as well as some idea of a prognosis for the alcoholic. Fourth, it should offer some reasonable theory about why some people become alcoholic and others don't. And finally, it must describe an effective method of treatment.

Let's ask these questions of the Disease model, and examine the responses.

What Kind of Disease Is Alcoholism?

First and foremost, alcoholism is a *chronic* disease, which means that it's long-lasting. Once it's established, we can safely assume it's not going to disappear. Like forms of diabetes and various heart, lung, blood and bone diseases, alcoholism represents an ongoing pathology which often appears early in the individual's life and lasts until he or she dies. We don't have a cure for it, although, as is true with cancer, there are frequently extravagant claims made for treatments which will supposedly restore the alcoholic's ability to drink without problems.

It's also a *progressive* disease, which means that instead of getting better as time passes, it seems to get worse. Quite a bit of personal experience on the part of alcoholics supports this observation. Time after time, alcoholics have attempted to rid themselves of alcoholism by changing their environments, jobs, and marriages, in the belief that the resulting reduction in stress would remedy their drinking. Instead, their alcoholism grew worse. Though there are extended periods of time in the lives of many alcoholics when they are able to drink without obvious problems, the general trend is towards more severe difficulties. This occurs even in cases where the alcoholic maintains abstinence for long periods between drinking episodes—each bout still seems to be more painful than the last.

Third, and most importantly, alcoholism is a *potentially fatal* disease, a fact which shouldn't require much elaboration. It can kill you directly through cirrhosis or some other disorder, or it can kill you indirectly, through traffic accidents, accidental overdose in combination with other drugs, and the like. If you combine all the direct and indirect deaths from alcoholism, it's our number-one killer among diseases.

What Are the Symptoms?

There are lots of symptoms for this disease. Some are primary and some are secondary, meaning they're the result of the primary symptoms.

The three common primary symptoms of alcoholism are *tolerance, physical dependence,* and *organ changes*.

Tolerance is the ability to drink without becoming intoxicated. It's something that occurs in almost every addictive disease, but is often confused with the popular term *capacity*. We tend to admire people who have a capacity for alcohol in our society, particularly if they're male; it's supposed to be a sign of character strength to be able to drink a lot without showing the effects. Additionally, having a tolerance is a social advantage because you don't have to monitor how much you consume as closely as someone who's worried about getting drunk and looking foolish.

Unfortunately, having a tolerance for alcohol often indicates the presence of alcoholism, or the eventual likelihood of contracting the disease. Tolerance represents not strength of will but physical adaptation to the intoxicating properties of alcohol. Although normally a large man will be able to hold more liquor than a small man, the development of high tolerance throws this off completely. A tolerant alcoholic who weighs no more than 120 pounds soaking wet can often drink a linebacker under the table —and then drive him home.

Not everyone who has a tolerance for alcohol becomes an alcoholic, but just about every alcoholic shows an abnormal tolerance for the drug. It changes over the course of the disease—often starting out relatively close to normal limits, ascending either rapidly or slowly depending on the individual, leveling off for a number of years, and then dropping—but it's always abnormal. In many cases, it's dramatically abnormal from the start; there are reliable accounts of alcoholics who were able to consume, without obvious intoxication, massive amounts of alcohol upon their first contact with it.

Ironically, the "advantage" of tolerance is that it enables the alcoholic to hide, from himself and others, the extent of his drinking after the appearance of the second primary symptom, physical dependence.

Dependence involves withdrawal symptoms. These come in stages: the first are mild, usually centering around anxiety, insomnia, nausea after eating. The intermediate ones are more disturbing: tremors, anxiety attacks, vomiting, diarrhea. The late ones are still more incapacitating, and may include convulsions and hallucinations.

Physical dependence is difficult to explain. It was once popularly believed that you were required to drink a great deal of alcohol over an extended period to become physically dependent, but there is increasing evidence that many alcoholics develop withdrawal symptoms early in their drinking career, before extensive drinking has occurred. One thing has become clear: it's this dependence, and not any situational or psychological stress, which motivates the bulk of alcoholic drinking. Once withdrawal symptoms begin, it's only a matter of time before the alcoholic discovers that more alcohol will eliminate, or at least alleviate, them. When the disease has reached the point where he drinks continually for extended periods, then his only real motivation for drinking, no matter what excuse he makes, is simply that the last drink has worn off.

The third primary symptom involves changes in the body's organs, which means that alcohol has done measurable damage to the body. This could be in the form of an enlarged liver, pancreatitis, kidney disorders, neuropathy, myopathy, and the whole range of alcohol-related health problems. Alcohol stands alone as a toxin among popular social drugs; it's certainly the most debilitating. More feared drugs such as heroin and marijuana are less dangerous. Physical damage, depending on its extent, plays a key role in alcoholic behavior, and in the progression of the illness itself. More on that later. For a summary of the stages of alcoholism, see the box on page 252.

When tolerance and physical dependence are firmly established, the effects on behavior are remarkable. The best way to illustrate this is by comparing the behavior of the alcoholic with that of the nonalcoholic when each is drinking.

Take a look at the following chart, which illustrates the effect of increases in blood-alcohol level (B.A.L.) on behavior. Be aware as you read that the B.A.L. isn't the same as the *amount* one drinks; it represents the percentage of alcohol in the bloodstream at a given time, so that people who are different sizes would have to drink different amounts to raise the B.A.L. to the same level. Nonetheless, a B.A.L. of .10 should have about the same effect on the behavior of any individual. And the effects of alcohol, unlike some other drugs, are directly related to this B.A.L.—the higher it rises, the more dramatic the result.

Now for the chart: the letters *LD* indicate lethal dose, which is measured on a scale of 1 to 100.

B.A.L.	BEHAVIORAL EFFECTS
.05	Diminished alertness, impaired judgment.
.10	Slowed reaction time and impaired motor function; this is legal intoxication in many states.

.15   Increasingly impaired motor responses.
.20   Obvious intoxication.
.25   Staggering; grossly impaired motor skills; "smashed."
.30   Stupor; inability to communicate or comprehend one's surroundings.
.35   Surgical anesthesia; about LD 1 (the minimal level at which death can occur through overdose).
.40   About LD 50.
.60   LD 100.

As you can see, the minimum lethal dose is around .30, and by .40, many people are in danger of death by overdose. Of course, very few people actually do overdose, because they simply pass out before the B.A.L. gets to these levels.

Anyone who's worked with alcoholics and had access to a B.A.L. meter will immediately notice that this chart simply doesn't hold true for most alcoholics. They don't behave in these ways at these B.A.L.s. If this is truly a representation of normal effects of elevated B.A.L. on behavior, then alcoholics are clearly abnormal.

Let's consider a man (we'll call him Alfred) who's been consuming around a fifth of vodka daily for six months to a year in what we call a maintenance pattern. He'll have to have an abnormal tolerance to alcohol, since a normal person would find it impossible to feed, clothe, and house himself while under the continual influence of this much alcohol.

He'll also have withdrawal symptoms which will force him to maintain a certain B.A.L. to avoid getting sick. He'll go into withdrawal as his B.A.L. approaches low levels, and come out of withdrawal (become normal, as he'll describe it), as his B.A.L. rises. A few drinks will therefore make him "well," just as the lack of alcohol makes him "sick."

With this in mind, let's make another chart, but one which describes *Alfred's* behavior at various B.A.L.s.

B.A.L.   BEHAVIOR EFFECTS ON AN ALCOHOLIC
.00   Severe withdrawal symptoms, including tremors, vomit-

ing, anxiety; possibility of seizure.

.05	Continued severe withdrawal.
.10	Some relief of symptoms; still obvious discomfort.
.15	Considerably better state of feelings; entering "normal" range. Dramatic reduction in tremor and gastric distress.
.20	"Normal" range; appetite begins to return, tremors not evident.
.25	State of being "comfortable."
.30	Upper limits of tolerance.
.35	Obvious signs of sedation, intoxication.
.40	"Drunk" state.
.50	State where he passes out from alcohol's effects.

Notice the disparity between the effect of alcohol on Alfred's behavior and that of the same drug, in the same concentrations, on the behavior of the normal individual in the first example. Clearly, Alfred is in another world altogether. His body sends him profoundly different cues about how and when to drink. Instead of improving in performance and judgment as his B.A.L. nears zero, Alfred gets worse, because withdrawal interrupts. Instead of weaving down the sidewalk on his way home from the corner bar at .15, Alfred is just beginning to feel like himself again. Rather than collapsing in a heap at .25, Alfred is walking quite nicely without assistance. And instead of falling unconscious before he reaches .30, this man is just beginning to show signs of intoxication, and probably feels like getting into a little trouble. It may be quite impossible to overdose him on alcohol alone.

All of us depend on cues given us by our own bodies to indicate when we should eat, sleep, drink, and the like; we sometimes choose to ignore these cues to a certain extent, such as when we diet or decide to stay up all night at a party, but for the most part, we obey them. Nor is Alfred, contrary to popular belief, ignoring the signals of his body when he drinks; in fact he's *following* them. His body directs his drinking. It punishes him when he doesn't drink a certain amount, and it rewards him when he does. Sure, Alfred's body instructs him not to overdrink, but only long after a normal body would have sent the same message. It even more dramatically prevents him from drinking too little. At the common .10 of legal intoxication, Alfred suffers from the *lack* of alcohol.

Far from punishing his body with alcohol as part of some bizarre need for masochism, Alfred is simply following directions given in the form of his own physiological response to the drug.

His body has adapted to alcohol, to enable him to function under its influence; paradoxically, he has become quite unable to function without it. He is now a physically abnormal person, in terms of his body's response to alcohol, and it is this which causes him to behave differently from a nonalcoholic.

Sometimes we hear objections, mostly from humanistic psychologists, about our use of the word "abnormal," but we apply no psychological meaning whatsoever. On the contrary, we believe that the personalities of alcoholics usually fall well within the "normal" range. It's a physical abnormality, in response to alcohol, which accounts for the alcoholic's legendary difficulties with the drug.

Another characteristic of alcoholic drinking is *loss of control*. Here, changes in tolerance and dependence as the disease progresses cause the alcoholic to lose the ability to accurately predict his own drinking behavior. He sets out to drink in one fashion; he ends up doing something quite different. Instead of stopping at two martinis—his New Year's resolution—he has somewhere nearer twenty. Instead of going without a drink for a week (to prove to his family he doesn't have a problem), he finds himself overwhelmed with craving and sneaking vodka in his study. There are literally thousands of stories about the symptoms of loss of control in AA and in all the literature about the disease.

Most people, though, are alcoholic for a fairly long time before they show many signs of loss of control. If they're able to arrange their lives in a certain fashion, they can continue drinking without obvious problems until they die—and many do exactly that.

By the same token, there are a considerable number who exhibit signs of loss of control from the onset of drinking. These alcoholics are the most spectacular in terms of behavior.

Another symptom of alcoholism is the *blackout*. That's a period of time which occurred while the alcoholic was drinking that he's unable to recall when sober. Blackouts are fairly definitive indicators of alcoholism, yet many alcoholics won't have experienced them—or if they have, simply won't be able to remember them. One of the most common—and silliest—answers to the question "Have you ever had a blackout?" is "I don't remember."

Last but not least among the common symptoms of alcoholism are the numerous *life problems* it generates. In some approaches, these are the primary diagnostic criteria. Alcoholic drinking so profoundly affects everything the individual does, thinks, or feels, that it quite frequently controls the lives of its victims more thoroughly than any dictator could. Alcoholics commonly lose jobs, families, marriages, and lives through the effects of their drinking. Once again, though, we should make it clear that the disease is often long established before these overt problems appear. They are a result of its progression.

Throughout their lives, alcoholics exhibit behavior which reflects the biological changes that occur during the disease process. Here are some examples of how alcohol influences the alcoholic's behavior:

• *Gulping and sneaking drinks*. This indicates drinking governed by increasingly severe withdrawal symptoms. Gulping raises one's B.A.L. faster, which is desirable if you're seeking to alleviate withdrawal. Sneaking drinks reflects the dilemma of someone who feels the need to drink regularly, yet lives in an environment where others don't approve. Sometimes alcoholics themselves disapprove of drinking—we once knew a woman who hid bottles all over her house, despite the fact she lived alone.

• *Broken promises and resolutions about drinking*. Of course they fail, if they contradict the realities of alcoholic drinking. If you promise to cut down when your B.A.L. is elevated, it will be hard to keep your promise when it approaches zero. If you're beginning to experience symptoms of alcoholic loss of control, it will be hard even to predict the results of your own drinking, let alone control yourself through will power.

• *Grandiose or aggressive behavior.* Again, this is a result of alcoholic loss of control; nevertheless, you can't reliably diagnose alcoholism from this behavior alone because millions of people become grandiose or aggressive due to the influence of alcohol, and most aren't alcoholic. Many alcoholics, on the other hand, drink addictively for a lifetime without showing these traits. Only when the individual drinks beyond his tolerance—thus leaving himself open for what we call drunkenness—do we see this kind of behavior.

• *Irritability, sleeplessness, neglect of food.* Withdrawal symptoms, all three. They are not the result of suppressed hostility, underlying depression, or lack of concern for one's health, to which all have at one time or another been attributed.

• *Failed efforts at control.* Especially as the disease progresses into later stages. What is it that the alcoholic tries to control? Usually, his withdrawal-related craving for a drink. No wonder he's so often unsuccessful. What he's fighting, though he probably doesn't know it, is not temptation, but rather the needs of his own body. We accept the impossibility of controlling a disorder like diabetes, but we have trouble accepting it with alcoholic drinking.

• *Fluctuating moods and emotions.* It never ceases to amaze us how often this is attributed to underlying psychological problems. Alcohol itself is a powerful depressant, and alcohol withdrawal is a potent irritant. The fluctuation between sedation and irritation on a daily (or sometimes hourly) basis is certainly enough to account for mood swings in an alcoholic— and don't forget, this up-and-down elevator often continues for a lifetime. Moods and emotions are as much the victims of alcohol as other brain processes are, such as memory and judgment. The emotions, remember, aren't centered in the gut, but in an area of the brain (the limbic system) which is richly exposed not only to the actions of alcohol, but to almost any drug.

• *Obsessive drinking.* An alcoholic in the grip of withdrawal. How could he not be obsessed with drinking? This behavior, along with the onset of what are commonly called "lengthy binges," simply means that the disease is growing worse. The alcoholic himself, however, generally regards this as the result of some particular current stress, which he then can claim causes him to drink in this fashion.

Simply put, the Disease model links behavior with physiology in a manner illustrated in the following diagram.

Visible and Invisible Changes As Alcoholism Progresses

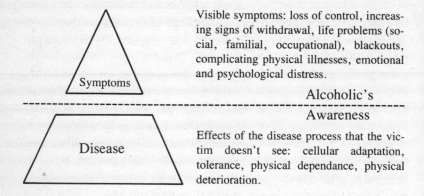

Symptoms

Visible symptoms: loss of control, increasing signs of withdrawal, life problems (social, familial, occupational), blackouts, complicating physical illnesses, emotional and psychological distress.

Alcoholic's

Awareness

Disease

Effects of the disease process that the victim doesn't see: cellular adaptation, tolerance, physical dependance, physical deterioration.

Alcoholic behavior, then, is simply what *shows* of alcoholism. What *causes* alcoholic behavior is an underlying disease with primary and secondary symptoms. The alcoholic's actions, even if seemingly mysterious, can be understood by learning how the disease works and what happens during the course of alcoholic drinking. When the alcoholic's family begins to understand this, they often lose a great deal of their confusion and resentment. When the alcoholic himself begins to understand it, and to recognize the influence of the disease on his own actions, it becomes a powerful motivation for recovery.

What Causes the Disease?

Ordinarily, we could discuss what causes alcoholism without preamble, but the vast mythology which surrounds this issue compels us to discuss several factors which are popularly supposed to cause alcoholism, but which, as far as we're concerned, don't.

First and foremost, we don't believe that alcoholism is the result of irresponsible use of alcohol. Though the disease produces much behavior which resembles irresponsible drinking, the true cause is the presence of the illness, and not any personal irresponsibility on the part of the alcoholic.

The fact is, there are almost as many irresponsible drinkers —who don't hold themselves accountable for monitoring their drinking when they plan to be driving, for instance—as there are responsible drinkers. Only a small percentage of these irresponsible drinkers suffer from alcoholism. On the other hand, many alcoholics, especially the type we call maintenance drinkers, monitor their drinking much more closely than any nonalcoholic does. We'd do better to assume that alcoholics come from both categories; some are irresponsible by nature, and others are not. The symptoms of the disease—which, after all, are how we determine who has it—make no mention of personal responsibility. That is simply a remnant of the moral models.

The second major misconception has to do with the relationship between alcoholism and stress. Again, as far as we can tell, stress—in this age, a sort of generic term for tension and anxiety—does not by itself cause alcoholism. It is, however, a wonderful excuse for drinking, which is how it gets bound so tightly into most people's concepts about alcoholism. We haven't seen persuasive evidence that alcoholics suffer from more stress, *before* the onset of the disease, than do nonalcoholics. Let's face it, everyone experiences stress—a great number of us use alcohol to treat it, yet only a small percentage develop any of the symptoms of alcoholism. And of course, though many alcoholics do link their drinking to what they regard as stressful situations, many others don't. It clearly isn't a requirement that you be under any kind of stress to become alcoholic.

Once the disease has progressed to a certain point, however, the alcoholic is bound to experience more stress than the non-alcoholic. He is most likely experiencing withdrawal symptoms, which tend to make normal anxiety and nervous tension seem pale in comparison, and he may well have a number of alcohol-related problems at home, at work, or with the law. Though the alcoholic almost invariably comes to the conclusion that his life is somehow more stressful than anyone else's, the fact remains that the biggest single thing any alcoholic can do to reduce the amount of stress in his life is to simply stop drinking, and stay stopped. Even if he believes, as some do, that he'll go absolutely nuts without the tranquilizing effects of alcohol, we have yet to see an alcoholic who wasn't healthier and happier without alcohol.

The third myth has to do with the role of that classic scapegoat, the unhappy childhood. Although many alcoholics did indeed have unhappy experiences as kids, that isn't the source of their present difficulty with alcohol. An equal number of the patients in our practice report no particular dissatisfaction with the way they were raised. This misconception about the importance of one's upbringing in developing alcoholism led some clinicians into the wholly untenable position that alcoholism was really dozens of different illnesses, each reflecting some error in parental judgment or flaw in childhood environment. This of course fed right into the alcoholic's conviction that somehow his particular problems were entirely different from anyone else's, and therefore justified his predilection for drinking more than other people.

What does cause alcoholism? Basically, two factors: being *physiologically susceptible* to the disease, and *taxing that susceptibility with alcohol*.

Although many researchers agree that there is a definite susceptibility which exists in some individuals but not in others, they sometimes disagree over the nature of this susceptibility. Does it, for example, represent adaptations in the nervous system, metabolic processes, or both?

Some researchers relate it to deficiencies in endorphins, which are opiate-like substances in the body that enable it to lessen pain. When alcohol is introduced into this flawed endorphin system, its response is to adapt, through the development of an addictive process. Other researchers relate susceptibility to the development of tissue tolerance in the central nervous system, or to metabolic tolerance through changes in liver processes.

The focus, then, isn't on the drug alone (as it was in the Dry Moral model), or on the personality of the drug user (as in the Psychoanalytic model), but on the *relationship between the agent* (alcohol) *and the biological system* (the alcoholic).

It follows, then, that whatever the alcoholic's original motives for his consumption of alcohol, if he taxes his susceptibility beyond its limits, he risks contracting the disease. What these limits are, of course, no one knows; alcoholics invariably fail to suspect that they, of all people, might develop alcoholism.

Because of space limitations, we'll end our discussion of the possible causes of alcoholism here, and refer you to our suggested reading list at the back of this book for further exploration.

Who Gets It?

The question of who becomes an alcoholic is the area where the Disease model's radical separation from other models becomes most apparent.

This is because the least important issue in the Disease model—determining who develops alcoholism—happens to be the most important issue in the Psychoanalytic approach.

And that is: the question of *why* people drink.

First of all, we've made it clear that once the addictive pattern is established, the reason the alcoholic drinks is because his body instructs him to—and this instruction becomes increasingly severe as the disease progresses.

But more importantly, we believe that the reasons the alcoholic started drinking—long before he couldn't stop himself—are exactly the same as the reasons every nonalcoholic drinks.

Which throws a slightly wet towel in the face of the addictive-personality theory.

It was assumed for years that alcoholics were different from nonalcoholics because they drank for "relief." This suggested that nonalcoholics somehow drank for reasons other than relief.

Which of course is ridiculous. Aside from professional wine-tasters, just about everybody who ever drank alcohol frequently did so to obtain relief from something or other. It doesn't matter what—relief from worry about bills, a hard day at the office, or to calm one's beating heart enough to call someone up for a date. These all constitute forms of mild stress which drinkers regularly treat with alcohol. In the early stages of the illness, where most of the important physiological adaptations begin and the disease itself is truly established, the alcoholic drinks for the same reason everyone else does: to relax, to be sociable, to feel good.

Where the alcoholic is different from the nonalcoholic is in his *response* to alcohol. Though we don't yet have a reliable method for measuring susceptibility to alcoholism in an individual, we do know that alcoholism very definitely runs in families. That doesn't mean that alcoholic parents teach their children to drink; instead, there seems to be a genetic susceptibility to alcoholism. If a child has an alcoholic biological parent, even if the child is orphaned and raised by nonalcoholic foster parents, that child's chances of alcoholism rise dramatically.

Perhaps the basic assumption of the Moral and Analytic models—that the same responses occur in the bodies of any two people who drink the same amount of alcohol—is simply incorrect. If so, then what we call alcoholism may stem from basic physiological differences between individuals.

If this is so, it would explain differences between rates of alcoholism in various racial populations. American Indians, for example, who have had little time to build up resistance to alcoholism, would be regarded as profoundly susceptible, while Orientals would have a much lower degree of susceptibility. It would be reasonable to assume that if you moved either group to an area where they interbred with each other, the rate of alcoholism over the next generations would probably fall somewhere between the two groups.

There's some debate over the role of social environment in the development of alcoholism. Our comment would be that an environment which was very conducive to drinking would be conducive to alcoholism only if the population was susceptible. Some cultures actually encourage daily drinking throughout life, and yet don't have high rates of alcoholism. Still other cultures censure drinking and drunkenness severely, and yet do have high rates of alcoholism. It's certainly not uncommon to find alcoholics who were raised in antidrinking environments; theorists have traditionally attributed this to a reaction to moral strictures against drinking. The problem with this idea is that there exists an even greater number of alcoholics who were raised in environments which were permissive towards alcohol use. What accounts for alcoholism in these instances? *Lack* of guilt?

It's important to remember, of course, that not all children of alcoholics become alcoholic themselves. It isn't unusual to find a family where only one of five offspring is alcoholic, just as it isn't surprising to encounter a family where all five children may be alcoholic. We could say, however, that all children of alcoholics have a statistically greater chance of developing the illness than children of nonalcoholics. They are more susceptible.

Treatment and Recovery

Once the disease has been defined—that is, once you've established clear criteria for identifying it, and removed it from the vague arena of "problems with alcohol"—an amazing thing happens: the disease itself shows how victims can be treated.

It's as though someone takes us by the hand and explains what alcoholics can do and what they can't.

For example, it's easy to see that if the cellular adaptations that result in alcoholism spring from an inherited susceptibility, then the disease is clearly not self-inflicted. Therefore, it isn't helpful for the alcoholic to spend years wondering why he did this to himself, because he didn't. His offense was the same as that of hundreds of millions of other people: he chose to drink alcohol.

It's also easy to imagine that if the key physiological adaptations took place before he drank "like an alcoholic," then they will still be there after he stops drinking. And since the first characteristic of the disease is its progressive nature, the same adaptations will probably produce even more severe symptoms if alcohol is reintroduced into the body. And since the illness is also chronic, there's no reason to suppose that it disappears, even after many years of abstinence from alcohol and superficial good health.

Thus, the treatment becomes apparent: total abstinence from all alcohol, permanently. The motivation for this dramatic step is the third characteristic of the illness: it's potentially fatal. As a lecturer once said so eloquently, "Autopsies seldom benefit those upon whom they are performed." One can go only so far to test whether or not alcoholism can kill a specific person. Alcoholics, despite the fact that their disease often shows itself very slowly, don't have forever to decide to do something about treating it. For each alcoholic (and everyone knows at least one) who drinks until he's eighty, there's another who doesn't make it to thirty-five. The alcoholic who's thinking about quitting drinking "some day" ought to ask himself: How lucky am I? How many chances am I likely to get? How many accidents can I afford? When is my last chance going to come?

And of course the disease sets one last important boundary on both alcoholic and helper: there isn't any reliable cure. Therefore, no amount of wonderful therapeutic technique, profound insight, or personal will power is going to remove alcoholism from the alcoholic. Sometimes it seems to us that it's harder for the helper to accept that than it is for the sick alcoholic (who always suspected it, anyway).

Nonetheless, alcoholism is an eminently treatable disease within these boundaries. In developing our methods, and in writing this book, we've tried to work within them, and we think that's why our methods are successful. We don't try to change the disease, and we don't try to find the legendary easier, softer way around it. Neither do we make moral judgments about its victims or what they have to do to recover.

But neither do we forget that effective counseling with chronic-disease patients has to fit not only the patient but also the illness. Anyone can help sick people feel better with sympathy, support, friendship, and kindness—but what can we do about what is making them sick in the first place?

Now that we've looked briefly at how the disease works, let's see if we can learn to recognize it in the haystack of the alcoholic's experience.

4

How Alcoholics Drink

J UST ABOUT EVERY ALCOHOLIC WE'VE MET HAS GONE
through a phase wherein he has examined his personal experience for signs of alcoholism, only to decide on the basis of this study that he doesn't have the disease.

He reaches this conclusion by discovering that there exist certain symptoms of alcoholism which he has not yet experienced.

For example, he might say to himself, "I read an article which claimed that alcoholics are people who get drunk every day. I, on the other hand, abstained for three whole days last week. Therefore, I can't be an alcoholic."

Or he may use this train of logic: "My father was an alcoholic, and whenever he had one drink, he couldn't stop himself until he passed out. I, however, never pass out, no matter how much I drink. So I'm obviously not alcoholic."

Thus reassured, he can resume drinking with a clear conscience. Even if drinking causes problems with his wife or job or health, he remains absolutely sure that it isn't alcoholic drinking.

And as he continues drinking, and continues to develop

symptoms of alcoholism, he always seems to stumble across one symptom that he still doesn't have. That absent symptom then becomes the focus of attention. "I'm not that bad yet," he thinks. "At least *that* hasn't happened."

We call this process *comparing out,* and it is the number-one all-time favorite alcoholic pastime, next to drinking. As long as there's a symptom or two the alcoholic doesn't have, he can insist he doesn't have the disease.

This is utterly harmless if he's right, and completely destructive if he's not—because this disease, which he's convinced he doesn't have, is inevitably going to get worse.

One of the great modern examples of real-life theater of the absurd can be found during a drinking alcoholic's usual visit to his physician.

"Doctor," the alcoholic says, trembling, "give it to me straight. I'm fine, aren't I?"

"Well, Mr. Smith, I wouldn't exactly say you were fine," the doctor responds. "You've got some pretty high results on your liver studies, which, uh, indicate you may be hitting the sauce a bit harder than you should."

"Wait a minute," the alcoholic responds, getting visibly nervous and upset, "you're not saying I've got liver cirrhosis, are you?"

"No, no, of course not," the doctor explains. "I'm just saying that you are overworking your liver to the point where if you don't quit soon, you might develop liver cirrhosis."

"Oh," the alcoholic says, "I *might* get it. Well, rest assured, Doctor, I'll watch it like a hawk. I guess I have been hitting the drinks harder than I should the last couple of weeks."

When this same man gets home, his wife asks him how his physical went. "Great," he replies.

"Did the doctor mention anything about your drinking?"

"I knew you'd ask that," the husband complains. "Yes, he mentioned it. He says I don't have liver cirrhosis, and he did *not* tell me I had to quit drinking. So there."

This entire comparing out process is based on the erroneous assumption that in order to qualify for alcoholism, one must have *all* the symptoms of the illness. Nothing could be further from the truth. Since the disease is progressive, one should assume that the persistence of a few symptoms implies the eventual appearance of many other, more serious ones.

We might say to the alcoholic: "Even if it isn't that bad yet, we can guarantee you it will get worse."

Of course, the fuel behind this comparing out process is the patient's natural resistance to diagnosis of this illness. The power of this resistance should never be underestimated.

For example, some months back we admitted to a hospital a patient who, in addition to his drinking, suffered from chronic obstructive lung disease. He insisted he couldn't be an alcoholic because he had driven a taxi for the past twenty years, and no alcoholic could have done that. We didn't get to discuss this, however, because his lung disease was so serious that he went into respiratory arrest and had to be transferred to the intensive care unit.

At one point during this crisis, he briefly regained his faculties and discovered that he was hooked up to an assortment of tubes, needles, and monitors. Seeing a nurse, he signaled for pen and paper, and soon was writing feverishly. He handed the pad back to the waiting RN.

Rather than asking questions such as "Where am I?" "What happened?" or "Am I going to die?" he had written: "Don't pay any attention to that doctor. I am *not* an alcoholic."

Having narrowly avoided death for the moment, his first priority was to convince a total stranger that he didn't need detox.

The opposite of comparing out, and the way out of this pit of self-delusion, is what we call *comparing in*.

Instead of concentrating on symptoms he doesn't have, the alcoholic begins to take note of the ones he does have.

In doing this, he will almost invariably come to the conclusion that he does have the illness. And his attitude towards treatment will change dramatically.

For example, a doctor might, on the day of admission, ask the patient if he believes he's an alcoholic, and get the following response.

"Well, I don't honestly see how I could be. I've had the same job for twenty years, been married to the same woman, and have three grown kids who are doing fine. I've never been arrested for drunk driving or anything. How could I have done all that if I were an alcoholic?"

Two weeks later, that same patient answers the doctor's question differently: "I could have sworn I wasn't an alcoholic, but now I'm beginning to think I may be. My wife is still with me, but it seems she's been going to Al-Anon for over a year. My kids say they won't bring the grandkids over on Sunday because they're afraid I'll be drunk. My family also claims they nearly die of fright every time I set foot in a car after five in the evening. There's *something* wrong with my drinking. I know that."

The key to this conversion is education. The alcoholic's first task is to learn something about how alcoholics drink. He can then recognize that his drinking qualifies as alcoholic drinking, even if it's not exactly like someone else's.

Once he accepts this, he'll have launched his own ship toward recovery. His new understanding will have two beneficial results: it will effectively ruin drinking for him, and it will motivate him to continue learning more about the disease.

No longer will he be able to kid himself that he suffers from "episodic alcohol abuse," or "occasional problem drinking," or "periodic stress-related, heavy, social, problem overdrinking," or whatever. Any further use of alcohol will have to be seen as part of the sickness, and a definite sign that he is not getting well. Liver cirrhosis will become a fixture in his dreams; AA will seem less boring and more informative.

In other words, this comparing in process is the difference between a patient who works to recover and one who sits around waiting for the next excuse to get drunk.

If a counselor wants his patients to identify their drinking as alcoholic, he'll have to learn to identify it as such himself.

Despite the fact that they have the same disease, not all alcoholics drink alike. They differ in amount consumed, rate of consumption, duration of drinking episodes, and behavior while under the influence. It's also inevitable that their drinking practices will have changed over the years, and their drinking will reflect whatever stage of the disease they are currently in.

Most alcoholics believe that their drinking grows to fit the stresses and strains of their everyday lives. But in point of fact, the typical alcoholic's lifestyle grows to fit his drinking. It protects, nurtures, and sustains the disease process.

In this chapter, we'll review the two patterns of alcoholic drinking. These patterns are intended to serve as general guidelines in understanding the experience of alcoholism but, as no two alcoholics will have precisely the same experience, these patterns will fit no single alcoholic exactly.

Maintenance Drinking

The maintenance pattern develops as a response to increasingly severe withdrawal symptoms.

Remember that an alcoholic typically has an exaggerated tolerance for alcohol: he can drink larger than normal amounts without becoming intoxicated. Somewhere during the course of the illness, he also begins to experience alcohol withdrawal. At first these symptoms are mild: anxiety, irritability, insomnia, nausea after eating. The drinker doesn't pay any particular attention to them since they seem to go away by themselves.

As the disease progresses, however, withdrawal becomes more severe, lasts longer, and is considerably more difficult to ignore. It begins to interfere with the alcoholic's lifestyle, making it harder for him to function in the usual way.

It's at this point that the alcoholic often makes a discovery: a little alcohol is the perfect medicine for what ails him. One person might find that a Bloody Mary is the ideal Sunday morning pick-me-up. Another will wake out of a sound sleep several nights in a row only to discover that a glass of wine will put her back to sleep in style. And someone else will find that a couple of beers makes it possible to hold onto breakfast.

And as this happens, the drinker's motive for using alcohol

changes from wanting to get high to wanting to treat the symptoms of withdrawal. Alcohol "mutates" from recreational to medicinal drug.

Of course, if he's careful not to drink too much at one time, the alcoholic's elevated tolerance will protect him from the signs of drunkenness. He won't look or act drunk, and certainly will take care not to *smell* of alcohol. He thinks, "If it isn't hurting anyone and makes me feel better, why shouldn't I drink?"

And like everyone else, alcoholics have "rules" about drinking. It might not be okay in one alcoholic's eyes to drink before noon, or during working hours, or in bars, or at home where the family can see him. If he experiences a real craving for alcohol during these forbidden periods, he'll most likely to try to white-knuckle it until it's once again acceptable to have a drink. He thus becomes a clock-watcher, constantly in a state of readiness for the next date with a bottle. Even while gulping one drink, he's beginning to plan how to get the next one.

As withdrawal becomes more severe, and physiological craving more pronounced, these interim periods between drinks will become quite painful. He'll be irritable, anxious, quick to anger, given to fits of depression. On what does he blame this almost continual state of emotional discomfort?

On stress. But when the alcoholic uses that term, he's not referring to the cycle of craving and withdrawal. He is either completely unaware of this physical process, or so minimizes it that he would find it impossible to believe that drinking had anything to do with the way he feels. He dwells instead on the stress caused by his job, family, or congenitally nervous disposition. Alcohol must remain the medicine in his eyes.

When the pain is too great, he begins to add small doses of alcohol to medicate it. He then moves naturally into the later phase of the maintenance pattern.

A working definition of maintenance drinking: using alcohol in such a fashion as to *maintain,* on an ongoing basis, a blood-alcohol level somewhere between the point where withdrawal begins and the upper limit of one's tolerance for the drug. In simpler terms, the practice of drinking so that one is seldom either completely drunk or completely sober.

As his B.A.L. descends, the drinker will experience a spontaneous desire for alcohol. When the B.A.L. drops too low, withdrawal will begin: he'll wake up in the middle of the night, nervous, perhaps with a film of sweat on his body, or discover during daylight hours that his hands shake when he tries to write a check.

Maintenance Drinking

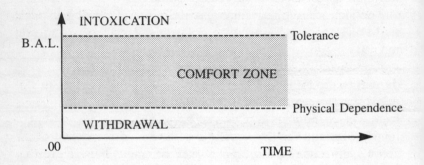

This shows an alcoholic in the middle stage, when the two dotted lines have not yet begun to approach each other. The time period here could be weeks or months, depending on the individual.

The area between the boundaries of intoxication and withdrawal is called the *comfort zone,* because that's where the alcoholic is comfortable.

If the alcoholic is able to maintain this pattern for a considerable length of time, we say he's a maintenance drinker. Not every alcoholic can do it; some aren't able to exert this degree of control over their consumption. More frequently, alcoholics drink in the maintenance pattern for a number of years, and then develop symptoms of loss of control.

The life of the maintenance drinker will differ markedly from that of an alcoholic who more obviously loses control over alcohol. This isn't to say that maintenance drinkers don't lose control—they most certainly do—but in comparison to other alcoholics, they're paragons of stability. In a way, this stability prevents them from understanding that they have the disease, and thereby interferes with chances of recovery.

For example, these drinkers experience fewer alcohol-related life problems as a result of their drinking. They tend to keep their jobs; they usually manage to hold their families together; they are routinely very ordered in their habits and may pride themselves on the discipline they show in the way they drink. Some of them measure, time, monitor, and otherwise control their use of alcohol for years on end.

Which means that neither counselor nor alcoholic can point to the usual array of destructive problems which should motivate recovery.

Secondly, the families of maintenance drinkers respond very differently to the presence of alcoholism than do the families of drinkers who lose all vestiges of control. The families of maintenance drinkers don't experience the same disruption of family life, and they're usually less aware of the extent of alcohol's influence on the drinker and on themselves. Nevertheless, they have adapted to alcoholism, and often in very profound ways.

A third difference is that maintenance drinkers, despite the lack of obvious problems, may experience even more physical damage than do loss-of-control drinkers. This may be due to the direct and indirect effects of exposure to acetaldehyde for long periods. (Acetaldehyde, the major byproduct of alcohol metabolism, is as toxic as alcohol itself.)

And of course, maintenance drinkers are even better defended than their more troubled brethren when it comes to seeing the need for treatment. They're the undisputed heavyweight champs at comparing out.

Here are some examples of how these alcoholics avoid recognizing alcoholism.

• *"I can function."* Here is the misconception that alcoholics are people who can't function. The definition of functioning, however, changes considerably as the alcoholic gets older, and the disease gets worse. At age forty, it means that he got his scheduled promotion despite the drinking. At age fifty, it might mean he hasn't gotten fired yet. At age sixty, it may mean that he can make it to the bathroom by himself.

• *"My drinking doesn't bother anyone."* This is based usually on the misconception that if no one's saying anything, that must mean they approve. In truth, the family has probably adapted to the drinking, and others may not be allowed to know its extent.

• *"I can stop after one or two."* Sure, if they're not too far apart, and if the next one or two are available in a few hours.

Curiously—because maintenance drinkers so often exclude themselves from the ranks of problem drinkers—this pattern bears a striking resemblance to heroin addiction. Like the heroin addict, a maintenance alcoholic seldom gets high from the drug, but is motivated to continue using it by the increasing severity of withdrawal.

Maintenance drinking is also the pattern of many in that most notorious of American alcoholic groups, skid row winos. With his often diminished tolerance for the drug, a wino may maintain his comfort zone on a relatively small amount of wine sipped throughout the day.

On the other hand, if reports are to be believed, some of the most stellar public careers have been built on a foundation of maintenance drinking. For some people, it seems, it's entirely possible to drink one's way through large portions of life without encountering any insurmountable difficulties, as long as one doesn't experience any sudden changes in tolerance or withdrawal.

And as long as the alcoholic doesn't make any foolish attempt to stop.

Of course, in most cases the maintenance pattern eventually breaks down because of changes in tolerance and withdrawal. We'll examine that process when we discuss how maintenance drinkers lose control, in the next section. But first, let's take a look at what happens when this maintenance pattern is allowed to continue for most of an alcoholic's life without interruption. In this event, a strange thing may occur: the alcoholic's body may become so dependent on alcohol that it literally collapses without it.

Bill was a postman who claimed to have been able to drink "successfully" in a maintenance fashion for thirty years. His average consumption, he said, was a bit under a fifth of whiskey daily. He denied any problems related to his drinking in all that time, and his family agreed with that assessment, describing his drinking as "heavy, but no problem for us, and he's a good family man."

Bill's postal route for many years ran through a section of the city which was known as a bar district. As the regular postman, he became friends with most of the bartenders in these establishments, and would usually have a friendly drink with them when he arrived with the mail. In fact, many of the bartenders would have Bill's drink waiting for him when he got there. "By the time I finished the route," he related, "I'd hate to think how many I'd put away."

Of course, he continued drinking when he got home from work, and normally started himself off with a few beers before he reported in the morning. We asked him how he managed to conceal this from his supervisors for so long, since there must have been some days when he overdrank his tolerance, and looked or acted a little drunk. "Maybe a few times," he responded, "but at that time, our office was very busy, and as long as you didn't fall asleep at your bench or fall off it onto the floor so they had to stop and pick you up, they wouldn't sent you home. The boss would just figure you had a bad night, or a personal problem, or something."

Bill eventually retired at age fifty-five and discovered that without the pressure to perform his job he quickly increased his drinking—to somewhere over a quart daily. One day, he was driving along a city street and was pulled over by a cop for driving too slowly. When the officer got a whiff of his breath, he tested Bill's blood-alcohol level and found that it was around .40—or four times legal intoxication. The officer noted in his report that the driver, strangely, was able to walk a straight line and touch his nose with his finger.

Bill was sent before a judge who, seeing his blood-alcohol level, strongly recommended that he seek treatment for alcoholism. So Bill dutifully enrolled in a program, and on the night he was admitted, sat through an AA meeting, accepted a sleeping pill from the nurse on duty, and went to bed. He slept soundly through the night.

The next morning was Bill's first without alcohol in thirty years.

He couldn't get out of bed.

His muscles, in fact, were so weak that he couldn't stand at all, even with assistance. He was unable to muster the strength to elevate his hips enough to let the nurse slide the bedpan beneath him. He had trouble making his mouth work well enough to chew his food. He couldn't sit up; he just collapsed wherever he lay. He couldn't slide himself to a more comfortable position in the bed.

He knew who he was, but he didn't know where he was or why he was there. He could remember almost nothing, and constantly asked the same questions over and over. On the second day, he began to see little bugs crawling all over his body and the walls of the room, and immediately began demanding an exterminator.

Several weeks later, when he was walking and talking again, we asked Bill what he remembered of his first two weeks in the hospital. Answer: *nothing at all*.

It was as though Bill's body had forgotten how to function without alcohol. Any attempt to quit, therefore, was life-threatening. It seemed that he'd been saving up problems for years, only to experience all of them at once.

We ought to caution you that it's easy, when discussing this pattern in a detached fashion, to get the idea that maintenance drinkers consciously adopt this comfort zone existence. They don't. They simply respond, like the rest of us, to what they experience as the necessities of everyday life, and as the disease progresses, so does their response. As withdrawal worsens, drinking increases.

The maintenance drinker adapts to the strictures imposed by the illness. Does he understand the real meaning of what is happening to him? No. He knows, to put it simply, that his body rewards him for drinking, and punishes him for not drinking. Each time he responds to this, it reinforces the maintenance pattern.

Loss of Control

The second major pattern of drinking involves a progressive loss of control over one's use of alcohol.

This means that alcoholics experience increasing difficulty in accurately predicting the extent, severity, and outcome of their drinking, principally in three key areas: the *amount* consumed at any one sitting, *the time or place* chosen for drinking, and the *duration* of drinking episodes.

Since most of our social restrictions on drinking fall into these three areas, the alcoholic who is losing control is constantly running afoul of other people. This isn't, however, because he has an antisocial personality (society's usual verdict) or because society's rules are unreasonable (the alcoholic's lament), but rather because the disease is sabotaging his ability to drink like nonalcoholics.

And since the progression through loss of control into the realm of total powerlessness is so spectacular, these drinkers make great subject matter for books and movies like *Lost Weekend* and *Days of Wine and Roses*. These are the alcoholics of whom friends and neighbors say: "Why would such a nice person want to do all that to himself? Can't he see what is happening to him?"

And of course the answer to that is *no,* he really doesn't see very much of what happens to him, and even when he does come to realize his predicament, he has a hell of a time doing anything about it.

We seldom hear of a case where the alcoholic awakes one morning to discover, to his chagrin, that he has become totally powerless over alcohol. The onset of loss of control is usually gradual. Interspersed with episodes of uncontrolled or inappropriate drinking will be periods of apparently normal consumption. This serves to further confuse him.

Take this example of an alcoholic who plans to attend a wedding. As has been his custom, he "primes the pump" with a few stiff whiskies before making an appearance at the reception. This practice has, in the past, enabled him to appear quite relaxed as he limits himself to several innocuous glasses of champagne during the party itself. But something goes amiss; despite his intentions, he ends up consuming most of the liquor supply, and passes out by the punchbowl. The next day, he recalls little or nothing of his behavior, and has to suffer through his wife's blow-by-blow account.

Upset with himself, he wonders what might have caused such an unforgivable lapse in discipline. "I must be overtired," he decides. "Whatever the reason, I'm making damned sure it never happens again."

He redoubles the monitoring of his drinking and, as the weeks pass without a repeat incident, grows confident that the matter is well in hand.

This, of course, is false assurance. Somewhere along the line—be it days, weeks or months later—another such incident occurs. Once again, he goes back on his best behavior and once again, still later, relapses. As the months or years pass, the episodes of "safe" drinking become shorter and farther apart. The periods of loss of control grow more frequent, and each one seems to last longer.

What's causing this change in drinking pattern? Simply, the disease—the one the victim would swear he doesn't have—is getting worse.

For example, his tolerance may have changed. Recall that for the past however-many-years this same tolerance has pro-

Loss of Control

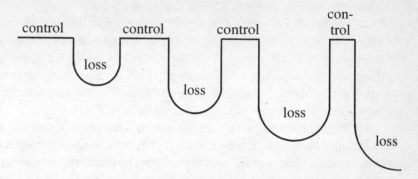

tected him from the obvious symptoms of drunkenness, and served as a kind of blanket to hide the extent of his drinking from others. Yet we know from observation that alcoholics often lose this tolerance as they grow older.

The Alcoholic's Decreasing Tolerance

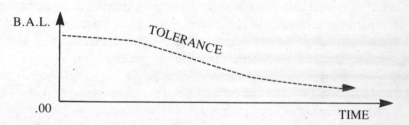

The line showing time could indicate years or even decades, depending on the alcoholic. The initial high tolerance drops as the disease advances.

What happens as this tolerance disappears? The alcoholic begins to experience problems. These may begin with the aforementioned episodes of obvious drunkenness, unplanned and unintended. They may include inappropriate behavior which causes great shame and a corresponding defensiveness whenever his drinking is discussed. He may find it difficult to perform simple daily activities. These are all signs that something is wrong with him and, by inference, with his drinking.

No one is more surprised by this turn of events than the alcoholic himself. He's accustomed to drinking without getting obviously intoxicated. He's worried about drawing attention to himself, which may even lead to a seemingly impossible choice: to continue drinking as he is accustomed, risking the censure of family and friends, or to quit and risk the pain of withdrawal and the loss of his favorite crutch.

Even if his tolerance remains intact, he may experience a change in the level at which withdrawal symptoms begin. As we have previously seen, withdrawal doesn't begin when the body is completely empty of alcohol, but at a point somewhere before that. As the illness progresses, the level at which withdrawal begins often rises, meaning that the alcoholic is compelled to drink *more* to allay the pain. His consumption may increase dramatically, and his drinking suddenly takes on an aspect of compulsiveness which wasn't there before. He now must rush to stave off the severe symptoms of mid-stage addiction—the stage when anxiety has become paralyzing fear, nervousness has turned into incapacitating tremors, and perspiration into the sheet-drenching night sweats. In mid-stage addiction the alcoholic often overdrinks his tolerance, again leading to episodes of drunkenness.

Note in the illustration how small the comfort zone becomes, and imagine how difficult it is for the mid-stage alcoholic to maintain a B.A.L. within it. In some cases, the level at which withdrawal begins becomes so high that it's nearly impossible for the alcoholic to consume enough alcohol to stay above it. Tolerance, at that point, may have dropped significantly *below* the withdrawal threshold, so the alcoholic could be actively drunk and yet in major alcohol withdrawal at the same time. Not long ago, we admitted a woman through our Emergency Room who was suffering major withdrawal despite the fact that she had a .60 blood-alcohol level. That shouldn't be possible, of course, but it nonetheless happens. At levels where a normal person would die of alcohol overdose, some alcoholics suffer from lack of the drug.

Diminishing Comfort Zone

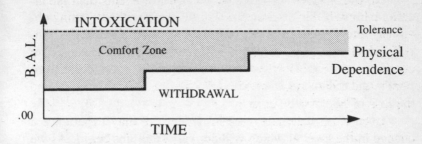

In other cases, physical deterioration interrupts the individual's ability to drink. An attack of pancreatitis or gastritis or a bleeding ulcer will render any once-resistant alcoholic completely amenable to treatment.

As the consequences of loss of control become more severe, alcoholics will most likely begin to abstain for as long as they are able. Periods of abstinence replace controlled drinking, and these are interspersed with the familiar binges. The illustration showing loss of control begins to look like this.

Abstinence-Binge Pattern

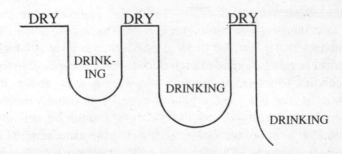

If asked at this point if he were alcoholic, the drinker would most likely categorize himself as an episodic problem drinker. This is really a way of continuing to compare out, since he is clinging to the belief that an alcoholic is someone who drinks every day. He deludes himself that during his periods of abstinence he is somehow no longer alcoholic, despite what occurs during his forays into drinking.

It's during this stage that the alcoholic's contorted explanations to justify his behavior become most obvious. Since the plain truth—that he is losing control over his drinking, despite efforts to the contrary—is unacceptable to him, his agile mind invents more pleasing explanations.

Perhaps he simply denies that any problem exists. He made the mistake of marrying a teetotaler (he tells his friends), and she becomes hysterical at the thought of any drinking in the house. There's no problem on *his* part.

Or maybe he rationalizes his difficulties with a parade of excuses: being overtired, preoccupied with other problems. Certainly, he claims, it was never any big deal.

Odds are that he commonly exercises a form of externalizing. He looks around his life for people or situations which don't quite meet his approval. He then exaggerates their negative impact on his psyche until, he believes, he has justified giving himself a good case of liver cirrhosis.

If he and his wife argue over the checkbook, it's grounds for divorce. If his boss asks him to work faster, it's a sure sign of an underlying personal prejudice. If the car has a flat tire, it's good for an orgy of self-pity at the local bar. Life becomes his enemy, and the imperfections of others are crosses he must bear.

Of course, after about two months of this, his family and friends are ready to string him up by the neck. "Aha," he says to himself. "I knew it all along. They hate me."

This, he tells anyone who will listen, would drive anyone to drink.

If he's one of that legion of Americans who frequently checks out the self-help shelf in the local bookstore, terms like "stress," "low self-image," and "depression" will begin to dominate his vocabulary. He might begin dropping over to the shrink's office for a bit of sympathy and quickly forgotten advice. Here he may find a new friend: the minor tranquilizer. Or anything else to help him "cope."

Meanwhile, loss of control proceeds apace. He'll drink

more than he intends to, with increasing regularity. He'll begin to break his own rules for drinking. If he's never had a drink at work, he'll begin to have powerful cravings throughout the day, and eventually give in to them. He'll start to sneak alcohol where he knows it will bring nothing but trouble, because he can't resist it. He will become the manipulative, sneaking drinker pictured by so many writers on alcoholism—a man whose word is worthless, whose promises are just delaying tactics.

Not only does the amount increase, but the duration of drinking episodes begins to lengthen. If the alcoholic has always been able to confine heavy drinking to weekends, he'll discover that he now drinks through Monday and maybe Tuesday, Wednesday, Thursday, and Friday. Then he'll go on the wagon for a month or so. When he starts in again, things will be worse than before.

This is the point at which those around him usually begin to seek help for him. Of course, by this time the disease is well into its crucial middle stage. If the family can be manipulated—through guilt or simple intimidation—into avoiding a confrontation, the alcoholic can keep drinking until some other factor, such as health, finally puts a stop to the whole process in one way or another.

An almost foolproof way of identifying the drinker who is losing control is through the proliferation of *control strategies*. These are behavioral devices designed to help the alcoholic drink as he imagines other people do, or at least keep him out of really severe trouble.

We knew one man who was given to taking his paycheck to a favorite country-and-western bar every Friday after work. The nice folks at the bar were only too glad to cash his check for him, and he found that after a few beers, he was eager to buy a couple hundred dollars' worth of drinks for the other patrons. This, of course, caused some friction with his wife when he arrived home in the wee hours of the morning, so he resolved to have only those precious one or two beers, and then go home to dinner and family.

The problem was, how was he going to get himself out of

the bar after only two beers? Here was his solution: he would park his truck at about 4 P.M. in a zone which was marked TOW AWAY AFTER 4:30. This would mean that he had only half an hour in which to drink before he had to come out and move his truck. "Once I get into the truck," he reasoned, "I'll just head on home." The first Friday of his experiment arrived, and at 4:30, after three drafts, he got up, left the bar, and went out to his truck—whereupon he drove to a zone marked PARKING ALL NIGHT, and returned to the bar to drink up the remainder of his salary.

Case Histories

To illustrate the various ways alcoholics lose control over drinking, here are three case histories. Note the difference in the rate at which the disease progresses and in the extent to which each person's life is affected. Such dissimilarities, along with differences in drinking practices, provide ammunition for comparing out, and interfere with self-diagnosis.

CASE #1: THE PURE ALLERGIC   A general rule is that the lower your *resistance* to a given disease, the sooner you develop symptoms following your first exposure to an activating agent. Though most alcoholics develop mid-stage symptoms gradually, after years of drinking have elapsed, some alcoholics appear to leap through early adaptations into later stages of the illness. Alcoholism dominates the lives of these victims from childhood.

Here is an example of such a case, as related by a thirty-year-old man.

I had my first drink when I was a little kid. I can even remember the taste of it. I was at a party with my parents at my uncle's house. I had a sip of wine, and everybody laughed at the sour face I made. Even though I didn't like the taste, about five minutes later I started to feel great. I had another sip, and felt even better. After everyone else went into the living room to play charades, I snuck into the kitchen and finished off what was left in the dinner glasses. I slept like a log and I remember being sick the next morning. Do you believe a little kid with a hangover? I never forgot that night.

I didn't have any more alcohol—I had an alcoholic grandfather, and my parents were pretty much against drinking—until I was in high school. One of the guys, sophomore year, had a couple of six-packs of beer that his brother bought him, and we took it to the beach with us. While everybody played volleyball, I snuck back to his camper and drank all the beer—about eight or nine cans. You can't believe how pissed they were at me.

I started going to parties with older kids, because my girlfriend was a year ahead of me. They all drank, and I began to realize how good I was at holding my liquor. I had a hollow leg. When I got my own car, I could go off by myself and drink, and that's what I did. The night we won the league football title, and I scored twice, I drank a case of beer. At least I think I drank it. That's how many empty cans were in my car when I woke up in the front seat the next morning.

I went to the state university on a track scholarship. It was a joke. I partied so much—every night of the week— that there was no way I could perform in meets. I lost my scholarship at the end of the first year, and transferred to another school about fifty miles from my home town.

I lasted another two years, very little of which I remember. I was pre-med for a while, so I could get student jobs in the lab and could sneak their supplies of alcohol. I smoked a lot of dope, and paid my tuition by dealing. My parents still thought I was on scholarship.

By my junior year, I was throwing up every morning like a pregnant woman. Drinking a glass of orange juice was a real adventure. Most of it wound up on the floor. I got arrested four or five times in bar fights, and two or three times for reckless driving. I spent a lot of days in jail, but drank all the way through my sentences. I'm not proud to say this, but there was a queer trusty I used to let give me blow jobs if he'd smuggle me in some hooch.

I finally moved back to my home town and went looking for a job. I must have been a sight. I always had a black eye or something from a fight. I ended up as a night watchman at a brewery. I sat around drinking every night.

Pretty soon after that, I got my first official drunk-driving arrest that wasn't reduced to a lesser charge. It was actually about my thirtieth arrest. I went to the school like they told me, and I was on time and made every class, and got 100 percent on their little examination at the end. I thought I did great. Unfortunately, I got arrested for two more drunk-driving offenses during the four weeks of the course. So I lost my license for good.

At that point I'm not working, because I can't drive the twenty-five miles to the plant. I'm not in school. I got no money, and the cops will pick me up if I so much as take a taxi.

I stayed totally drunk for about three months. Around the clock: drink, sleep, drink, sleep. Stopped eating entirely after a while. TV on all the time. Taxi drivers brought the booze. My parents collected me finally, when I was in a state of total collapse, and when I hit the hospital, I went into the screaming meemies, they tell me. It took them about two weeks to get me down. I remember nothing of it.

As soon as I could walk, I snuck out. That started my string of traveling drunks. I'd end up in some different mental hospital in some new state, talking to some shrink about my upbringing. Maybe twenty times this happened.

About two years ago, I started to get these terrible attacks of pancreatitis. I can't drink at all without getting it. So now I quit for three months at a time, and then something sets me off, and after one drink, I'm just like a runaway truck.

CASE #2: "BUT I'VE NEVER BEEN THAT MUCH OF A DRINKER..." Another general rule in alcoholism is that the longer the alcoholic has been able to get away with drinking—reinforcing his image of himself as a social drinker—the more difficult it will be for him to accept that he can no longer drink as he has in the past. This is especially true if that alcoholic has lived with someone who drinks more, or with more disastrous effects, than himself. That other individual, in his mind, is the alcoholic. But could this disease touch *him?* Never.

This story was told by a forty-year-old woman.

I had my first drink on my eighteenth birthday. Turning eighteen was a big deal in my family, because to them it meant you'd get married and start producing children for them to take pictures of. My dad poured my first glass of wine. It made me dizzy and I didn't even finish it.

I talked my family into letting me go to college, on the grounds that I'd meet more eligible men. I was very proper at school, and drank only socially, if at all. I got married when I was twenty and didn't finish school. Within five years, I had three kids.

My husband was an officer in the military, and we moved a lot. I hated that. You had to leave your friends as soon as you got used to them. Besides, my husband was drinking too much. He'd stay with his buddies till all hours on weekends, leaving me stuck with the kids. When we went to parties together, he would always get drunk. I'd try to make excuses for him, but he'd always make a scene about driving when it was time to go home. I could usually get the keys away from him, so I could drive us home. I was never drunk once.

Then he started taking off for several days at a time. It was usually over the weekend, but he'd miss a lot of Mondays and I'd have to call to make some excuse for him. I was terrified he'd lose his job and we'd get transferred again to someplace like Korea. When he was out of the house I'd get nervous wondering if he was even alive or if he'd been killed in some kind of car wreck. I'd sit up at night and sip table wine, which I'd grown to like. Sometimes I'd get pretty stoned and the next day I'd be angry that I'd let him drive me to drink.

Finally, he did get transferred. We decided I'd stay in the States with the kids. But when he left, I was very lonely. I admit I cheated on him a couple of times, but I'm sure he wasn't entirely faithful to me, either. He always liked the ladies. But I lived in a small town, and I couldn't go out like I wanted to, because of the gossip. I had to stay home a lot, which encouraged more drinking. Some weekends I'd get all dressed up and tell the kids I was going out with friends. Then I'd drop them off at the baby sitter's, and come back home and drink. I'd learned about vodka gimlets by that time, and those were my favorite.

It was during this time that I had my first problems with alcohol. If I drank during the week, I felt awful when I got up the next morning. So I made a vow never to drink except on weekends. Since the kids were in school, I went out and got a job in a department store, to keep busy. I was really going to change my life.

But on Friday night, at dinner, when I had my first drink of the week, I found I couldn't stop myself. I'd keep right on going through the weekend. I was so scared of losing my job I could stop myself on Sunday night, but it took all my will power. I felt like I was losing control of myself.

I was nervous all the time, and I couldn't sleep. So I went to see a psychiatrist. She explained to me that I was suffering from stress, and gave me some tranquilizers to help me. I was fine for a while, the best I'd been in three years.

But then I started having trouble again. I was still in therapy, and working on my low self-image, but I was having problems remembering what I did on weekends. I'd go to bars and wake up the next morning with men I couldn't recall meeting. After one of these times, I freaked out on the guy I was with, started yelling and calling him names. He beat the hell out of me, and I took all the tranquilizers I had in the medicine cabinet.

I wound up in a mental hospital for a month and a half. My husband came home on special leave from the Phillipines, and the bastard had been sent through this program in the military and had quit drinking. He was in AA, if you can believe that.

All he wanted to do was take me to meetings. I told him to forget it, that what happened to me was his fault, *he* ought to be trying to kill himself with guilt, not me. We lived together for about three months, and I kept drinking (I'd lost my job) and he took care of the kids. Well, it was his turn.

One day he packed up the kids and left. Moved about a hundred miles away. I called and begged him to come back, and my shrink said he was obviously a sociopath. I overdosed again, this time on antidepressants.

Now I drink because I want my kids back. I'm their mother. If I had them back, I wouldn't have a drinking problem. I drank like everybody else till I was thirty-five. I'm just depressed.

CASE #3:   "I'VE ALWAYS BEEN A DRINKER, BUT LATE-LY . . . " Here's an example of a maintenance drinker in the process of losing control. Note how he has come to regard himself, over the years, as a heavy drinker, concentrating on the lack of disruption in his lifestyle as proof of his ability to control alcohol. Thus, it's very difficult for him to understand the increasing difficulties he experiences.

I've always been a drinker. Started in high school like everyone else. Drank whatever rotgut we were making on board ship in the navy, and drank cheap whiskey and beer on shore leave. I was never the guy to get drunk or pass out or make a fool of himself. I was a good sailor who liked his booze and could handle it.

I got out of the service and went into the restaurant business. By the time I was thirty, I managed my own place. I'd drink in the evenings with the customers at the bar. I maybe had six or eight drinks a night, or a few more, but nothing excessive.

Then I started to get insomnia. I'd wake up nervous and sweaty, with a bad dream in my head. I went to two doctors about it, but they didn't do anything. Then I discovered that if I had a couple of beers, I felt good enough to go back to sleep. I figured that even though it was five or six in the morning, it was the middle of the night for a guy with my schedule, so a few beers was okay.

But I didn't feel very good even by noon. So I started having a few with lunch, as a pick-me-up, you know, and that helped. So I guess I was pretty much drinking all day long. But I wasn't ever drunk, remember, and I made it to work every single day. I was the Rock of Gibraltar when it came to working.

Then I started to have this problem with my hands shaking. When I wrote something, my hand would just tremble something awful. It was embarrassing. I went to a nerve specialist. He said it was probably inherited from my family, and put me on tranquilizers.

The medicine didn't help that much, though I took it every day. I discovered a couple of swigs of vodka were a lot better than the pills. I tried to alternate them, though, so I wouldn't overdo either one.

My big mistake was on my fortieth birthday. I got stinking drunk at the party they gave for me at the restaurant where I was working. There was a guy arguing about his check, and I went out to the main room, and they tell me I hit him in the mouth. He hauled me up on assault charges.

I thought I'd lose my job, but they kept me on. I just had to promise I'd never do it again. It occurred to me that I was so valuable they couldn't replace me.

But about three months later, I threw a party at my own house. One of my neighbors had borrowed a lawnmower from me and never returned it. I apparently got real mean about this, and when he talked back to me, I got a gun and went looking for him. Thank God I never found him. I recall nothing of this.

After that, I swore to give up drinking. I remember looking at the glass in my hand, and promising God that it was my last. Two hours later, I was in front of the liquor store ready to kill for a drink. I knew then that something was wrong with me.

My boss fired me a few weeks after that. I was doing a lot of stuff that you can't do in business, like disappearing for hours at a time. Wasn't indispensable after all.

After I got canned, I stayed drunk for a month. My wife, who hadn't said much through all of this, went home to her mother. I'd thought my drinking hadn't bothered her, but I guess I was wrong. She wouldn't even talk to me on the phone.

I ended up in the hospital for detox. They let me out in five days and I was drunk that night. My neighbor brought me back the next week, and I left against medical advice in two days. Got picked up for drunk driving and spent a night in jail. Drank again the minute I got out and was arrested for being drunk in public in the lobby of the courthouse. Spent another five days in jail before my brain worked well enough to recall I could post bail. Got drunk in the bar across the street from the jail, and ended up picking such a fight with the bartender that I got hauled in again. This time, they took me to the county nut ward. After about a week there, they gave me a pass. I got drunk and never went back. Stayed drunk about a year. Have no idea how I survived. My mother would stop over every day to check on me, and it was her who filled me in on much of what I just told you.

When I ended up in the hospital the next time, the doctor talked me into going to an AA house. I've been sober about six months now, and I'm starting work as a cook next week.

Looking back on it, it seems like problems hit me all at once. Just lost my capacity for the stuff, I guess. But why, I couldn't tell you.

5

Mixing
It
Up

Problems on Top of Problems

SOME OF THE THORNIEST PROBLEMS ENCOUNTERED IN alcoholism treatment involve the use of drugs other than alcohol.

There are a number of ways in which these problems may appear. A certain percentage of patients will arrive on the counselor's doorstep in possession of full-blown histories of narcotic or other drug use. These patients will as a rule be more difficult to diagnose, detoxify, and treat than the average, garden-variety alcoholic.

Another group will encounter some sort of drug-related problem during the course of treatment, usually because of protracted withdrawal symptoms such as insomnia. This involvement will make their chances for recovery more difficult.

Still another group will develop drug problems long after they give up alcohol, and will quite likely relapse because of it.

The use of other drugs in addition to alcohol is nothing new, but it has been steadily on the increase over the past few decades. Many treatment programs can foresee what treatment problems will be coming up simply by dividing their patients according to age: in patients over forty, only a minority will be involved in any drugs besides alcohol, while patients under forty are highly likely to have histories of multiple-drug use, although alcohol will still be the drug most commonly used.

Alcoholics have always used other drugs (many of them prescribed) to support and to counteract the effects of their drinking. There's no mystery behind this. Other drugs simply fit neatly into the developing addictive pattern.

In other words, multiple-drug use is a natural response to the disease, and the extent to which a counselor finds it in his caseload is simply a question of how many patients managed to stumble upon the "advantages" of other drugs during their drinking careers. Once they have, however, their lives can change to a remarkable degree.

We believe the best way to look at alcoholism is as one of a group of addictive diseases that are more alike than different. Some clinicians prefer to lump all addictions under catch-all titles such as chemical dependency, but we try to avoid that. In the first place, the experience of someone whose primary addiction is to alcohol can be very different from that of someone whose primary drug is cocaine or heroin. Better to illustrate how these addictions are *related* than try to convince someone that they're all exactly the same, when that directly contradicts the person's experience.

Second, we prefer to use the term *disease* wherever we can, because there is such a long history of mistaking alcoholism for something else. The term *dependency* can be applied to a variety of conditions including the feeling of loss when someone's TV set goes on the blink. In our estimation, the term "chemical dependency" trivializes the experience of alcoholism, as well as other drug addictions. When we treat alcoholics, we don't simply deal with behavioral conditioning; we address a *chronic, primary, hereditary, physiological disease process*.

Since the focus of this book is on alcoholism we'll confine

our discussion to the ways in which people whose primary drug is alcohol use other substances as part of the addictive pattern. We'll look at ways to get someone who is mixing drugs to compare in with the symptoms of alcoholism and initiate the recovery process.

In our practice we have seen five basic patterns in alcoholic patients who are using other drugs in addition to alcohol.

Alcohol with Sedatives and Hypnotics

The drugs listed below are pharmacologically similar chemicals which generally do one of two things: the sedatives *sedate*, relieving whatever nervousness the user might feel, and the hypnotics *induce sleep*. Some are stronger than others, and there are significant differences in some of their effects, but all *depress* the central nervous system, which carries messages to and from the control centers of the brain. These drugs slow that activity down. When under their influence one's responses and reactions are more sluggish, and it is usually advised not to do anything physically complicated or dangerous while taking them.

Chloral hydrate
Paraldehyde
Meprobamate (Miltown, Equanil)
Methaqualone (Quaalude)
Doriden
Placidyl
Phenobarbital
Secobarbital (Seconal)
Pentobarbital (Nembutal)
Amobarbital (Amytal)
Tuinal (combination of amobarb and secobarbital)
Chlordiazepoxide (Librium)
Diazepam (Valium)
Clorazepate (Tranxene)
Lorazepam (Ativan)
Oxazepam (Serax)
Flurazepam (Dalmane)
Xanax

All of these drugs are very similar in effect to alcohol. One of their primary uses is in relieving the pain of alcohol withdrawal. They're considerably better at this than narcotics, which, though also depressants, act differently in the body. The preferred drug for detoxification has changed several times in this century, but doctors seem to return consistently to this category as new additions to it appear.

Because of the similarity between these drugs and alcohol, two related phenomena emerge: *cross-tolerance* and *cross-addiction*.

Cross-tolerance refers to the way the alcoholic's abnormal tolerance for alcohol seems to carry over to his use of other sedative or hypnotic drugs. Just as it requires unusual amounts of alcohol to sedate him, so it will require atypical doses of sedatives to get that same effect. Normally prescribed amounts simply don't do the job: he thus has a built-in incentive to increase the dose of any sedative or hypnotic drug.

We also found out—the hard way, as usual—that the same disease which affects the alcoholic's use of alcohol affects his use of any of these drugs. In case after case, alcoholics who have used them have developed the same kinds of symptoms that dominate their drinking. Besides tolerance, they appear to rapidly develop symptoms similar to alcohol withdrawal, as well as experience the same kinds of problems controlling their use of the drug that they've had with liquor. We call this process cross-addiction.

Alcoholics customarily use these drugs to ease withdrawal symptoms. For example, we recently treated a woman who took great pains to confine her drinking to the socially acceptable hours after work. She drank heavily every evening, from her before-dinner cocktails to her pre-bed nightcap. After a few months of this, she began to notice that she woke up a few hours after she had fallen asleep, and couldn't get back to sleep without a brandy. She also discovered that she was nervous and temperamental all morning long, had no appetite until dinner, and generally felt bad throughout the day. It would never have occurred to this woman to use alcohol during the day to treat these symptoms, because she firmly believed that people who drank during the day were "in trouble," as she put it, so she instead diagnosed herself as suffering from job-related stress and paid a visit to a psychiatrist, who agreed with her assessment. He prescribed a liberal dose of a sedative to help "support her coping skills." With this medical blessing, she felt free to use the tranquilizer during the day and to return to her regular diet of alcohol each night. She told us that this regimen had worked admirably for about three months, when she began to experience a return of the same symptoms she'd had before: sleeplessness, worry, bad temper, loss of appetite. She increased her dose of the tranquilizer to treat the symptoms, and got to the point where she was calling her doctor every week or so for a renewed prescription. After a few over-the-phone renewals, he insisted she come into his office to talk. She angrily refused, saying she "didn't need that kind of grief," and called another doctor, who prescribed the sedatives for her over the phone.

Her symptoms continued to get worse, however, no matter how many of the sedatives she took. She began to approach still other doctors to avoid making excessive demands on the prescription pad of any one physician. Finally, she was fired from her job for appearing drunk at the office. She was amazed by this; after all, she'd never had a drink before five o'clock in her life.

Here, sedatives were never anything more than a substitute for alcohol in a maintenance drinking pattern. If she couldn't drink at work, she could take pills. Once her withdrawal passed a certain point, however, she wasn't able to keep the symptoms at bay unless she dramatically increased the dose. Eventually, she passed the level of her tolerance, and started looking and acting drunk.

Here is a clear case of a psychiatrist inadvertently participating in the progression of the disease by treating stress instead of alcoholism. It really didn't matter what his diagnosis was—it could just as well have been lower-back pain, a hysterical personality, or Bolivian birdwatcher's disease. It wasn't alcoholism and he resorted to sedatives to treat it.

Occasionally, this pattern develops backwards, with sedative use preceding, and perhaps laying the groundwork for, alcoholism. We knew a man who suffered from chronic back pain, the kind that never goes away and periodically afflicts him to the point where he's unable to live normally. The only medicine that seemed to relieve his pain was meprobamate, one of the sedative hypnotics. He used it faithfully, several doses daily, for about ten years. Several times he attempted to stop using the drug, but his pain soon returned until his doctor put him back on it. One day he happened to volunteer for an experiment, conducted at the college where he taught, to test volunteers for their tolerance to alcohol. Though he'd never been much of a drinker, he decided to test himself. To his considerable surprise, he exhibited by far the greatest "capacity" of any subject. Somehow, he had become tolerant to alcohol.

Several years later, he read a book about meprobamate which described it as an addictive and possibly dangerous drug. This unnerved him, since he didn't like to think of himself as a drug addict, so he approached his doctor for help in getting off the drug. Another tranquilizer was prescribed to tide him over the initial period without his medicine, but he didn't want to substitute one drug for another, so he didn't use it.

The first three months without drugs were very difficult for him. He slept badly, ate poorly, snapped at everyone around him, and woke up every single night with cramps in his legs. After about ten days of this he began to have a glass of wine when the symptoms became irritating, and this seemed to help. His doctor agreed with him that one or two glasses a couple of times a day would probably do the trick. The doctor was pleased that at least his patient's back pain wasn't unbearable.

A year later, this same patient was admitted to the hospital for liver disease, and his wife estimated that he had been drinking as much as a bottle of whiskey a day, while still complaining of nervousness.

Here, the initial signs of alcoholism—sedative tolerance and active withdrawal—were probably established before alcohol was ever added. The patient and doctor simply switched the sedative of choice to one which neither believed was a dangerous drug.

A chart in the back of this book offers a treatment plan for the recovering alcoholic who has used sedatives.

Yet another cross-addiction problem occurs when drugs are used to treat alcoholism itself. This is discussed in Chapter 11, on page 236. For now, let's move on to another drug combination: alcohol and marijuana.

Alcohol with Marijuana: "Oh, marijuana isn't dangerous."

Cannabis is the name of the plant which yields marijuana, hashish, and hashish oil. Its active ingredient is THC (Delta-9). Marijuana is used all over the world by hundreds of millions of people of all backgrounds, and in some areas it is more popular than alcohol. Difficult to place in a pharmacological category, it is usually grouped with hallucinogens.

Our most common alcohol/other-drug pattern among people under the age of thirty is alcohol plus marijuana.

We would like to state immediately that we have no interest in whether or not cannabis becomes legal. Most young alcoholics have used it, and would continuc to do so in spite of any legal sanctions. Therefore we don't care if it's legal or not; neither, for that matter, would the alcoholic who wants to smoke it.

For most users, marijuana provides a pleasant high which doesn't dramatically impair their mental or physical capabilities, and allows them to pass an hour or two in a pretty relaxed state. It isn't as powerful as opium or alcohol, so most people who use it regard it as utterly harmless. You don't get "stoned-driving tickets" (at least it's rare), and you don't end up on a slab in the morgue after a grass overdose, so many people feel free to at least experiment with it. Lots of them quit after one or two of these experiments but others become quite attached to the drug.

During the turbulent sixties, experimentation with drugs was the rule rather than the exception, and marijuana was the least scary, the most available, and, as a result, the overwhelming favorite. Many of today's rising young businessmen got their first exposure to commerce through selling marijuana to friends and classmates.

When the sixties died, marijuana didn't. It filtered from colleges to high schools to, in some cases, elementary schools. Dope-sniffing police dogs left the customs desks and moved into high-school locker rooms. This seemed to do absolutely nothing to decrease its use.

The result, as far as alcoholism is concerned, is that, especially in the cities, where it's so available, most young alcoholics incorporate grass into their drinking patterns as they grow up.

Here's an example, a patient we'll call Teddy, a twenty-five-year-old liquor-store manager. Teddy started using marijuana when he was fifteen, and by the time he entered college, he was smoking five joints a day. He claimed this didn't interfere with his functioning in any way but simply relaxed him. He experimented with other drugs, but marijuana remained his favorite. When he graduated, he got a job as a liquor salesman and for the first time began to hang around people who drank regularly. He discovered he liked alcohol's effects, and within a year was drinking about a half-pint of bourbon every evening, along with his ration of marijuana during the day. On some days, he'd have as many as ten joints before he switched over to alcohol after work. He'd smoke in the back room of the store when there weren't any customers.

After about six months at this level of use, he discovered one morning that he had terrible pains in his stomach. His doctor told him he had a case of gastritis along with the beginnings of a stomach ulcer, and advised him to stay away from alcohol until it cleared up. He found, however, he couldn't manage to stop using marijuana. He continued to smoke until, one night at a party, he began drinking again. In another two months, he was readmitted to the hospital with an even more severe case of gastritis. He realized he couldn't avoid alcohol unless he also gave up grass, because sooner or later he would get high enough that he'd forget about his resolve not to use alcohol.

Alcohol and marijuana, obviously, can work together to complicate a given individual's drug usage. Anyone who's having trouble getting through a day of withdrawal can at least mask the discomfort with dope. Sure, a couple of tranquilizers would do a better job, but they aren't always as available, and someone who's mistrustful of pills often won't think anything of taking marijuana, even though it's illegal. Paradoxically, it seems that there are indications that the use of alcohol and marijuana together will produce tolerance to both faster than the use of either drug alone. Thus the combination may *hasten* the appearance of alcoholism in some cases.

People like Teddy, who use it regularly, don't get the same effects from marijuana that occasional users get. Instead of getting high, most chronic users report that they use grass to relax in the same way a nicotine user relaxes with a stimulant drug. In alcoholism, therefore, marijuana can fit neatly into the developing sedative pattern.

For example, to help Teddy compare in, we asked him to estimate, from his own experience, the relative sedative power of a joint as opposed to an alcoholic drink. He decided that one joint was roughly equivalent to one drink. We then asked him to convert the whole of his drug use to drinks, so he could get some idea how much sedative he required to get through a typical day. Here's his result.

7 A.M. to noon	3 to 5 joints =	3 to 5 drinks
Noon to 5 P.M.	3 to 5 joints =	3 to 5 drinks
5 P.M. to 12 P.M.	6 to 8 oz. alcohol =	6 to 8 drinks
	2 joint =	2 drinks
	2 sleeping pills =	4 drinks
		18 to 24 drinks

Teddy actually consumed the equivalent of between a pint and a fifth of alcohol daily, just to make it through the day. This, he could see, wasn't quite normal.

Teddy did develop alcoholic gastritis on a rather frugal amount of alcohol, so there is a good chance he may have been understating his consumption. Nonetheless, we believe him when he says that he relied on marijuana during the day and that it would be as difficult for him to give that up as it was to give up alcohol, if not more so. For him, the two drugs were inseparable partners in the disease process.

Alcohol with Stimulants: Life in an Elevator

Certain common drugs acts as stimulants: for example, cocaine and various amphetamines.

Where alcohol depresses central-nervous-system activity, these drugs stimulate it. Their original value in recent years was to those who wanted to feel sudden bursts of energy, stay awake for extended periods, or diminish appetite.

Coca, the plant from which cocaine is derived, has been used for centuries by South American Indians for exactly these purposes. When food wasn't available, they could chew coca leaves until they weren't hungry. In battle, they could avoid fatigue and sleep, both of which are very dangerous if someone is lurking about with a stone axe. The Europeans who conquered their homeland shipped the plant back to Europe, where it was refined and used to treat narcolepsy, a neurological illness which causes its victims to fall asleep at unpredictable moments. Like many other drugs, cocaine was added to a number of patent medicines to treat common ailments. Though never as widely used as opiates or alcohol, it was also a target of the prohibitionist movement which resulted in the proscription of those drugs in the early years of the twentieth century.

Amphetamines are a much more recent invention, providing a cocaine-like stimulant effect that made them applicable in the same situations: whenever one needed to stay awake, eat less, or get a sudden burst of energy. Synthetically manufactured, amphetamines were used by all the major combatants in World War II to combat battle fatigue. Their greatest popularity was with the Japanese, who picked up on another property of these drugs: if you take them in high doses for an extended period, they make you, and your central nervous system, very irritable. Hence the name among the Japanese: the drug to inspire fighting.

In America, amphetamines became part of popular culture.

Several profiles of users emerged: the student staying up for the weekend to cram for final exams; the trucker on a long-distance haul, eating "beans" all the way; the eternally dieting housewife, strung out on speed for years. Perhaps the most memorable was the appearance, in the late 1960s, of the methedrine-injecting "speed freak," wandering the streets of the Haight-Ashbury looking to kill someone he imagines may once have burnt him in a drug deal.

How, you may well inquire, do stimulant drugs play a role in alcoholism, when they have an opposite effect to alcohol?

Basically, their importance springs from the fact that they do have an opposing effect.

Cocaine, for example, is our most popular recreational drug, outside of marijuana and alcohol. One of our patients was a thirty-year-old man who had been using cocaine recreationally for about ten years. He bought it every weekend and used it to spice up his parties or his Saturdays on his sailboat.

He drank socially during the week but denied any problems due to that. Then he adopted a practice known as free-basing, which involved refining the cocaine with a solvent to produce a more powerful concentration, as well as enabling the user to smoke the cocaine. Free-base is what psychologists regard as a powerful reinforcer, which is the next best thing to saying it's addictive. People who use this method of refining the drug often become *very* attached to it. When our patient began to use free-based cocaine, he quickly developed all the symptoms of cocaine toxicity: visual hallucinations, loss of appetite, sleeplessness till exhaustion, suspiciousness to the point of paranoia. He also felt completely nervous and irritable all the time, due to the presence of such nervous-system hyperactivity.

Each time this man used the drug, the level of stimulation went up dramatically. As the drug wore off, he would experience a crash—what's known as a *reactive depression,* which follows the effects of the stimulant. If you don't use too much of a stimulant, the crash isn't too painful or distressing, but it's there, nonetheless. If, on the other hand, you use a considerable dose of a potent stimulant over an extended period of time, as this fellow

Mood Changes in Cocaine User

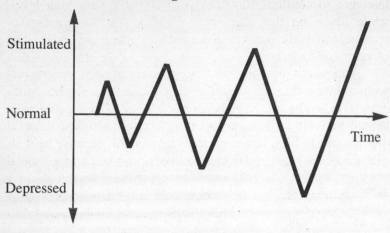

Fluctuations in nervous-system activity resulting from cocaine use.

did when he began free-basing, then your crash is going to be very real. So what he did, and what lots of others do in the same situation, was to avoid letting the stimulant wear off. He just kept getting higher and higher, as the illustration indicates. Now he was on a coke "run."

But this method isn't foolproof, either. So much stimulant over that period made him toxic. His irritated nervous system produced hallucinations, especially formication (with an *m*), a particular kind of toxic hallucination that involves seeing bugs. In order to counteract this and other toxic symptoms, he began to use a handy depressant drug: vodka. In this state of nervous-system hyperactivity, he was able to consume enormous amounts without getting drunk. In fact, he reported that he could "take a pint of vodka and tilt it up and nearly drain it without a stop." His nervous system, irritated by coke, was capable of absorbing huge amounts of sedative without intoxication.

So every time he went up too high, he brought himself back down to manageable levels with vodka. The cocaine toxicity mimicked alcohol withdrawal—which is also nervous hyperactivity—and gave him essentially the same motivation for drinking that an alcoholic in withdrawal has. It also provided him with the tolerance to continue functioning, if not at a very high level, while living on this elevator. He called his combination of cocaine and vodka—since he never used them separately—an elevator cocktail.

After about three months of this, he ended up in the hospital with a dandy case of alcoholic pancreatitis and alcohol withdrawal. When he was released from the hospital he went to great lengths to avoid cocaine, not wanting to repeat his experience. It didn't occur to him, however, to avoid alcohol, because he'd attributed all his problems to the free-basing. So he resumed social drinking. To his chagrin, within two weeks he was back on a drinking binge, the only difference being that now no stimulants were involved. He developed all the alcoholic's symptoms—tolerance, withdrawal, and organ change—without any cocaine use.

He was more surprised than anyone by this occurrence. Had he somehow managed to induce alcoholism by his use of coke? His physician explained that what had caused his alcoholism was his use of alcohol *in response to* his use of cocaine. When he reflected on it at length, he could point to an elevated tolerance in his drinking history for years before he began free-basing, but since it had been an asset rather than a problem, he'd ignored it. It may also be that he was a person susceptible to alcoholism, and that the cocaine use overtaxed his resistance to the illness. Either way, he ended up, as he described himself, a "stone alcoholic" —street language for very addicted.

Similar stories come from people who develop amphetamine habits. They treat the increasing irritability of chronic amphetamine use with alcohol. There's an interesting reversal of this among some alcoholics: a young woman patient told us that when she began to lose control over her drinking, getting drunk when she didn't intend to, she could always perk herself up with a diet pill, so she didn't look as sedated.

So far, we've concentrated on the role stimulants play in counteracting the sedative effects of alcohol, but alcohol in lower doses also seems to have a less publicized stimulant effect which may turn out to be significant in changing the way we view how alcoholics use these drugs. There may be some kind of interplay between the *stimulant* properties of alcohol and cocaine (and the others) which is as important as the *sedative-stimulant* interaction. Again, research will show us the answer to that.

Alcohol and Mixed Drugs:
The "Garbage Syndrome"

The use of several drugs at a time is an effective disguise for alcoholism, and the best of all such disguises involves simply taking every drug one can get one's hands on.

This is what we have come to call, for lack of a better term, the "garbage syndrome." We believe it usually features many of the symptoms of alcoholism, a fact which becomes progressively more evident as time passes. However, for considerable portions of the drinking career, the presence of alcoholism is obscured by concurrent use of many other drugs.

In adolescent alcoholism or drug-treatment programs, teens are asked on admission: "What drugs have you used during the past few weeks?"

A typical answer, preceded by a bit of head-scratching, goes like this.

Well, let's see . . . I been drinkin' beer all week, because my brother's home from college, and his friends are buying for us. And one of my buddies stole a quart of vodka from his dad's liquor cabinet (his old man is a stone drunk) and we split it last weekend. Then, there were some pills on the street last week, and I got hold of a bunch of them, but I don't know how many I took . . . I gave some away . . . and then my girlfriend had some Dilaudid last week, and we got stoned on that, and of course, there's a lot of acid around, and I do favors for this one guy, and he gives me all I want. And I like to smoke boat or joints with a little green* on

---

*Boat: a cigarette or joint sprayed with PCP. Joints with green: joints made of parsley that has been sprayed with PCP.

120

'em, and I'm always smoking dope, because it's easier to get than beer. All you got to do is go to the boys' bathroom at school, and you can get about anything you want. Oh, yeah, there's coke around on the street now, and it's not that expensive, so I bought some of that. And then I was in the doctor's office last week gettin' the cast off the wrist I broke jumpin' off that roof, and when his back was turned, I took some stuff that was on his desk, and ate that later. It was pretty good, man, but I don't really know what it was. I guess that's it. Lots of beer, lots of grass, and anything else that's around at the time.

All jumbled together in the same nervous system. Take a look at the drugs mentioned and their differing effects.

Beer and vodka (depressants)
Cocaine (stimulant)
Pills (amphetamines?) (stimulants)
Dilaudid (narcotic depressant)
Marijuana (mild depressant)
LSD (hallucinogen)
PCP (dissociative depressant)**

Plus assorted other chemicals we can only speculate about.

It's not hard to imagine what will happen to this adolescent following such an all-out assault on his brain.

First, he'll probably fail in school. He may even take a swing at another student or a teacher, and get suspended.

He'll quite possibly see a lot of the inside of the local police station, because these kids have behavior problems outside of school as well as within it, and he'll accumulate a retinue of probation officers, caseworkers, and guidance counselors with the same ease that a top athlete collects varsity letters.

If his parents are able to get him to a psychiatrist, he'll most

**A drug that suppresses pain by causing dissociation from physical sensation. Dissociative depressants are often used as anesthetics.

likely be diagnosed as having a character or behavioral disorder, or perhaps, if the drugs he uses disrupt his thinking enough, an underlying psychotic illness.

Trouble will be his middle name. His parents will be alternately enraged and guilt-ridden, depending on whether they believe they are responsible for their child's actions.

But the real problem here, it seems to us, lies in the fact that adolescents in this pattern are so seldom diagnosed as suffering from an *addictive* disease. Like adult alcoholics earlier in this century, they don't recover because they never receive treatment for what's really wrong with them.

Instead, they get treated for an array of psychological and character illnesses which they may or may not have, simply because professionals cannot bring themselves to believe that alcoholism, that scourge of the adult population, can appear in one so young.

As the years pass, however, the situation clears of its own accord. It's too difficult for the typical twenty- or thirty-year-old alcoholic to function under the influence of this bewildering variety of drugs, so he begins to drop them, one by one. And by his thirties, he uses alcohol or heroin as his drug of choice, usually with marijuana thrown in.

Here's an illustration of such a history in a young male alcoholic.

Ages 12 to 15: 3 joints of marijuana daily; 3 to 6 cans of beer on weekends when available; experimentation with stimulants and sedatives when available.

Ages 15 to 17: 3 to 12 beers three or four days per week, mostly after school; regular marijuana use; LSD and a variety of pills, including narcotics; experiments with heroin, cocaine, etc.; hard liquor when affordable or obtainable.

Ages 17 to 22: increasing consumption of beer, along with continued reliance on marijuana; use of stimulants and sedatives, street or prescription; decrease of LSD, PCP, etc.

Ages 22 to 30: 12 to 24 cans of beer daily; use of marijuana daily but in diminishing amounts; increasing use of vodka or other liquors, if needs are not met with beer.

In this instance, it would have been difficult to diagnose alcoholism during the prime multiple-drug-use phase, which was between the ages of twelve and sixteen. After that point, it becomes a bit more apparent, but this young man had been to four specialists by the time he was fifteen, who diagnosed him on the basis of his presenting problem. Curiously, even though he gave all of these clinicians the same history, all of them diagnosed him as something other than alcoholic. In fact, they came up with four different opinions as to what was wrong with him—none of which had anything to do with alcohol.

Obviously, with this kind of patient, one can't focus exclusively on alcohol to explain behavior or to encourage self-diagnosis. One has to be a bit creative in linking all these drugs into a somewhat coherent pattern of usage. PCP, for example, seems to fill the role of a sedative, masking any incipient withdrawal; they are both often called *dissociative anesthetics* because of their marvelous capacity to lessen awareness of even the most extreme discomfort. Stimulants, as the teen-ager's history indicates, can be used to pep up a sedated alcoholic, so he can go on getting loaded, or to smooth out the effects of a powerful downer such as alcohol or a barbiturate. Even LSD, used sparingly, seems to allow the user to occasionally space out when things begin to get hairy. After a while, this person gets so confused that it would be a challenge for him to tell you exactly what he had used on a given day—or during a given month. Just anything that came near him, usually.

The younger the average age of the caseload, the more likely the counselor is to come across this type of alcoholic. Because they're so difficult to identify, as well as to work with, they often get shuffled off to psychiatric units to wait until they're old enough to get help for their drinking. They usually spend the intervening years getting loaded at home or in the hospital while learning how to say the right things about their feelings and poor self-esteem. It makes sense for counselors to learn how to work well with them. There are certainly new ones showing up in treatment every day.

Alcohol with Narcotics: Dual Addiction

Opiate narcotics (opium, codeine, and morphine) were originally derived from the opium poppy; now many are synthesized by man. These include "euphoriants" as well as cough suppressants and our most reliable and effective pain-killers; all produce tolerance and dependence, and some, like heroin, are among our most addictive drugs. They are the subjects of numerous anti-drug campaigns and much legislation against use and sale. This is the group of drugs most people think of when drug abuse is mentioned.

At one point, most treatment professionals believed that narcotics addiction and alcoholism were incompatible. This was largely due to the fact that very few heroin addicts admitted using alcohol, and very few alcoholics gave any history of narcotics use.

But this assumption of incompatibility was incorrect, as we've since discovered. The first real indication of this came as methadone maintenance programs began to proliferate. (Methadone is a narcotic developed by the Germans during World War II because of a morphine shortage.) When heroin addiction became widespread, researchers decided that one possible solution to the problem of relapse among heroin addicts (which is far more common than among alcoholics) could be the substitution of methadone. This potent addictive narcotic has two advantages over heroin: it could be manufactured and controlled by the government (unlike heroin), and it could be administered orally, so the addict wouldn't get high (as he would after an IV injection). So chronic relapsing narcotics addicts were given the option of enrolling in methadone maintenance, and many of them did. It was at least easier than hustling every day for dope.

Since methadone features a cross-tolerance with heroin, it

acted as a blocking agent against any further heroin use; maintained on high doses, addicts couldn't shoot enough to "get off." But it didn't seem to interrupt their ability to drink alcohol, and many began to do just that.

After anywhere between six months to two years on methadone, some of the same people who reported no alcohol at all on their initial drug histories were drinking prodigious quantities and exhibiting all the symptoms of alcoholism. One former patient of ours, an ex-convict who'd been a heroin user since age sixteen, entered methadone maintenance at about age thirty-five, and within a year was in the hospital for alcoholic pancreatitis. We saw so many of these "newborn" alcoholics that alcoholism counselors used to say, "If you get a patient who turns out to really be a heroin addict, send him over to the methadone maintenance people. They'll send him back to you in six months drinking a fifth a day on top of his methadone."

We began to hear, as well, about people who overdosed because they used the combination of alcohol and heroin. Shooting heroin while drunk seemed to increase one's chances for misfortune.

This is an area where more research is necessary, but meanwhile these patients are showing up in alcoholism treatment again. How does the counselor handle them? Primarily by teaching the narcotics addict to recognize the presence of a *second* disease process in addition to the first. Chances are, if the treatment he's received is typical of modern approaches, he may not know that narcotics use represents the first disease process. Thus, he'll view his present problems with alcohol as a response to stress, or character weakness or whatever, and expect to treat alcoholism with will power.

This will result in the same problem faced by any alcoholic who relies solely on will power: a much increased risk of relapse. The farther advanced the illness, the less likelihood that this approach will bring even temporary abstinence.

So we recommend that the counselor start by educating the patient about how alcoholism works, just as he might with someone who had no narcotics history, but making use, if possible, of the addictive history to help the addict to understand the disease process. Anyone who's been addicted to narcotics has no doubt at all that such things as tolerance and withdrawal and a comfort zone exist, and knows from experience that quitting is no piece of cake. All that information can be used in teaching about alcoholism.

What do we recommend for someone who's currently using both heroin and alcohol in addictive fashion? Separate treatments for separate ailments. Naltrexone, an opiate antagonist, looks promising. (An opiate antagonist blocks the effect of an opiate, preventing an addict from experiencing any euphoria.) Then AA *and* Narcotics Anonymous.

We've also encountered a fair number of recovering alcoholics who've become narcotics addicts during periods of abstinence from alcohol. In those cases, the predisposing factor that encourages the alcoholic to start using narcotics is chronic pain, and the medications involved are usually codeine, Darvon, and Percodan, narcotics commonly prescribed for pain.

We recently had a patient who had been sober five years when he injured his back and was placed on a narcotic for pain. Within about six months, he was largely out of control, taking enormous amounts, and suffering acute withdrawal. This kind of dual addiction is relatively rare among alcoholics, but very troublesome when it occurs. After we detoxed him, he was able to return to AA without relapse and treat his addiction in the same way he treated his alcoholism. By some good fortune he didn't begin drinking while on his narcotics escapade, as many others in his situation would have. In this type of case, we recommend educating the alcoholic about the nature of the medicines he's been taking, getting him to accept some alternate solution for pain relief (or accept living with pain, if that's the case), and getting him involved in AA again as though he were a newcomer. To live without narcotics, especially in the presence of a good reason for taking narcotics, such as pain, requires adopting a program for living. AA's Twelve Step program, which probably worked for him before, is an obvious suggestion. Work it again, we'd advise.

6

Enabling and Provoking

A FRIEND WHO WORKS IN THE ENGINEERING DEPART-
ment of a large firm in the Northeast tells us that he's recently come to the realization that his boss is a practicing alcoholic.

Actually, he's suspected this for a good long time. He just
wasn't completely certain. Lately, however, the boss's behavior
has become so erratic, and so obviously alcohol-influenced, that
our friend (along with everyone else in the office) has set aside
his doubts.

Here is a typical day in this boss's working life.

He arrives at the office before anyone else and seems to be
working feverishly by the time the others arrive. He's noticeably
tense and irritable, and often exhibits a pronounced hand tremor.
About eleven-thirty in the morning, he goes to lunch in the bar
that is conveniently located in the basement of the building. This
bar does serve sandwiches but, more importantly, it serves liquor, and allows him to run a tab on what he drinks.

On the rare occasions when his employees have ventured

127

into this darkened den to have lunch with him, they've usually marveled at the quantities of beer he can consume during the course of a hamburger.

His mood improves remarkably after these lunches, which last anywhere from one and a half to three hours. When he returns to the office, he smells overpoweringly of alcohol, and is generally unable to do any work before he leaves. Of course, he leaves early; often, he stops off for "one or two" on the way home.

The employees used to keep a cooler in the boss's office, which they stocked with beer so they could sit around and have a few after work at the end of the week. It was one of those silly alcohol-oriented socialization activities that people often believe bring co-workers closer together. The employees grew bored with it and stopped filling the cooler a long time ago, but it continues to sit in his office. Now, as his drinking becomes an issue, they're beginning to suspect that he stocks it (and empties it) by himself.

All of the boss's work is done during a two-hour stretch in the morning. The rest of his day is taken up by drinking.

How, you might reasonably ask, does this man manage to get away with this, given the fact that he works as an important supervisor for a busy, rather staid corporation, where a conservative image is necessary and deadlines must constantly be met? The answer is simple: his employees protect him.

They do this in two different ways. First, there's a group of what we might call active defenders of the alcoholic boss. These are the people such as his secretary and assistants who make excuses to the company directors and the other department heads when they come with a question about a project. They say he's out of the office and take a message. If the call is really important, they can phone him in the bar and tell him to rush back upstairs to return it. They're the ones who try to make sure he has some idea of what's really going on in the office so he can look knowledgeable at meetings and so the necessary departmental tasks are done on time. They also put the muzzle on any complaining which might come from other employees, and make sure the office maintains a facade of functioning smoothly under his supposed direction.

The rest of the employees practice a sort of benign neglect, which means that if he doesn't bother them, they don't bother him, or mention anything about his drinking.

So the people in the office are a great help to their boss. He literally couldn't get along without them.

As a result of this help, the boss has managed to continue drinking through two heart attacks and a dangerous ulcer. He slurs his speech so badly that he is completely unintelligible after lunch. He weaves about the office, unable to navigate between two rows of desks without bumping into something, and there is a standing office joke about his memory. "I told the boss I was going to do that," one person will say. "Yeah," says the other, "but did you tell him in the morning or the afternoon?"

Everything passed on to the boss after his noon drinking session, you see, is lost to posterity.

The boss's health is so bad that even though he did quit smoking, he's still a medical disaster area. Even though they'd be horrified at the suggestion, the people who work with him are waiting for him to be felled by another attack, and perhaps die.

This situation has been worsening steadily for at least three years, and probably longer.

Why haven't the people around him done something about it? Why haven't they at least recognized it for what it is?

There are several reasons. First of all, like most Americans, they're ignorant about alcoholism. They've heard that alcoholism is a disease, but that's about as far as it goes. They neither know what the symptoms are nor understand the peculiar nature of its progression. Thus, they have no way of differentiating an alcoholic from a heavy social drinker, or whatever other phrase is current.

Second, like most Americans, they get wrapped up in the supposed causes of his drinking. We're all amateur psychologists, and this alcoholic, like most, invites speculation: a miserable marriage, kids who've run off to join bizarre religious sects, whatever. Instead of talking about his drinking, people in his office tend to concentrate on the stress he must be experiencing.

And of course, there have been some practical tradeoffs made between boss and employees. With the boss so preoccupied with his own difficulties, the workers are allowed to set their own hours, schedule their own vacations, work virtually without supervision. They get all the work done, and they do it well—and they don't have to worry about any rules which might inconvenience them. They don't have to adhere to the boundaries that a more active supervisor might impose.

Last, and perhaps least logical of all, they go along with this pattern because they really like their boss and think they're *helping* him—there's that word again—by showing loyalty and sticking up for his behavior, no matter what it might be. Their intentions are basically good, and this makes it all the more difficult for them to understand how their actions (or inaction) fit into the progression of this disease like a hand in a glove.

Enabling the Alcoholic

It is the peculiar nature of this illness which takes help and loyalty and turns them into something called *enabling*.

In the beginning of this disease, remember, the rewards of drinking far outweigh the penalties for the alcoholic. As the disease progresses, the penalties begin to overcome the benefits. This shift in balance is what ultimately leads the alcoholic to consider quitting drinking. Anything which prevents him from experiencing or being aware of those penalties is going to effectively prolong the drinking and thus the active, dangerous phase of the disease.

The help provided by those in his office enables the boss to continue drinking in spite of the consequences. That's a good description of enabling behavior: that which helps the alcoholic avoid the negative aspects of his drinking.

Obviously, enabling can be found throughout society. We once sat in a courtroom and listened to a judge chastise a prosecutor for insinuating that a prominent local citizen be evaluated for alcoholism simply because he'd received three DWI violations in two years.

"This man is a respected figure in the community," the judge admonished, "and he should not be treated in this courtroom as though he were a common thief or alcoholic." The respected figure was let off with a slight fine and wound up in that same courtroom for yet another alcohol-related charge less than nine months later.

Another example was a sheriff's deputy who, during the twelve years of his active alcoholic drinking, was stopped by police and found to be drunk behind the wheel no less than twenty times. He never received a single ticket. The word had been passed among his fellow officers to simply drive him home and put him to bed, rather than give the department a bad name.

Some of the most effective enablers are physicians, who for years have hospitalized alcoholics under any diagnosis *but* alcoholism. We recently encountered a twenty-five-year-old woman who'd been treated three separate times for ulcers and gastritis, and was never asked by her doctors about her drinking — which happened to be at the rate of about two gallons of wine per week. This happened more than twenty years after the medical establishment formally recognized alcoholism as a disease.

The worst examples of this misguided enabling by doctors are sometimes found when the alcoholic they're treating happens to be a physician also. Legitimately concerned that their patient might lose his license to practice medicine, attending physicians often go out of their way to keep any reference to alcohol or drug use out of a medical record.

Of course, in the process, they never get around to treating alcoholism itself, but continue putting band-aids on its most severe symptoms. Meanwhile, the alcoholic gets worse and new problems appear even before the last ones are resolved. We heard about one alcoholic psychiatrist who was admitted by his partner to various psychiatric units under diagnoses such as depressive neurosis and agitated depression to cover what was really a case of chronic alcoholism. In no instance was alcohol or drug use ever mentioned in any hospital chart. After about twenty of these admissions, the alcoholic killed himself, accidentally or deliberately, with an overdose of barbiturates. On the death certificate, his partner asked if the coroner couldn't change "abuse of secobarbital" to "suicide after depressive illness."

The worst sort of enabling by far occurs within the alcoholic's family, because family members are so much closer to the disease process. If they are fortunate enough to learn something about alcoholism and overcome their own resistance to recognizing it in someone they care about, the family could probably take steps to end the active drinking much earlier than usual. But most families instead fall into a pattern of destructive enabling which prolongs the alcoholic's drinking and causes no end of problems for everyone. In fact, this enabling often leads not only to the demise of the family unit, but of the alcoholic as well.

"Buddy" was a construction foreman whose wife had died several years earlier and left him responsible for the care of their two young daughters. He received quite a bit of help in this from his sister, who lived down the street and was unmarried.

Buddy also happened to be an alcoholic. His particular pattern was to limit his intake during the week, and then really cut loose on weekends. Every Friday night, he'd hit the workingmen's bars, paycheck in hand, and by two the next morning he'd have gotten in a fight and wound up in jail (if he'd won the fight), or in a hospital emergency room (if he'd lost).

He'd inevitably call his sister, who would get out of bed, get dressed, and drive downtown to retrieve him.

She considered this to be her sisterly duty, and though she constantly complained about it, she never failed to bail him out of whatever jam he'd gotten himself into.

As a result, Buddy managed to get roaring drunk, get in a fight, and get arrested nearly every weekend for several years without once spending a night in jail.

That's enabling. Observers are often fooled, because of the enabler's loud complaints about the drinking and open criticism of the alcoholic, into thinking that this enabler is the only one who stands between the alcoholic and still worse drinking. But in fact, the enabler directly contributes to the duration of active alcoholism by preventing the drinker from experiencing the results of his own behavior.

Enablers fool themselves as well: they often can't believe that they (of all people) are actually part of the problem. They see themselves as victims of the drinking, or as the drinker's last hope for recovery. They see themselves as charged with holding the family together, whatever the cost; many enablers will tell you, "At least we've got each other." And in some cases, this type of behavior is seen as selfless or Christian, and thus gains the enabler a measure of gratifying praise within the community. People said of Buddy's sister: "She's just so much more (check one: patient, kind, loyal, giving, loving) than I'd be in that situation." She was actually admired and respected in some circles for this very behavior.

Changing Directions

How is this net of enabling that supports the drinking alcoholic to be broken? As in the other aspects of treatment, the first step is to *educate* the enablers. They need to understand two things from the outset: that alcoholism is a chronic, progressive, and potentially fatal disease which must be treated, and that their good intentions have become part of the problem rather than part of the solution. Thus, basic education about the disease and about enabling behavior can lead to self-awareness on their part—meaning that they recognize what they've been doing and what could be done to change that.

This is important because it's entirely possible that they've been looking the symptoms of alcoholism right in the face without recognizing them as symptoms. You get queries from them like, "What causes her to shake like that in the morning?" and "Does drinking cause those gaps in his memory?"

Like as not, their only exposure to alcoholism information has been through magazine articles on the warning signs, which dwell on irrelevancies like "drinking for the effect" and "drinking to feel better" rather than on the actual symptoms and mechanisms of the illness.

With professional help, these misguided helpers can participate in an intervention which usually results in an otherwise hopelessly resistant alcoholic entering treatment. (Intervention, discussed in the last section of this chapter, involves an organized effort on the part of others to get an alcoholic into treatment.) Even if the intervention is unsuccessful, the education of the enablers (and their resultant change in approach) often leads to the sudden collapse of the alcoholic's control over his drinking, which *then* leads to treatment.

Either way, it's nearly impossible for the alcoholic to continue drinking without the help of others; it's simply too debilitating. Left on his own, the drinker succumbs to the progression of the illness. Illusions about his own ability to function independently are quickly eroded.

In a series of six meetings, we educate families, friends, employers, and employees of alcoholics with the following points.

- *How alcoholism works*. Why we call alcoholism a disease; what kind of disease it is; why it keeps getting worse, despite everyone's efforts to control it; drinking patterns; loss of control; how it's treated.
- *Alcoholism and the body*. Medical effects of alcoholic drinking; alcohol-related diseases; how alcoholic drinking affects the alcoholic's behavior through its effects on his physiology.
- *Enabling and the family*. What enabling and provoking behaviors are; stages in the family's response to the illness; how to change.
- *Drugs and the alcoholic*. Alcohol used with other drugs; drug use and relapse.
- *Normal recovery symptoms*. What happens to the alcoholic's body after he quits drinking; the post-acute-withdrawal

syndrome; how to treat symptoms such as insomnia and periodic impotence.

• *How to live with the recovering alcoholic*. Recovery and relapse; the family's role in recovery; friends and co-workers; living with a disease you can neither cure nor control; getting better yourself.

The last two sessions are of most interest to the people involved with the alcoholic after successful intervention has occurred and treatment has been initiated. The first three are useful before the intervention.

For supplemental reading, we usually assign James Milam's *Under the Influence*.* Though they're too numerous to name, there are also a number of excellent films about alcoholism both from the perspective of those who live with it and those who work with it. All may prove helpful, and we encourage people to search out what's available in their own communities.

Behavior That Provokes Alcoholism

There's yet another form of behavior that develops in response to another person's alcoholism. It's usually called *provoking:* behavior which directly encourages an alcoholic to drink.

One of our former patients worked for a man with whom he'd developed a much closer relationship than is normally found between a boss and an employee. This man had helped our patient get ahead in the company, making sure he got every raise and every chance for advancement that came down the pike. They went to lunch together every day, played golf together on weekends, and our patient had even asked his boss to be godfather to his first child.

When this relationship was about four years old, the patient was admitted for alcoholism treatment, and decided to give up

*James Milam and Katherine Ketcham, *Under the Influence*: Seattle, Madrona Publishers, 1981.

drinking. He had experienced a rather severe bout of pancreatitis, so he wasn't reluctant to quit, though he was concerned that others at work might regard him as somehow different and therefore shun him. He believed, however, that with the support of his friend the boss, he could overcome any prejudice against him.

The first day he arrived back on the job, his boss took him to lunch. Great, thought our patient; at least I'll be able to be myself with *him*.

To his surprise, the first thing the boss did was to order drinks for both of them.

The employee sat there stunned. "John," he said, "what are you doing? You know I quit."

"Yeah, but now you can control it," the boss replied. "That's why the company paid for that expensive treatment you went through. You aren't seriously saying you can't handle one lousy drink, are you? You're not some kind of cripple, you know."

Our patient managed to refuse, despite continued promptings from the boss, but was shocked at the complete lack of understanding from the man who was supposed to be his friend. Indeed, their friendship never was the same again; that was because, now that he was sober, the employee noticed that his boss drank as much as he himself ever had, and exhibited quite a few of the symptoms of alcoholism.

After all, they'd done quite a bit of their drinking together. It seemed they had even more in common than our patient had first realized.

The most dramatic, and destructive, examples of provoking behavior occur within the family. The syndrome usually makes its first appearance during the period of alcoholic drinking where the family is actively trying to get the alcoholic to stop, but before they've gone to get any professional help—what's often called the home remedy stage. Here, the spouse and kids may resort to such Dry Moral model tactics as pouring liquor down the sink, throwing it out of the house, or searching around for the alcoholic's hidden bottles. There are inevitably loud arguments over the drinking and the unpredictable behavior that results from it, and all this hullabaloo only serves to incite the alcoholic into still more drinking, because now he can legitimately feel that everyone in the household is persecuting him. Thus the feverish campaign to get him to stop has simply provided him with a new set of excuses to continue.

Provoking behavior is usually rooted in resentment over the alcoholic's drinking and in a misunderstanding of the illness itself. It often extends beyond the alcoholic's drinking and sabotages his efforts to stay sober. In some families, it's one of the major obstacles to recovery.

Let's go back to the case of Buddy and his sister.

As Buddy's drinking got worse, his sister was forced to take over more and more of his duties within the family, for the simple reason that he couldn't perform them. Due to lack of time, she had to give up most of her own interests, and devote himself to Buddy's kids. At some point, he lost his job; she then had to arrange for him to receive aid, and even dipped into her own savings to make up for his lost income.

And she was still having to take care of Buddy as well, cleaning up after him, cooking for him, and the like. Since he was drinking heavily all the time by now, he was actually more difficult to handle, and more dependent, than the children. It was a bit like living with a two-hundred-pound infant, and she didn't like it.

As happens when one person gives up her own life to take care of someone else, she grew more and more resentful of Buddy. She didn't often confront him directly—he was usually too drunk to hear, anyway—but she developed a terrific hostile glare that, in his lucid moments, even Buddy knew meant that life was intolerable and that it was his fault.

Eventually Buddy got so sick that he realized he had to put a stop to his drinking. He sobered up, joined AA, and started living without alcohol. But even though he was able to put the past behind him, his sister wasn't. She was profoundly unimpressed with this new Buddy; she told him flatly that he'd get drunk any day now, because that's just the way he was, and there wasn't anything he or anyone else could do about it (a perfect example of the impaired model).

Somehow, Buddy managed to hang on to his sobriety. His sister, however, went from selfless saint to nagging harridan. She criticized every move he made and fought him every time he attempted to take back his responsibilities.

The sister caused problems despite the fact that Buddy was at long last doing what she supposedly had been trying to get him to do for years. Now, it seemed, she was trying to prevent him from doing it.

As so many alcoholics do, Buddy stayed sober despite her negative response, using AA as his support and being as hardheaded about his abstinence as he had been about his drinking. A lot of less stubborn alcoholics, however, would have thrown in the towel.

What motivated Buddy's sister to behave in this fashion? Simply the accumulation of resentments that she'd developed during her years of servitude to her brother. These were years of sacrifice which she justified by telling herself that Buddy was incapable of getting sober—and that his drinking was a sort of test of her worthiness as a person, which she believed she was passing with flying colors. Certainly, no one could have accused her of selfishness. She held the family together through thick and (mostly) thin.

And now, her no-good drunken reprobate brother had gone and gotten sober, simply because his drinking was starting to make *him* feel bad. If he could stop, she thought, then why hadn't he done it years ago, when she had begged him to? What right had he to subject his family to all this grief? To ruin her life and not even have the courtesy to feel guilty about it? Who would repay her for the lost years?

Instead of loving Buddy, she slowly realized, she now hated him. She was afraid of his new-found independence: suppose he decided to remarry? What would become of her? She'd given up so many of her own interests that she had no idea what she could do to support herself. Even though Buddy's drinking was intolerable, it was at least familiar, and she felt that it was better than nothing. And without realizing it she set out, through provoking behavior, to get him drunk, and dependent, again.

People get used to living with drinking alcoholics. Invariably, they don't know at first that they're dealing with alcoholism, so they adapt to the lifestyle dictated by the progression of the illness, while believing that something else is behind their difficulties. Then, once they know that drinking *is* the culprit, they set out with their program of home remedies, which involve them even more unproductively in the disease process. Finally, as it becomes obvious that the loved one's actions are outside their control, they give up and learn to live with, or around, the progressing pathology. That is, if they stay.

It's no surprise, then, that some of our patients find that their families liked them better drunk than they do now that they're sober. Drinking is familiar to the family, and they've probably, through painful experience, learned how to manipulate and control the drinking alcoholic so as to limit his interference in their lives. Then, when he returns home with plans for rebuilding the family according to his own desires, they rebel.

Unless the alcoholic is prepared for this, it can come as quite a shock. We knew one man who'd pretty much spent the year before he entered treatment in a chair in the living room, drinking Scotch and trying to finish reading a scholarly work on the Civil War. Every evening, he'd discover that he was unable to remember most of what he'd read the night before, so he would have to start all over again; he devoted about a year of his life to reading over and over the same hundred pages of the same book.

His wife and five children at least preferred this to the days when he'd get arrested for being drunk in public and come riding home in the back of a police cruiser. As long as he was willing to sit quietly in his chair, they were willing to go on living their lives around him, as though he were a piece of furniture.

Eventually, by some miracle, he ended up in treatment, where he discovered that he felt so much better when sober (he even finished his book) that he wanted to try staying that way. He became very enthusiastic about life, and went home with high hopes for a grand restoration of family life.

The first thing he noticed was that his family didn't spend much time together, that everyone seemed to do his own thing, independently of everyone else. So he drew up a schedule of family activities which he felt would substantially improve things.

One night after dinner, he called the family together and read over his new schedule of activities. When he was finished, he looked around for their response. His eldest son said simply: "We're not going to do that stuff." When the father asked him why not, he replied, "We like things the way they are. You weren't around when we needed you, so you don't have any right to tell us what to do now. As far as we know, you could get drunk again tomorrow."

That's a direct, but very painful, statement of exactly how the alcoholic's family felt about his drinking and his recovery. Their defenses were still up, and he would have to wait for them to come down, just as they had had to wait for him to decide to do something about his problem.

Getting the Family into Treatment

When the family members have reached the point where their lives have been dramatically affected by another member's alcoholism, they belong in Al-Anon. That's a self-help group for anyone whose life has been affected by another person's drinking. It is similar in structure and philosophy to AA, offering many of the same advantages: ongoing practical advice and support in changing behavior.

Families, however, often resist this kind of help. They may take the position that the alcoholic is the one with the problem, not them. Why should *they* learn anything about the illness?

Or they may adopt the attitude that it's the counselor's job to fix the alcoholic, much as a surgeon fixes a ruptured appendix or a mechanic repairs a carburetor. A dead giveaway is when the family drops the alcoholic off at the hospital and then flies to Hawaii for a three-week vacation; they either have no understanding of the disease, or they have completely given up on the alcoholic and just want a break from him for a few weeks. Treatment, to them, is like the boarding the family schnauzer at a kennel.

The first attitude (that it's the alcoholic's problem) is essentially correct, in that the ultimate solution does lie with the person who has the disease. But it denies the truth that most families develop enabling or provoking behaviors, which promote relapse and interfere with recovery. That part of the problem can only be rectified by the enablers themselves.

Second, as we've pointed out again and again, this disease is treated by the patient, not by the doctor, because we don't have any reliable cure for it. No magic is available to alter the alcoholic's response to alcohol, from abnormal back to normal. Like the diabetic, the alcoholic is given a regimen to follow, and like the diabetic, generally does well as long as he follows the regimen. When he deviates, he gets into trouble.

Thus, the family's role becomes even more significant than if he was merely being asked to recuperate from some kind of surgery. In this case, the alcoholic is required to make substantive changes in lifestyle *in order to recover*—changes that the family will influence, and be influenced by. Just as the alcoholic's drinking affected their lives, so will his recovery.

The counselor needs to point out to the family that their choice is whether to continue as part of the problem, or move towards becoming part of the solution.

In Al-Anon, the focus shifts back towards the individual being responsible for his or her own happiness, regardless of what the alcoholic does or doesn't do. Alcoholism is regarded as something beyond the control of even the most strong-willed family member, and so, like the alcoholic, the family member is encouraged to quit fighting and acknowledge the need for help.

With accompanying education, membership in Al-Anon generally serves to overcome the remaining defenses, and the destructive cycles of enabling and provoking are broken.

How to Ruin an Intervention

Certainly, the most striking single technique in the field of counseling is the *intervention*. This method, described in the book *I'll Quit Tomorrow,** by Vernon E. Johnson, allows those around the alcoholic to present their concern to him in such a dramatic fashion that he's motivated to seek help for his drinking problem. Since the popularization of this technique, many alcoholics have entered treatment who otherwise might have continued drinking and perhaps died.

In AA, popular wisdom said that an alcoholic had to hit bottom before he would accept help; intervention was designed to dramatize how much alcohol had *already* affected his life, and the lives of those around him. As Johnson pointed out, the alcoholic's limited awareness of events outside of himself was primarily responsible for his failure to understand the seriousness of his condition, and intervention could quickly increase this awareness.

Intervention, if done correctly, usually works. The alcoholic is impressed by the concern shown by others, sees that things are not what he believed them to be, and at least consents to subject himself to some form of evaluation for alcoholism. For information regarding successful intervention, we suggest the numerous publications of the Johnson Institute of Edina, Minnesota and of other specialists (see Suggested Reading at the back of this book).

Since we find that we usually learn more from mistakes than from successes, however, we'll confine ourselves to an example of an intervention which, despite the good intentions of everyone concerned, was messed up to the point where the alcoholic practi-

*Vernon E. Johnson, *I'll Quit Tomorrow*: San Francisco, Harper & Row, 1980.

cally had to force the counselor to let him get help. You'll be able to see from this what not to do during an intervention, and therefore may save yourself some painful experience.

Let's introduce Marty, a bright, concerned, experienced social worker for a community service agency. Marty had recently attended a two-day workshop in intervention techniques at a local college. He was impressed with the new concepts and eager to put his knowledge into practice. So, he was excited when a woman visited his office to complain about her husband, a retired military officer, whose drinking drove her crazy.

Marty explained the concept of intervention to her; it would center, he said, around a meeting attended by significant others who are willing to confront the alcoholic, in a loving fashion, with the seriousness of his dilemma. She was impressed by this, especially by his reassurance that she wouldn't have to face her husband alone. He asked her to make a list of people who might be able to help in such an undertaking. She said that her two children might be willing to join in, along with her husband's boss at his new job, one of his co-workers, and his doctor, who'd mentioned to her on one occasion that her husband's liver was enlarged and who wondered about his drinking.

"I didn't say anything at the time," she told Marty, "because I didn't want to embarrass Bob. But I know the doctor was concerned."

The two daughters, it turned out, lived close by, and had complained to their mother a number of times about their father yelling at his grandchildren when they come to visit. His co-worker had brought him home from the office Christmas party where he'd gotten drunk and embarrassed everyone, and probably, she thought, had seen more of his drinking than anyone besides herself. His boss was a recovering alcoholic himself, active in AA and open about his history of drinking problems, and might be willing to involve himself.

Marty went over the list, and decided that the intervention should include the three immediate family members and the co-worker who was familiar with the husband's drinking. He was reluctant to involve the boss because he felt that the inclusion of such an authority might make the alcoholic very uncomfortable and resistant. Besides, the boss wasn't personally involved with the alcoholic, and therefore wouldn't carry as much emotional weight.

Marty had them all think of evidence, from their experience, that something was seriously wrong with the intervention's subject. He advised them to express their concern repeatedly to the subject, so that he would know they cared deeply for him, and were only doing this for his own good.

Marty did place a call to the physician who'd been mentioned, but Marty didn't hear back immediately, and decided that they should go ahead with the intervention the following day.

At ten o'clock, the daughters and friend arrived. Marty briefly reviewed their presentations with them, and reminded them to try to make the alcoholic feel really cared about.

When the alcoholic arrived with his wife, he was really shocked. His wife had told him they were going to a counselor to talk about *her* menopausal depressions, which he said had been irritating him for months. As soon as it dawned on him that he was the subject of this meeting, he was ready to walk. But his wife burst into tears, and his daughters pleaded with him to listen, so he reluctantly, angrily, agreed.

The first presenter was his eldest daughter. She told her dad that his temper was frightening her children and they didn't want to visit him anymore. "You snap at everyone," she said, "and never let anyone disagree with you without implying that they're idiots." Several times, she told him, she'd tried to talk to him about these problems and he'd refused to even listen.

He looked at her coldly. "What right do you have to wash our dirty laundry in public? If a father and his daughter have a disagreement, does the daughter run to some counselor and criticize her father? Frankly, I expected a bit more loyalty than that. If the tables were turned, I wouldn't be running to other people with stories about *you*."

Tears were in her eyes. "But it's because I care about you, Daddy," she pointed out.

"Then why don't you show it once in a while," he said,

"by doing what *I* want you to do, rather than what other people tell you to do. No wonder you can't hold a job and your husband left you—you don't know what it means to be loyal."

She dissolved into helpless weeping. Marty was at a loss for words. The second daughter rushed to her sister's defense.

"Stop picking on her, Dad," she snapped. "You are such an intellectual bully. You find people's weaknesses and jump all over them."

"*I* do?" her father shouted. "What about *you,* getting me here under false pretenses, ganging up on me like a bunch of jackals, directed, I suppose, by this grinning moron here"—this was for Marty—"as though you had no more concern for your father's feelings than the man in the moon?"

"*I'm* not concerned?" the daughter responded. "You have the nerve to talk about *my* lack of concern? Where were *you* when I was growing up? Stuck on some stupid tour of duty somewhere, so that we never saw you."

The shouting continued. Marty tried desperately to intervene, but couldn't get anyone's attention. Finally, the wife screamed, "Stop it, both of you! I'm sick of your constant arguing!"

As soon as they quieted, she began talking softly, crying all the while. "I wish I'd never consented to this," she said. "I only thought it might get you to do something about your damned drinking. You yell at everyone, you threaten me constantly, I can't sleep at night because of you. Every time I try to bring up the subject of your temper, you blame it on my menopause. Nothing is ever your fault. Well, I'm sick of it. If you don't do something right now, I'm leaving you. I mean it. It's up to you."

The husband was clearly shocked. He appeared to have no idea she was willing to divorce him after thirty years of marriage. He looked at her and said quietly: "Martha, I don't want that. I'll do whatever you want. If it means that much to you. . . . I don't agree with you, but I don't want to lose you." He looked towards Marty.

"I guess you're the one who knows about these things. What am I supposed to do?"

Marty was greatly relieved. He felt that the day had been rescued from complete failure. "You need help," he said. "It's hard for you to see it at this point, but you have a disease of feelings, which is causing all your problems with your family and with alcohol. Instead of facing your feelings, you drink to escape from them, and this has led you to the point where you're dependent on alcohol. Unless you receive some kind of help, it will get worse, to the point where your life is seriously damaged. Recovery isn't easy, but it's possible. First, you have to admit your problem; then you have to begin to look at your own feelings honestly, on a gut level, so that you can understand your own anger, fear, guilt, and emotional pain, and can deal with those without resorting to alcohol. You'll learn to grow emotionally and spiritually, to become a more loving, giving, expressive person, able to give and receive love freely. You're entering a period of great growth as a person." Marty said this with great feeling. "And I want you to know," he added, "that *I* care about you as a person, too, and want only the best for you."

"Look," the alcoholic said, "I don't mean to be rude, but I'm fifty-six years old, and I don't want to grow any more as a person. What you're saying makes no sense to me. And I don't see how you can care so much about me. You've never even met me before, and I called you a moron twenty minutes ago."

"You'll understand what I mean after you've been in treatment for a while," Marty responded.

"I hope so," the alcoholic responded. "Where *is* this treatment I'm supposed to go to?"

"There's a facility down the road which is known for its alcoholism treatment," Marty said. "It's very expensive, but very effective."

"My insurance won't cover it unless it's in a hospital," the alcoholic said.

"It won't?" Marty said weakly. "But it's an excellent residential program, even though it's not a medical facility—"

"No go," said the patient. "Didn't you people check this out before this little session?"

"No," the wife said. She looked at Marty. "Isn't there a hospital he can go to?"

"There must be," Marty responded. "But I don't know where, exactly. I could check for you," he said, even more weakly.

"You do that," said the alcoholic. "In the meantime, I'm going home. In fact, I'll call my doctor and ask him what he thinks. He told me my liver was too big last year, but I didn't pay any attention to it. Maybe *he* knows where I could go."

"Come along, Martha," he said to his wife, and left the office, his family and friend trailing along after him. As they left, Marty realized that the friend had said absolutely nothing throughout the entire session.

Let's take a look at what Marty did wrong. There's plenty to see.

First of all, Marty chose *not* to include in his intervention team the two people who, along with his wife, had the most authority over the alcoholic—his boss and his doctor. Given the fact that the boss was himself a recovering alcoholic, and that his doctor would be able to offer some hard evidence of alcohol-related liver problems, the oversight is even worse. Marty chose, in effect, to rely on speaking loudly while carrying a small stick. Instead of having three people at the meeting who had actual leverage over the alcoholic, he chose to limit himself to only one.

Second, Marty did not make it plain that primarily *drinking-related* behavior was to be pointed out to the alcoholic. Generalized observations about his irritability and changes in mood are easy for him to rationalize and blame on others. But it's not his personality which is the problem; it's his drinking. Wherever possible, his behavior should be related to his drinking.

Third, these people were not adequately prepared for resistance. When attacked, the elder daughter simply collapsed. Her father found her weaknesses in a way that only someone who had lived with her could, and completely immobilized her. The second daughter immediately rushed to her rescue (as she'd probably done for years), and was also rendered ineffective for the rest of the intervention by her own obvious resentment against her father. Thus, he was free of having to listen to either of them; two down, one to go.

Fortunately, that one had the good sense to raise the ante. She wasn't going to get into the same old arguments; something was going to change, or she was leaving. If she hadn't been willing to do this, the intervention would have ended right there.

Once the resistance had been broken, Marty jumped in with a lot of theorizing about the causes of the alcoholic's drinking, and a lot of emotional talk that was as out of place as a fish in a bicycle race. This just confused the issue, and confirmed the alcoholic's opinion that he was dealing with an idiot. Marty's protestations of caring were equally out of sync with the situation at that point. He thus divested himself of any effectiveness he had as an intervener.

Finally, and most embarrassingly, he was completely unprepared for closing the deal: he didn't know where his patient could get the treatment he needed. The patient would have to do the research himself. Had he been more severely out of control over his drinking, he would have relapsed as soon as he left the office, and simply would never have followed through.

Fortunately, this patient decided on his own to get help, as a result of his wife's words. If he hadn't, there's no way Marty's intervention would ever have convinced him.

Oh yes, about the co-worker: what do people usually do when they find themselves in the middle of another person's family dispute? They shut up. And that's exactly what this poor soul did.

7

Getting Started

The Counseling Process

B EGIN AT THE BEGINNING: SUPPOSE THE COUNSELOR has his first patient sitting there in front of him with that trademark expectant look on his face. What comes next?

Whether the initial contact takes place in an inpatient or outpatient setting, it's impossible for a counselor to work with someone who is intoxicated, so we'll assume this alcoholic has entered treatment at the point most do: either very recently sober, or in that stage of controlled intake which we call "being between problems."

We'll try to address issues that confront counselors with either brand of alcoholic.

The counselor knows nothing about the patient except that he has some type of alcohol- or drug-related problem; nor does he know how the alcoholic got to this point, or what he hopes to accomplish. In fact, no one could prove so far that treatment is necessary at all.

Obviously, the counselor needs to obtain a history from the patient.

Now this history is not a life story. Taking such a history doesn't mean prying into the locked closets of the individual's upbringing. It does mean inquiring into his drinking with an eye to finding out what, if anything, is wrong with it. There should be more concern with the extent and severity of his use of alcohol than with his feelings about Mom and Dad.

Unfortunately, the patient may not want to discuss drinking at all. He's probably more willing to talk about the big kid who pushed him around in the fourth grade. In fact, it's this very fondness for irrelevant detail which is responsible for many alcoholics getting deeply and unproductively enmeshed in past-oriented psychotherapy. Though this type of therapy seldom reaches completion—drinking interrupts it—it nonetheless holds endless fascination, and represents a classic wrong turn in recovery.

Therefore, it's essential for the counselor to confine early conversation to drinking and its effects and, if the patient strays, to bring him back to the issue at hand.

It's equally important that discussion be centered on *recent* drinking. Patients also like to talk about how they drank ten or fifteen years ago, which isn't germane to the moment.

If the alcoholic is still drinking or has only recently quit, then appropriate first questions have to do with how much he has consumed on a daily basis over the past few weeks, as well as about symptoms of withdrawal he may have experienced. Undoubtedly he will have to be taught how to recognize those symptoms, by selecting from a list read to him. This gives the counselor an idea of the severity of the addiction.

Then, returning to the question of amount consumed, the counselor asks if recent drinking is appreciably more or less than it was, say, six months ago. He asks too about any drinking-related illnesses experienced during this period; when complete, he will have a preliminary drinking history.

Many counselors become very concerned about the accuracy of this history. They suspect, often correctly, that the alcoholic is understating the true extent and severity of his use of alcohol.

Some counselors abandon the alcoholic's version entirely, preferring to rely on what the spouse or family tell them. Unfortunately, this is often as inaccurate as the alcoholic's story. Thus the old saw: "To find out how much an alcoholic drinks, take the amount he claims to drink and double it, or the amount his wife says he drinks and divide it in half."

Right along with the investigation of alcohol use, it's crucial to look for any concurrent drug use. Again, the counselor simply goes over a list of drugs, and asks about the patient's use of them. If he's been using tranquilizers, for example, that substantially changes the withdrawal experience. Most alcoholics who've been through several treatments have a bottle of tranquilizers that some doctor gave them along the way; if they've not used the drug, of course, it's of no importance, but if they have relied on sedatives to medicate alcohol withdrawal, that is essential information.

There is more denial encountered in this area than in the discussion of drinking itself. But if the patient is under twenty-five years of age, the odds are that other drugs, particularly marijuana, are involved. This must be ferreted out now. It will be extremely important later in recovery.

The Counselor-Patient Relationship

Some psychologists have made a fortune advising therapists as to what must be done to make their patients feel comfortable and therefore allow them to start therapy off on the right foot. In our experience, most of this advice is unadulterated nonsense. What *is* required in establishing a solid relationship is knowledge, directness, and common sense.

Any counselor recognizes the advantage of being seen by the patient as competent, as knowing what he's doing.

There are many ways to give this impression. It never hurts to show the patient that, indeed, the counselor has experience to draw on. We do not refer to the very personal experience of recovery from alcoholism, but the experience of working with people—as counselor, or counseling intern, or AA sponsor.

But most helpful is a simple demonstration of knowledge of

this disease. The patient must be shown that the counselor understands, better than he does, how alcoholism works.

Suppose the patient describes the experience of waking up every night with horrible nightmares. He can be filled in on the role of alcohol withdrawal in causing that. Since he's usually assumed that nightmares are due to stress or underlying depression, he is probably surprised to hear that drinking may be the real source. The counselor may promise further details of the mechanism of discomfort. This ties him to the patient a bit, and also establishes him as the authority, from whom the alcoholic might learn something very useful.

For recovering people who have entered the counseling role, we once again advise that it isn't necessary that the patient feel they've both had exactly the same experiences. We knew one counselor who continually claimed to have done about everything imaginable during her own drinking career. If her client told her he'd received three drunk-driving arrests, she claimed to have been picked up four times. If the patient swore he puffed nitrous oxide every morning with his scrambled eggs, she would state that she'd been down that road herself. One day, to test her claims, we asked her if she'd used a fictitious drug, "narcoamphetadone-X." Of course, she'd been stoned on it twice in Milwaukee.

It's only important that the patient understand that the counselor earned his position. We did know one psychiatrist whose patients refused to believe on initial contact that he was really a doctor. "It's just that he acts like he doesn't know what he's doing," one said. A three-piece suit and wall full of diplomas won't make up for that.

The second beneficial counselor trait is to appear to be safe to talk with. Being safe simply means that the counselor won't run out and tell everyone what the patient said, or won't make him feel like he's crazy, or some kind of retarded person, for having said it. This is simply the basis of trust.

It's also essential that the counselor appear to be secure in his own beliefs. That's evidenced by a willingness to listen to the patient's beliefs—even if they're a tad on the wild side.

To become confrontive on the first or second interview is a mistake counselors frequently make. They operate on the assumption that if they don't manage to reach the alcoholic immediately, he'll leave treatment. More often, this tactic serves to drive him away. If the patient has already taken the step of seeking treatment, the counselor should try not to scare him off. It probably took him years to get to this point.

We believe the most effective approach simply involves letting the patient know that he has a fatal disease and it therefore shows extremely good judgment to come for counseling. Since this is a true statement, no particular technique is involved in making it. It also helps in reassuring the patient that there is no intention of taking a moralistic perspective towards his actions.

The third counselor trait we recommend is simple friendliness. There isn't any need to be especially authoritarian with these patients. If the counselor really knows more about their illness than they do, that knowledge will bring with it an air of authority which will carry him through the initial stages. Then he's free to treat alcoholics without worrying about whether or not they respect him.

Above all, it's important at this point to keep the conversation from straying off into areas which don't have anything to do with the matter at hand. This is emphatically the counselor's responsibility because the typical alcoholic isn't able to do it by himself. His scattered brain won't allow it. Left to his own devices, he'll cheerfully ramble off into various wars and college experiences, none of which will bring him any closer to recovery.

When the patient explains what he believes is wrong with his life, the counselor can then begin to set the boundaries for the counseling relationship, by indicating along the way what he thinks he might do during the sessions. That will give the patient some anchors into the relationship.

Even during the history-taking, a process is being set up which will have to be strong enough to pass through the initial stages of treatment. The relationship can be changed at any point, but the foundations should be laid from the outset.

The reason is because with this, as with other chronic diseases, the counselor ultimately has to sell the patient on the idea of recovery. To do so effectively, he'll need some of the same skills possessed by a good life-insurance salesman.

As our friend Lee Silverstein says, "To sell life insurance, you have to back the hearse right up to the door and let the customer get a whiff of the flowers."*

That is exactly what the counselor will be doing over the next weeks: introducing the alcoholic to a program of change that he will be motivated to follow by simple fear of the alternative.

Finally, the counselor should be sure to compliment the patient on his or her decision to do something positive. If his patients are like ours, they are genuinely proud of themselves for making the effort, and in many instances, it's the only thing they've been proud of for a long time.

Emotional Augmentation

The term *emotional augmentation,* coined by Dr. James Milam, is one of the keys to understanding alcoholic behavior during the period *after* the alcoholic quits drinking.

Everything we know about the nervous system indicates that withdrawal activity continues for some months or even years following drinking. The nervous system itself—a network of some billions of cells which have been profoundly affected by the addictive process—does not function smoothly, and seems to augment its own responses. In terms of gross behavior, this means that the alcoholic will fly off the handle at small irritations, become frightened at imaginary dangers, and in general make life difficult for himself. It is the behavior which the psychiatrist may unsuspectingly identify as signs of underlying depression, and medicate unnecessarily.

In addition, most alcoholics have a hidden agenda which they won't acknowledge to their counselors and often don't acknowledge to themselves. That agenda centers on proving that he

*Lee Silverstein is the author of *Consider the Alternative*: Minneapolis, CompCare Publications, 1979.

or she is *not* alcoholic. If this can be demonstrated, he reasons, then perhaps he can return home, get his job or driver's license back, skip all those AA meetings, and prove his wife wrong forever.

The combination of emotional augmentation and this hidden agenda dominate the patient's initial experience of treatment. As a result, he doesn't see treatment as fun. This is why he so often drops out.

It's also why dropping out doesn't work. Patients drop out of treatment in order to drink. They just don't realize it at the time. In the middle of this confusion stands the counselor. His challenge is to help the alcoholic hold on to sobriety until his befuddled brain allows him to see what has been wrong with his life. Once again, the concept of task becomes important. Somebody has to remember the work which must be done. More than anything else, this is the counselor's job.

During the course of treatment, the patient has to accomplish three basic goals:

1. He must learn what alcoholism is, and how it works.
2. He must self-diagnose, recognizing a disease process in his experience.
3. He must learn how to treat the disease effectively.

And when he completes those three goals, he must cement his recovery with the fourth and final one:

4. He begins to take *personal responsibility* for the continuing treatment of his disease.

Now: here we must present a precept of treatment in the Disease model which we find is often difficult to understand or accept for those taking the moral or psychological approach. Nonetheless, it is essential to effective treatment of this illness.

If the patient accomplishes these four primary goals and begins to implement them in his daily life, then treatment for alcoholism is successful.

The counselor has been a good, nurturing counselor. The treatment program is a successful one. The patient has been a motivated worker.

This remains true even if the patient hasn't found the Holy Spirit, developed a perfect support system, become content within himself, reconciled with his family, regained his status in the community, gotten in touch with his feelings, become a long-distance runner, paid his bills, or been signed to star in his own TV series.

If any or all of these goodies come to pass, then more power to him.

But when push comes to shove, what does any of that have to do with the disease?

Learning about the Disease

All treatment begins with education. That's due to the peculiar nature of chronic diseases like this one, which seems to be able to conceal itself from its victims even as it progresses. Though most counselors underestimate the role of education, it's the first and most effective weapon against the web of intellectual and emotional defenses the alcoholic has woven around his drinking.

A therapist once asked us: "How can you teach anything about alcoholism to somebody who's in total denial of any sort of alcohol-related problem?" Our answer was: "What else are you going to do with him?"

Nonetheless, most counselors have trouble knowing where to begin when it comes to this sort of education. Even if they have the requisite knowledge of the disease, they don't know how to bring it to bear on the situation at hand. Here's how we do it.

First of all, when we evaluate our patients initially, we make a serious attempt to obtain several pieces of information.

• *The alcoholic's current drinking pattern.* Once we know this, we can make some educated guesses about the rest of his experience, including the stage of the disease he's in, and then we can begin to explain this experience to him. We also make an educated guess about the rate of his recovery, based on his physical health.

- *His motivation for coming to see the counselor.* This is almost always the result of a combination of internal and external pressures. He'll usually emphasize the fact that he came of his own free will (if he didn't, we'll hear about *that*), while behind his decision to seek help may lie a solid external consequence—divorce, legal problems, loss of job—which is strong enough to overcome his resistance.
- *His model of alcoholism.* What does *he* think it is? Does he believe alcoholism is the product of stress, loss of will power, problems with his family, or what? If he's been treated before, unsuccessfully, he'll probably have two models (one superimposed on top of the other). The counselor must find out what these are.

  For example, if he talks about how he's involved in attempts to control his drinking, and wants help with this struggle, then it's fairly likely he's in the Wet Moral model. If he talks about what a sinful fellow he is, and how joining a church will save him, he's in the Dry Moral model. If he acts as though treatment is hopeless, or claims he'll probably always drink because he's "just that way," he's operating from the Impaired model. If he talks about how his family makes him drink, or how he wouldn't drink so much if it wasn't for them, he's in his own version of the Family Interaction model. If he talks about his low self-esteem, his poor coping skills, and his fear of success, or if he appears to spontaneously enter a state of rambling self-investigation, that is evidence of therapy, where he undoubtedly learned the Psychoanalytic model. It's certainly possible to be in more than one model at a time.

- *His defenses.* This will be easy, since the patient will show them with very little prodding. Alcoholic defenses are the same as any other defense mechanisms, but they are magnified and distorted by toxicity and by the disease experience itself. Initial defenses include:

Denial ("That never happened," or "I don't care how big my liver is—I can't be alcoholic!");

Rationalizing ("Okay, my liver is too big, but I had hepatitis as a teenager," or "I know I drank too much, but I was nervous about that interview");

Externalizing ("He—or she—made me," or "If you were in my place, you'd have done the same thing");

Minimizing ("Okay, I yelled at her, but I didn't hit her," or "That DWI was two years ago, and my B.A.L. was just barely over the limit, so I don't think it's such a big deal..."); and sometimes

Intellectualizing ("Wait a minute... exactly how do you define liver disease?")

In using these defenses, the patient unconsciously educates the counselor about himself.

Most alcoholics also have one or more problems of attitude or approach which will interfere with treatment. In other words, the patient is inclined to think or act in ways (or patterns) which will make it difficult to complete the tasks of early recovery. No doubt these patterns have been around so long that he is completely unaware of them, and of their negative influence. Some examples:

• *Living in the future or past to the exclusion of the present*. It's impossible to change any repetitive behavior such as drinking or drug use without devoting attention to what's going on in the present. Alcoholics often slip from the present into the past or future, probably as a result of their struggle to account for the problems they've experienced and to reassure themselves about what's yet to come.

• *Holding grudges or resentments*. Also the result of too much time spent in an alcoholic haze, where events are lived and relived until they come out the way the alcoholic wants them to. If the patient has spent any length of time in past-centered psychotherapy, this bad habit may have been refined to an art. Such grudges and resentments fuel relapse and serve to distract the alcoholic from the real problems of recovery.

- *Overemphasis on feelings rather than actions.* Contrary to conventional psychiatric wisdom—which insists the alcoholic is out of touch with his feelings—alcoholics in the early stages of treatment are dominated by their emotional responses, often to the exclusion of rationality. The newly recovering alcoholic is buffeted about by exaggerated emotions, and may operate on the assumption that he can't change anything until he feels better. In reality, very little will make him feel good *until* he makes several basic changes in his behavior.

- *The presence of any coexisting mental illness.* This does not mean that the counselor's job is to diagnose any such illness, because it isn't. Nevertheless, he will encounter, on occasion, alcoholic patients who have disturbing signs of mania, depression or psychosis. In that case, it's important that he not try to treat those conditions himself. He should send the patient for evaluation by psychiatric staff, since that problem will most likely require attention first. The alcoholism isn't going anywhere; it'll still be there when the patient gets back. About 5 to 15 percent of a typical caseload, depending on its makeup, will have some type of psychiatric problem. If the psychiatrist says that the psychiatric illness is under control, then it's appropriate to go ahead and treat alcoholism.

The Treatment Plan

Once a client has been evaluated, a treatment plan can be written to indicate both treatment needed and ways for the alcoholic to follow the plan. One can't be done without the other, so they should be written at the same time.

If the counselor can't do the treatment plan right away, he must give some kind of assignment to hold the patient's attention until they meet again. This will serve two purposes: it will motivate the alcoholic to begin doing something, and it will establish the working relationship. The real benefits will come not from extended discussions about the whys and wherefores of life, but from his own actions on his own behalf—so those actions should begin as soon as possible. He should be told when the next meeting will be. If he's still drinking, or has only recently quit, then contact with the counselor should be frequent, whether in person or by phone.

This frequent contact is important because his motivation for sobriety, no matter how good it may appear, is really very weak. The counselor wants to strengthen it.

So a commitment is made to work together. At this point we want to emphasize the importance of the counselor urging the alcoholic to follow directions. The counselor is not going to ask anything unreasonable, so there's no cause for the alcoholic to be afraid of doing what he's told. On the other hand, if he doesn't do what he's advised, then the help is worthless. It's good for the alcoholic to know that if he doesn't think he can follow one of the directions, it can be changed so that he can, within certain boundaries.

Above all, the counselor should not let the patient pick a fight. If the patient is able to fight, that will provide him with all the excuse he needs to quit treatment. If he had his way, life would always be "personalities over principles," to reverse an AA slogan. He'd never have to face up to his illness, since he'd always be in the midst of some personality conflict with his doctor, his counselor, whoever. The counselor must take care not to provide the excuse.

The key to treatment planning is identifying the most important problems—those that, left untreated, would interfere with recovery.

In the evaluation the counselor conducted, he looked for answers to the following questions.

1. What model (or models) of alcoholism does the alcoholic use?
2. What's his attitude towards AA?
3. If he doesn't recognize alcoholism in his own experience, then how does he compare out?

Getting Started

4. If he is self-diagnosed, yet is still drinking, or relapsing, then how has he managed to avoid treating the disease?

These are the most common initial problems in treatment. If the patient's operating in an unproductive model—meaning one which will make it difficult for him to recover—there is the first problem. If, for example, he blames all his drinking on members of his family, then it will be difficult for him to get better unless *they* do—and as we mentioned earlier, families frequently refuse to recover before the alcoholic does. If he blames all his drinking on low self-esteem or stress, then he'll be tempted to treat those rather than his drinking problem, and it will be that much harder for him to believe that quitting drinking might improve his lot.

If he tries to restore his ability to drink without problems through will power, or through self-punishment, the problems he'll encounter should be obvious. If he drinks every time his liver improves, and thus quickly returns it to a state of disrepair, then that represents a flaw in the model. He's trying to get sober by treating the symptoms rather than the disease.

The second common initial problem has to do with the way the alcoholic uses, or rather doesn't use, AA. If he has no experience at all with the organization, the problem is simply lack of exposure. If he's been to AA meetings for a while but hasn't gotten involved, or hasn't been able to stay sober, then it's probable that something he's *not* doing would help AA work for him. Perhaps he doesn't go to enough meetings, or he avoids a sponsor or use of the Twelve Steps. He may have religious objections to the AA literature. Whatever it is, if there is a problem, it should be addressed right away so he can begin making use of that organization.

The third common problem area—that of comparing out- —refers back to the extent of his knowledge of alcoholism. It's not uncommon to come across an alcoholic who has some idea of what alcoholism is (though frequently not a very good idea) but who doesn't really think he has it. He might be rationalizing, minimizing, or externalizing his behavior to exclude himself from the diagnosis. He might be telling himself he's a "border-line" alcoholic, and thus can return to controlled drinking after taking extra precautions. He might fail to recognize at all that his particular drinking pattern is an alcoholic one.

If, as the fourth problem indicates, he has compared in but continues to drink, either steadily or intermittently, there is a problem with the way he aproaches treatment of the disease. Usually, it has to do with the degree of personal responsibility he's willing to take for treating his own illness.

He might, for example, be waiting for some all-powerful therapist to make him stop drinking. In that event, the counselor must point out he has no such power—that the steps for recovery, simple as they are, can be taken only by the person who has the illness.

For whatever problems emerge, an appropriate goal should remedy each. Take, for example, a problem such as the patient believing that alcoholic drinking does not affect his health. A goal to treat that problem might read: "Teach the patient about the toxic effects of alcohol in body systems; help him identify any alcohol-related health problems he has experienced." The treatment plan will include the following questions.

- What does the patient have to learn in order to reach that goal?
- Where does he go—to what educational resources—to find the necessary information?
- Through what method will he best learn—reading, talking with others, discussion with the counselor? How will he communicate his new knowledge so the counselor can see what he's learned?
- In what sequence should he take the various tasks he is given under each goal? Do they build on each other? If they do, he'll have to do them in order. If not, he can skip around.
- What are appropriate time boundaries? When is he to have learned the new information? When will he use it in treatment?

Several of these problems and their attendant goals add up to a treatment plan.

The counselor must go over it with the client to make sure he understands it, then ask the all-important question: Will he actually do what he is asked? Is he *capable* of doing it and is he *willing* to do it?

· The alcoholic should be left with the expectation that the counselor will later go over his work with him to evaluate his progress. Built into the plan, if possible, should be the experience of teaching the new knowledge to someone else, since the best way to learn is to teach.

All this works most effectively in some kind of group situation, since groups are really the best setting for treating illnesses like this one. A group removes the sense of uniqueness which works against the alcoholic's recognition of his problem. A group also helps him to learn about the experience of others in similar straits. Mind you, this should be a group of alcoholics. A couples discussion group composed of people with communication difficulties will just distract from the real problem.

Basically, the treatment plan assumes his experience will be within a group. The group provides peer support, structure, pressure, and supervision. It gives instant reinforcement for positive actions and instant discouragement for negative behavior.

Common Early Problems in Treatment

Following is a list of common problems in the initial phases of treatment, based on the Disease model. We have provided in the back of the book two sample treatment plans with appropriate tasks, which illustrate how a treatment plan looks when it's finished. These ought to be adaptable to individual case needs.

Problems with the Model

If there are problems with the model, it's because the patient misunderstands the nature of his problems with alcohol. Unless clearly identified and changed, his misconceptions will undermine efforts at recovery.

Following are examples of patients' misunderstandings when problems arise with the Disease model.

1. *Alcoholism is seen as the result of situational stress.* Here the alcoholic attempts to remedy alcoholism by eliminating all sources of stress from his life. Besides being an impossible task, these efforts to control his environment produce numerous conflicts with other people and eventually make him so nervous he gets drunk. He doesn't realize that alcoholic drinking—accompanied by withdrawal, emotional augmentation, and very real life-problems—is the primary source of stress in his life.

2. *The alcoholic believes excessive drinking to be the result of a weak will.* In this case the alcoholic becomes obsessed with eliminating signs of weakness from his character and struggles to devise a strategy for "disciplining" himself while drinking. He becomes rigid, intolerant, and self-hating, as well as impossible to live with. He doesn't grasp the absurdity of insisting that he can control his nervous system's response to alcohol.

3. *Family problems are seen as the cause of alcoholism.* The alcoholic who believes this devotes his efforts to changing his family rather than himself. Of course, the family disagrees with this assessment and resents his efforts. If he does abstain, he will blame relapses on family disharmony and fantasize about how good things would have been if he had been born to different parents, married someone else, had better children, whatever. He doesn't understand that his disease has undermined family life and disrupted all his relationships, rather than the other way around.

4. *Alcoholism is temporary.* This alcoholic convinces himself that the disease goes away after a few weeks or months of abstinence and superficial good health. Then he resumes social drinking, and redevelops problems. This is an offshoot of the Old Medical model.

5. *An unhappy childhood was the cause of alcoholism.* Someone who believes this operates on the assumption that the key to controlling drinking lies in identifying and eliminating the hidden resentments and disappointments of early life. Of

course, this epic search through the locked closets of the psyche takes years, costs enormous amounts of money, and justifies innumerable relapses. The alcoholic doesn't realize that alcoholism is physiological in origin, and that the secrets of early childhood will probably remain hidden long after he himself has died of liver cirrhosis.

Problems with AA

Since most alcoholics who recover do so in AA, any problems in using the AA program will affect treatment Usually, the problems turn out to be linked to the way the alcoholic approaches AA. These can be remedied with a little education. Here are some of the most common that arise. (A treatment plan in the back of this book shows how an alcoholic who has not made sufficient use of AA can become involved in it.)

1. *The alcoholic doesn't understand how atheists or agnostics can use AA.* Here's the classic religious objection. AA, though very definitely oriented towards the spiritual, isn't a religious organization. The fact is, about 25 percent of the sober people in AA are atheists or agnostics, and the rest don't agree about what God is.
2. *The alcoholic doesn't use the Twelve Steps for recovery.* This is a major factor with people who have been members of AA and relapsed. Although many alcoholics get away with this half-measure, many others don't.
3. *Meetings are rarely attended.* Frequently, an alcoholic will attempt to treat the disease which has dominated his every waking moment for a number of years by dropping in on a meeting every so often. If that was how AA worked, those meetings would be a lot smaller than they are.
4. *The alcoholic doesn't find a sponsor.* This is a problem that severely limits involvement in AA's program, although many people get away with it.
5. *The alcoholic doesn't know how to use AA to stay sober.* This

is the basic problem for newcomers; they don't know AA terminology, where the meetings are, what reading to do, or how to find out.

Problems of Self-Diagnosis

Problems of self-diagnosis are most common with patients who are just starting treatment. Common examples are the alcoholic who:

1. *Doesn't understand the nature of alcoholism as a disease.* This person doesn't know he has the illness because he has no idea what alcoholism is, or even that it is an illness. He needs the most basic education before anything else.
2. *Denies* (or rationalizes, externalizes, minimizes) *the effects of his drinking.* If he says it didn't happen and it obviously did, he's denying; if he says it happened but there was a reason for it that isn't reasonable, then he's rationalizing; if he says it happened but only because forces outside himself made him do it, he's externalizing; if he says it happened but it wasn't that bad, he's minimizing. These are all ways of saying a drinking problem doesn't exist.
3. *Has symptoms of alcoholism but doesn't identify the disease.* Here's someone who's probably comparing out by telling himself the symptoms he doesn't have are more important than the ones he does have.

Problems with Other Drugs

Alcoholics having problems with other drugs are appearing in ever greater numbers in treatment centers. Examples are the person who:

1. *Doesn't understand cross-addiction.* Most alcoholics don't even if they've used drugs for years. Unfortunately, many doctors don't grasp this either.

2. *Doesn't understand how other drug use interferes with recovery*. This applies to the marijuana and cocaine and narcotic users in treatment who plan to continue on their merry way.

Problems of Relapse

People who are suffering relapse problems have attempted recovery before but were unsuccessful. Contributing factors are that the relapser:

1. *Doesn't understand the nature of recovery*. In other words, he doesn't get the idea that it's an extended process, involving ongoing effort towards personal change.
2. *Doesn't understand the need for personal responsibility in recovery*. Although similar to the above, this usually implies that the alcoholic is operating under the erroneous assumption that somebody else can treat the disease without his help. Thus he is prone to making sobriety dependent on those around him. Some get away with this.
3. *Doesn't understand the need for continued abstinence*. This relapser probably believes that alcoholism goes away when he stops drinking, and thus is tempted to experiment with controlled social drinking.
4. *Doesn't follow directions for recovery*. In other words, he finds out what to do, but doesn't do it. Probably he is better at thinking about what he's going to do than at actually doing it (as are most of us).
5. *Doesn't recognize symptoms of approaching relapse*. Most relapses come only after weeks of not-very-subtle signals which, if the alcoholic recognized them, would have enabled him to avoid relapse.
6. *Doesn't know how to prevent emotions from interfering with recovery*. As far as we know, there isn't any law requiring alcoholics to get drunk every time they get upset about something. Nonetheless, many act as though there is. There are ways to approach one's own emotional difficulties which will

help prevent relapse. There are also plenty of things one can do to improve the quality of life if one is a member of that group we call the chronically unhappy.

These of course represent only some of the problems occurring in the initial stages of treatment. Just remember, what is being treated is alcoholism, and the treatment should always reflect that. It's easy for counselors to get lost in the alcoholic's various complaints—be they about his relationships, his emotions, or whatever—while forgetting that the real goal is to teach the alcoholic how to avoid suffering from the effects of alcoholism. The only way we know for him to accomplish this on an ongoing basis is to stop drinking and stay stopped. If that happens, then treatment is successful.

Evaluating Progress

To figure out how well a patient is doing, it helps to have a way to evaluate his work in a group setting. If the counselor sees him in an outpatient or inpatient group, then he can evaluate him personally; if not, it helps to know what questions to ask the person who is leading the group. Here's what the counselor needs to know.

First of all, *does the alcoholic use group time to work on the problem areas* and the appropriate treatment plan objectives? In some forms of group therapy, a casual observer might easily get the impression that members were teaching each other how to drink, rather than how to stay sober. This is because the group is unfocused; usually, neither the group members nor the group leader know precisely what to do with group time. The alcoholic, however, has a treatment plan to guide him. It represents what the counselor, in his professional judgment, thinks the alcoholic needs to learn in order to stay sober. Therefore, he's in a position to maintain his own growth even when the group strays off into the hinterlands.

Second, *does the alcoholic seem to make recovery a priority?* Is he starting, as every alcoholic must, to put his recovery ahead of personal comfort and convenience?

For the third progress marker, we go back to what happens within the group itself. *Does the alcoholic seem to progress from attentive listening* (even if reluctant or hostile) *to questioning to discussion to leadership* within the group? Does he begin to show the signs of that particular brand of enthusiasm for his new experience that will carry him into recovery?

And last, though most important, *does he abstain from alcohol and other drugs?* These, after all, are boundaries set not by counselor, family, or employer, but by the illness itself—and therefore can't be violated.

We feel that the best direction in which to push the newly recovering alcoholic is towards AA. The reason for our emphasis on AA is entirely practical. The advantages over other forms of treatment are legion. First of all, there isn't any problem with finding the right therapist (which many alcoholics simply never do) or with what to do when that therapist moves away. There's the availability of instant associations with people who really do empathize with the sick alcoholic and can offer practical suggestions on how to live without alcohol. There's the incredible convenience: it is difficult to live anywhere in America where there isn't at least one AA meeting. It's right there in the phone book, usually on the first page, under AA Alcoholics Anonymous. And finally, of course, it's free. You don't need employment, money, insurance, or any other form of payment to make use of it.

Coping with Toxicity

There's another factor that must be taken into consideration in the early stages of treatment, and that's the degree of residual alcoholic toxicity the person is experiencing.

Something that is toxic is destructive or poisonous; the result of alcoholic toxicity is intellectual and memory-related difficulties. For example, most of our patients seem to have problems with short-term memory, probably due to deficiencies in thiamine. Your short-term memory is what enables you to remember what you had for breakfast this morning. Just about everyone we know who's worked with alcoholics has noticed that their clients are able to remember the details of their childhood homes, but have great difficulty recalling appointments made only several hours before, or the content of a conversation conducted only that morning.

In some cases, alcoholics also have one or more liver disorders which can produce confusion or disorientation, and which take time to correct.

The result of these factors is that the typical alcoholic is experiencing a learning disorder at precisely the time when he's most ready and willing to learn about what's wrong with him.

Therefore, we try to gear our counseling and education to three standards which we believe will minimize this learning disability. They are:

- *Simplicity*. We believe that every interaction between the counselor and the newly recovering alcoholic should be a simple one, and every kind of educational material used should be readable and direct, both in language and content. The AA "Big Book,"* for example, was deliberately written, we're told, at a fifth- or sixth-grade level, which makes it excellent initial reading. The same is true of the slender book *Living Sober,*** which is really nothing more than a basic discussion of how to use AA and of what it's like to live without alcohol. At this point in treatment, everything should be simple enough to boil down to two ideas: *don't drink* and *go to meetings*. If the patient gets these two messages, he'll probably make it through the initial stages with flying colors.
- *Repetition*. What else would you recommend for people whose major problem isn't that they can't understand what they learn, but that they can't remember it? Don't be concerned about complaints that treatment is repetitious; the complainer still won't be able to retain as much as he should.
- *Self-Reinforcement*. Because sobriety is so new to the recover-

Alcoholics Anonymous: New York, AA World Services, 1955.
**Living Sober*: New York, AA World Services, 1975.

ing alcoholic, the idea is to cram as many little victories into
this stage as possible. The counselor should get into the idea of
"one day at a time" with the client, making each day spent
sober a kind of victory. It may not sound like much to you, but
it will to someone who hasn't had many sober days in recent
years. We once observed an interesting phenomenon at a DWI
school in California: one of the students in the class that night
came to the session boasting that he hadn't had a single drink
("not even a beer") for the entire interval since the last
meeting—approximately a week. The rest of the class gathered
around him, asking him how he managed to do it, congratulat-
ing him, and telling him what a paragon of will power he represented. The unusual thing was that these same students completely ignored their instructors, most of whom had gone at
least two years without alcohol. They seemed to believe that
anyone who went without a drink for that long was probably
some kind of religious nut.

The best time-frame for initial treatment tasks is the single
day. Most counselors know how easy it is for an alcoholic to get
lost (and subsequently drunk) by ruminating over the events of
the past—but it's really just as easy for him to fall by the wayside
because of his preoccupation with the possible happenings of the
future. Do-this-every-day directions are very helpful in getting
him to stay "on task."

We *don't,* however—and this is very hard for some counselors, physicians, nurses, and others to understand—advise letting the patient become dependent on the helper. He does need
friendship and guidance about a lot of things at this point and, of
course, will want that helper to meet all his dependency needs.
The fact remains, however, that a counselor is not the ultimate
solution to his problem. It's most likely that the only thing that is
going to enable him to maintain *long-term* sobriety (and while he
sticks with the short term, the counselor should be keeping an eye
on the long term) is Alcoholics Anonymous. It's been well documented that a major difficulty for people using AA is that they
find it hard to get involved during the initial months; nonetheless,

that involvement must happen sooner or later. Given their choice, most patients will prefer to lean on the counselor rather than go through the work of meeting and getting to know strangers in AA. But ultimately, it is doing a disservice to allow an alcoholic to believe that a counselor can replace AA.

If that were true, then all those sober alcoholics would be trotting off to counselors rather than to AA meetings.

The big excuse for not involving oneself in AA is usually comfort. "I'm not comfortable with those people," says one alcoholic. "She can't be comfortable," agrees her therapist, "so what's the point in going? If she isn't comfortable, she won't get anything out of it."

Want to bet?

Did you ever meet a recovering alcoholic with less than three months' sobriety who was really comfortable *anywhere?* The fact is, the majority of people who recover from this illness sacrifice a degree of personal comfort in order to do so.

If, for example, you had been drinking alcohol for ten or twenty years, could you expect to be immediately comfortable in its absence? Wouldn't you anticipate an adjustment period involving some discomfort? And wouldn't you be able to learn despite that discomfort, if it was important enough to you?

People do it every day. It's how they get better.

Some alcoholics don't make it past the initial stages of treatment.

These are the ones who are able to come up with excuses good enough, as far as they're concerned, to stop seeing their counselors. Soon enough, if they *are* alcoholic, they'll either get involved in some other kind of treatment (rare) or they'll resume drinking (common). Once they start drinking, that's all the reason they need to keep going.

The most common excuse is that the alcoholic has other, more pressing problems to take care of. As soon as those are resolved, he says, he'll return to treatment, with a clear conscience and the ability to concentrate on his alcohol problem.

This approach often results in his return to treatment, all right, but on a stretcher rather than upright.

In 90 percent of these cases, the important problems that the alcoholic was intending to take care of seem to fade from consciousness, to be replaced by a truly gigantic desire for a drink.

What can one do in the face of these excuses? Be direct.

"No matter what you think is going to happen when you get home," a counselor might tell him, "the most likely result is that you're going to start drinking again. Then instead of being sober and facing problems you'll be drunk and unable to do anything about them."

About half the time, if the patient doesn't quit treatment and makes it (sober) through to the next day, the problems won't seem so awesome anymore. If he still insists on terminating, however, that's no sin and may be just the thing to convince him he really *does* have an alcohol problem, at least after the next binge. There's no need for anyone to punish him for leaving—he just doesn't understand the illness. If he wants to rejoin the "research division," trying to drink without creating even more problems, that's his right.

8

Working in Groups

F OR SIMPLICITY'S SAKE, WE DIVIDE ALL ACTIVITY IN any treatment group into two broad categories.

First, there exists what we simply call *work*.

This refers to any interaction within the group that serves to advance the goals of treatment. These goals, you'll recall, are:

- To instruct the patient in the nature of the disease;
- To facilitate self-diagnosis;
- To teach alcoholics how to treat their illness successfully; and
- To encourage the patient to assume personal responsibility for continuing recovery.

On the other hand, there also exists a much larger collection of activities we call *non-work*. These do little or nothing to advance the goals.

This division is especially important because we determine the relative success or failure of a given group session by the ratio of work to non-work activity which has occurred.

We should point out that in all our years of practice we have never been lucky enough to witness a group that had an entire hour of work-related behavior. In most cases, the amount of work which transpires represents only 30 to 50 percent of group time.

The rest of the session is spent in activity which, however busy it may be, does nothing to further treatment.

A group in which participants spend even 40 percent of their time working will seem pretty dull to a group leader. A bunch of alcoholics helping each other understand and live with their disease requires little intervention from trained facilitators. Such a group virtually runs itself. Still, we have faith that the human inclination to waste time in treatment is strong. There will always be plenty of opportunities for professionals to test their skill.

What does worry us is the fact that so many counselors, despite having graduated with advanced degrees, seem unable to distinguish work from the rest of the activity in a treatment group. Because of this, groups can flounder and treatment often stops cold.

In most cases, the group members get the blame for such difficulties. Leaders are always talking about how their groups aren't motivated—the alcoholics in them don't really want to change. Frequently a leader will decide not to waste effort on such uncooperative patients, and will simply endure them until the composition of the group changes.

Yet, time after time, we have found ourselves co-leading such "resistant" groups at the request of the leader only to find that the group miraculously seems to work again.

Knowing that we have no magic wand, we suggest that this occurs because of one or more of the following:

1. We happen to be a lot better-looking than the previous leaders;
2. The previous leader was unable to recognize and overcome the various kinds of resistance the group presented;
3. The group was doing a certain amount of work all along, but the leader hadn't recognized it because of preoccupation with some other agenda;

4. The group members had heard in advance of our reputation for cruelty, and believed that if they failed to work, we would simply have them all shot.

Now despite the fact that we really are unusually handsome, we suspect that numbers 2 and 3 were the important factors. In fact, we believe that these two problems are responsible for most of the "stuck" and "hopeless" groups we encounter.

We've written this chapter to explore the nature of work and non-work in groups, and to give a few simple suggestions for turning resistance into recovery.

How to Run a Successful Alcoholism Treatment Group

The leader of an alcoholism treatment group will need, among other skills, three particularly important ones: the ability to assign tasks to the group, to recognize and deal with group resistance, and to set boundaries.

A Specific Task for Each Session

Obviously, no group can work on all goals of treatment at the same time. There are too many of them.

This is why we recommend assigning each group a specific task which somehow directs it towards accomplishing the larger goals but presents a more manageable objective for the single session.

A task, then, is something to be worked on during the course of the group. It lends focus to discussion and minimizes the rambling dialogue which ordinarily wastes much group time.

It also establishes a useful boundary for behavior in the group. If the task of a meeting is to discuss self-diagnosis, then a group member who insists on grieving for her departed cocker spaniel is "off-task." The group leader, or an individual member, has a responsibility to point this out to her.

That way, sessions are devoted to issues that benefit the

group *as a whole*. Vocal members are less able to dominate the group with personal agendas, and shy types are less able to fade into the woodwork while others ramble.

Here is a list of suggested tasks for treatment groups, all of which will direct and focus activity and therefore maximize work:

1. Discuss how defense mechanisms (such as denial) interfere with self-diagnosis;
2. Examine how enabling or provoking behavior from those around the alcoholic might influence recovery;
3. Review the symptoms of alcoholism and their role in the progression of the disease;
4. Discuss the First Step (or any others) of AA's Twelve Steps;
5. Discuss how drinking affects sex;
6. Examine the role of other drug use in alcoholism;
7. Explore the factors involved in relapse.

And so on. As you can see, a task is not awfully different from a topic, but there's one important difference: while a topic may be selected simply because it's interesting or stimulates discussion, a task must advance the goals of treatment.

Sometimes there's disagreement about what constitutes working on a designated task. For example, we have one meeting set aside in our inpatient program for the specific purpose of handling the kind of problems which arise within a treatment community. That goal is reflected in the meeting's task: solving community problems.

Thus if a particular patient has a predilection for practicing the trumpet at 4 A.M., the others have an opportunity to point out to him how irritating this can be. Then the community as a whole can pass a "community boundary" that it is emphatically not okay to play the trumpet at that hour. The trumpeter and everyone else will know that if such behavior occurs again, the community will likely dispatch a delegation to dismember him.

Occasionally, however, a disgruntled patient will decide that this meeting should be devoted to listening to his complaints about institutional meatloaf. When someone points out that this is off-task, he replies: "What do you mean? We're supposed to discuss community problems, aren't we? Well, I'm a member of the community, and that's my problem."

At which point the counselor might interject: "In that case, I'd like you all to listen to my complaints about the cockroaches in my kitchen at home, because that's *my* problem."

It must be clear to you, as it is to us, that a group which has *no* task—witness 90 percent of psychotherapy groups—is a group in which everything that occurs must be considered work. Even if, as is often the case, it has absolutely nothing to do with what brought the patient to treatment in the first place.

Think how impossible it is to measure the success of such a group. What standards would you adopt? Our motto, derived from bitter experience: If nothing is *supposed* to happen in a group, then by and large, *nothing will.*

Group Resistance

During any session, events flow back and forth between work and non-work. Remember, it is much easier to do nothing than to work, which accounts for the variety and popularity of non-work activities.

Two typical non-work diversions are helplessness and hostility.

HELPLESSNESS   In the helpless phase, the group acts as if all knowledge, wisdom, initiative, and creativity must come from the designated leader.

As a result, group members see their role as simply to sit around and wait for the leader to do something.

And since the assumption of group helplessness has been made, if the leader fails to come through with the desired commands, the group will do one of three things:

• Sit silently until the session ends, the leader says something, or the building is washed away in a flood; or

- Begin trying desperately to get the group leader more involved through questioning, pleading, manipulating, or threatening; or
- Turns the group over to the most talkative member, who will bring up a "problem." The group will then bat this problem about until the meeting is over.

It's easy to see why this is a non-work pattern: the group's unstated agenda involves getting an all-powerful healer to use magic to cure them. Since group leaders possess no such power, the effort is doomed to failure.

Of course, a leader can always *pretend* to such potency, in which case he will become extremely popular. Leader-worship will then carry the group through several weeks or months of infatuation, before someone brings the leader a problem which he simply has to admit he can't solve. At this point his fallibility will be apparent and everyone in the group will be entitled to feel misled, and, if alcoholic, to get stinking drunk.

In that event, guess who gets the blame?

Of course, all groups *begin* in the helpless phase, and seem to keep trying to get back into that position whenever they are having a rough time in treatment. There's nothing sick about this, but nobody is really getting anywhere by doing it.

The leader's success in promoting work without allowing the members to remain dependent on him is, in fact, the yardstick by which we measure the leader's effectiveness.

Some group members will drop out of treatment as soon as they discover they have to take responsibility for their own behavior. No leader can prevent this. But we do hope that leaders who *want* alcoholics to become dependent upon them—usually at great cost and little benefit to the alcoholic—will move out of treatment and find other vocations.

Recognizing helpless behavior in groups is easy. Rambling, off-task discussion—which forces the leader to direct—is a dead giveaway. Constant questioning of the leader, or excessive eye contact as though the members are checking out what the leader thinks, indicate helplessness.

Helpless groups will always be forgetting the task, or "not

understanding" the meaning of various terms. People will complain of being confused, thus requiring assistance from the leader. Above all, a helpless group won't broach an on-task issue without specific clearance from the leader, leaving him with the responsibility for deciding the course of treatment and, therefore, for the group members' recovery.

HOSTILITY: FIGHT AND FLIGHT   Hostility comes in two forms: active and passive—fighting or taking flight.

Suppose a group leader reminds the group at some point that he doesn't have any magic cure for alcoholism and can't be expected to provide answers for all the members' problems. One member might respond angrily,

> Well, if you don't have any answers, then what the hell are we doing here? What are we paying for? I mean, what's your background, your training? Are you an alcoholic yourself? What do you know about how we feel, unless you're an alcoholic yourself?

The leader can answer the charges, attempting to establish his leadership, which of course feeds the group right back into helplessness. Or he can become defensive, which wastes everyone's time as he and the angry member slug it out while the rest of the group catnaps. Either way, work stops. The real issue—the patient's responsibility for himself—isn't addressed.

The opposite of this active hostility is flight. Here, something threatens the group to the point where members go into full-scale retreat. They try to avoid attention and may even claim the leader wants to trap them into damaging admissions. A group-wide paranoia develops, and work grinds to a halt.

Another form of passively hostile behavior involves the introduction of irrelevant subjects. Bring up impotence in a group of alcoholic men, and see how many develop a sudden urge to go to the bathroom. Bring up child neglect in a group of newly sober alcoholic mothers, and see how many women volunteer to get coffee for everyone.

If the leader points out this avoidance, the other members are likely to accuse him of being overly suspicious, and shift into active hostility.

A lot of time is killed in this process.

On the other hand, it's easy to fall into the trap of singling out one or two members of such a group as ringleaders. But if the whole group is tolerating this behavior, then on some level those two members are simply expressing the group's sentiments.

When the group decides to work, the members will effectively silence resistance themselves. They will, for example, respond to the fight behavior of one member, and tell those in flight to stop fooling around.

They, in effect, will lead the group.

In order to work as a group, members must learn to cooperate with each other in performance of the task. No such cooperation is necessary in order to *avoid* work. All the members have to do is simply go their own ways.

There may also be what writer/psychologist Wilfred Bion calls pairing—alliances between members that are supported by the rest of the group as a way of avoiding work. An alliance can dominate interaction, direct the group in active or passive resistance to the leader, or provide a convenient focus for discussion while the task itself is ignored. Sometimes pairing takes the form of a love relationship between two members. The inevitable ups and downs of such relationships are endlessly fascinating to the other members and permit them to disregard the issues which brought them to the group in the first place.

Effective Boundaries

To promote work, we believe it's necessary to establish and protect boundaries, which in turn direct the group's focus to the task at hand.

For example, we insist that groups begin and end on time.

This is to discourage two classic interruptive maneuvers which, taken together, have probably wasted more group time than all others combined.

The first of these is lateness.

When someone arrives five, ten, or fifteen minutes after a group has begun, all eyes go to the door while the latecomer makes an entrance. Discussion usually halts. Half those present greet the new member with questions about whether or not it's still raining outside. Two or three others take advantage of the interruption to get coffee or use the bathroom. Extra chairs have to be found, and people have to make room within the circle. Somebody remembers to ask someone else about a ride to the next group. Another ash tray must be found. Do you take cream in your coffee?

By the time the group resettles, poor George's problem with his wife is long forgotten, even by George. "Where were we?" someone asks. And slowly, painfully, the group starts all over.

Until the *next* latecomer, that is.

Many leaders operate on the assumption that people can't help being late. That's ridiculous. Any members who aren't hallucinating or comatose can make effective use of a clock. But they might not bother, unless they understand its importance. Once the leader and majority of members decide that being on time is an expectation, lateness will disappear.

Just as devastating to group functioning is what we have come to call the bomb syndrome.

This occurs at the end of a session, after discussion winds down, and people are beginning to look for their car keys.

"I don't know if I should bring this up," some fellow who's been silent all evening will say, "but my wife moved in with her lover this week, and my terrier was put under quarantine for infectious hypoglycemia, and I was arrested for income tax evasion, and I have all these fantasies about going home and swallowing all my antidepressants and just dying." This inevitably results in the whole group staying for another hour to comfort the poor soul.

When the appointed time for ending the session arrives, we leave. In the middle of a sentence, if necessary. Our patients know that if they need to discuss something, they'd better do it during the group. There is no other opportunity, as far as we're concerned.

One more word on the issue of time. We agree with many other clinicians that groups should never exceed ninety minutes in length. Nobody works that whole time as it is. We know people do attend weekend marathons, but even there, we see work stop frequently—for hours at a time, though the members are still talking. If you want to study non-work, on the other hand, a longer group session is ideal, because that's mainly what you'll get from the participants.

But time is not the only area where clear boundaries assist work. Here are several other boundaries we recommend:

- *Everyone has to know where the meetings are held*. You'd be surprised how many programs, afflicted with schedule conflicts, move groups around without telling the members. It's also the members' responsibility to make sure everyone in the group knows the location of the meeting.
- *Group membership is closed for a specific period*. This is so that members do something other than introduce themselves to newcomers.
- *Everyone should know the task*. We once attended a five-day workshop in which no one thought to ask the leader for the task until the last day. Everyone just assumed they were there to talk about their childhoods. That, it turned out, was off-task.
- *The number of meetings should be set*. In treating this illness, we don't believe in open-ended long-term groups. Why sit in a group for years on end just because you can't decide whether or not you're really well yet?

Once the necessary boundaries are established, the group leader spends most of the time simply maintaining discussion. Here are some typical maintenance activities which help keep the group on course.

- *Encouraging everyone to contribute*. Talkative types monopolize discussion and wallflowers inhibit it. It's up to the leader to

point out to each their effect on the group.
- *Assisting members in assuming leadership*. When working, members share leadership as their skills allow. The leader should help this process.
- *Compromising and reconciling*. The group needs to avoid silly personality conflicts which interrupt work.
- *Active teaching*. Nondirective leaders often become so involved in noninvolvement that they forget they have information which may not be available to the group. If you're a leader, don't be afraid to teach the group how to work.

Dealing with Resistance

As we discussed, groups constantly move from work to non-work and back again. Here are the simplest ways to get any group from non-work to work.

Step one: Point out to the group that they are not at this moment working on the task.

Step two: Suggest that they might do something to change that situation.

If the task and boundaries have been established adequately, this should present no problem.

Let's return to the example of the angry patient who confronts the leader with demands for credentials. Here's a good response: "Feel free to ask me about that after the meeting. But during the meeting, that's clearly off-task. We're here to discuss (whatever), and anything else will just waste our time."

Case closed. No arguments, no accusations, no defenses. Just a statement of the truth.

Or suppose the group is stuck in the helpless phase. They insist, for example, that no matter how clearly the leader has explained it, they just can't understand how to work on the task.

They might be advised thus: "It seems as though this group is waiting for me to say something which will make everything instantly clear. That's too bad, because I've already told you everything I can to clarify it. We now have a choice: either begin to work on the task to the best of our ability, or sit around waiting for everyone to get drunk. Take your pick."

Or as an option: "People seem to be waiting for me to begin the group. Actually, the group is designed to encourage all of you to work with each other, rather than with a leader. That's why I didn't simply schedule individual appointments for all of you."

This represents nothing more than a swift kick in the psychological pants. That's exactly what a group may need.

And of course a counselor should feel free to give suggestions to facilitate work. There are lots of handy techniques devised by therapists over the years to facilitate discussion.

Sometimes a resistant group will have a very good reason for its balkiness—one or more members is drinking or using drugs, for example, and everyone but the leader knows it. If he suspects this, he should bring it up. If no one admits it, at least someone may tell him after the meeting.

Here, then, is a simple list of actions which support the task and hold the group in the work phase. The leader (or leaders) should:

1. Define the task, and clarify it if necessary;
2. Suggest methods for discussion;
3. Give information which facilitates work;
4. Present options to standard approaches;
5. Share opinions if appropriate;
6. Summarize what's been accomplished;
7. Help the group to look at things in different ways.

How to Tell When a Group is Working

The group is working if:

1. Members are on time;
2. If somebody is late, other members point it out;
3. Everybody knows the task;
4. If one person doesn't know the task, the others teach him;
5. Nobody is allowed to remain a silent wallflower throughout the meeting;

6. No one is allowed to totally dominate discussion;
7. Others intervene if someone becomes overtly resistant or interferes with the work;
8. Nobody spends ten minutes in the bathroom, unless he's been given a powerful laxative;
9. Nobody sleeps;
10. The group spends the bulk of its time actively discussing the task.

Get the picture? In a working situation, the only silent person is likely to be the leader.

The better the group learns to work, the less they need the leader.

Personalities

Occasionally, personality conflicts develop within a group.

One member will be in a state of chronic disagreement with another. Rather than resolving their differences, these two will attribute them to an innate opposition in personality.

Interestingly, a group leader often sees two such combatants as being remarkably *similar* in attitude and behavior. But this observation is usually to no avail. Once the group has diagnosed the presence of an irreparable personality conflict between two of its members, it clings to this as stubbornly as a belief in will power or its fascination with two members' romance. Such disputes are viewed as outside the realm of its individual choice.

Thus, the only thing the group can do is choose up sides. Therapy begins to resemble the Red Sox versus the Yankees at Fenway Park.

After a few hours, days, weeks, or months of this, the group dies a natural death, or perhaps splinters into factions.

To the amazed, often helpless leader, this situation, despite being played out within the supposedly dignified confines of an adult therapy group, resembles a child's game.

The most important part of any elementary-school sport is choosing up sides. Each child desperately hopes to identify with one side or another—to belong. It's more important to the child to be on the "right" team than the winning team.

It seems to us that in groups torn by such conflicts, individual personality has very little to do with it. The underlying issues are privilege, recognition, and seniority: the stuff we're all out to get for ourselves.

The odd thing is, we can't see any reason for such conflicts to destroy the work of the group. What difference does it make that two group members dislike each other?

What does that have to do with accomplishing a given task? What relation does it have to the common need to treat a disease?

We can't help but recall that the dominant baseball teams of the 1960s and the '70s—the Oakland A's and the New York Yankees—were also two of the most conflict-ridden organizations in baseball history. Players would get into fistfights in the clubhouse and then go into a state of almost total cooperation for the length of time it took to win a baseball game.

If personal conflict always precludes work, how was this possible?

It's our belief that disagreements within a group cause no harm whatsoever as long as the group is able to come together for performance of the task. It's only when the group is polarized around *individuals* that personality conflicts are truly incapacitating.

To prevent this, the leader must repeatedly emphasize the pre-eminence of the task. And it never hurts to boldly state that personal dislike is no excuse for not working.

Feelings

Perhaps an even more serious threat to the work of a group is a therapist's emphasis on feelings.

We've already mentioned that most group leaders receive training at the hands of teachers who believe that the path to individual growth lies through the uninhibited expression of feeling.

In addition, publishers have produced a formidable number of books based on the importance of understanding one's own emotions. We have no quarrel with this until we find it applied to the treatment of alcoholism.

When we began working in this field, we were taught that alcoholic patients suffered from a profound inability to get in touch with their feelings. It was this deficiency, we were told, which necessitated their attempts to drown themselves in Jack Daniels.

As instructed, we geared our groups to assisting these poor souls in overcoming their handicap. Expression of feeling, preferably on what we liked to call the gut level, became our dominant agenda. If patients could have this kind of emotional breakthrough, then life would be great, and they wouldn't have to drink any more.

After about two years of this (we're slow learners), we noticed that instead of being incapable of knowing how they felt, our patients seemed to be so completely involved in their own feelings that they had real difficulty doing anything which wasn't directly based on emotions.

We found ourselves wishing that our patients would get *out* of touch with their emotions for a while. Give *us* a break, at least.

Emotion, it turned out, was the dominant theme of many early-stage recovering alcoholics. It was this generalized emotional discomfort which fueled the resentments, frustrations, and conflicts that led to relapse.

Then it occurred to us that emotions, far from being solely the product of external circumstances, were dramatically influenced by the disruption of the nervous system which inevitably follows years of drug addiction. Thus the term coined by James Milam: *emotional augmentation,* to refer to a nervous system that has been affected by chemicals and therefore exaggerates emotional responses.

What cures this hyperactive response to the travails of ordinary life? Time, abstinence, and whatever simple program of living seems to help the individual.

Soon after this realization, we began to see that what we did in therapy—through our emphasis on feelings—actually *fed into* the process of augmentation, and into the excuses which eventually led to relapse.

We hadn't understood that recovery from this disease is based first and foremost on actions, and that it is quite possible for an alcoholic to improve his morale, through expressing feeling in a group, without actually making much progress towards achieving the goal of sobriety.

As slow as we were to grasp this idea, we believe there are thousands of professionals out there who still don't grasp it.

The truth is, one doesn't work on the alcoholic's feelings in the hope that someday he just won't feel like drinking anymore.

One works on his drinking, knowing that if he sees the need to change that behavior, and is able to do so, he'll eventually adjust emotionally to life without alcohol.

Counseling can help this adjustment, but only after the patient stops drinking. Relapses just point out how utterly futile it is to complain to a therapist about your unhappiness when you aren't even willing to give up something which is actively threatening your life.

We certainly don't pretend that alcoholics have no feelings. We know they fluctuate from joy to depression to frustration to lust to grief and back to elation, and so on. But our question is: are these feelings what we're here to treat?

When a patient comes to us with the complaint that he still feels like drinking, we say: "So what? If you've been at it for ten or fifteen years, what do you expect to feel when it's taken away from you?"

We think a recovering person is one who recognizes this desire as part of the problem. A relapser is one who believes that simple desire justifies more drinking.

Change always requires action. Most of the time, we all take steps like this because we have to—because we can't think of a better alternative. We adapt to that change somewhere down the line, and that's when we become comfortable with our decisions.

The alcoholic's great advantage during the first months of recovery is his ability to set aside other concerns in favor of the overriding necessity of treating alcoholism. To the degree he's able to accomplish this, he will be successful in recovery.

We think therapists should help him in this and stick to that task alone.

Problems

Why do so many group leaders begin a session by asking if anyone in the group has a problem they'd like to work on?

This makes no sense to us. Aren't they all there because of alcoholism? Why don't they just work on *that?*

Instead, somebody inevitably volunteers that they don't feel comfortable with the boss, spouse, eldest kid, Mom, or whoever, and the group launches forward to resolve this difficulty.

First, somebody has to get the person with the problem to describe the boss so that everyone will have a picture of what this boss (who, it's assumed, is causing the problem) is really like.

Then several people have to offer observations of their own on the group member's personality.

Then, someone always wants to know what was *really* said on a specific occasion, which means that the group has totally lost its way and is now functioning as a grand jury.

At this point, the leader must intercede, and begin asking more appropriate questions about the nature of the problem. This is done in the interest of saving time.

When enough time has been spent, the leader helps the Member With The Problem get in touch with his underlying feelings towards the offending boss so that he will not be so negatively affected the next time.

Or, failing this, the member will at least have something clever to say at future encounters.

In groups such as this, the bulk of time is spent gathering information the group can't really use, followed by an extended period in which the leader/therapist carries on a dialogue with one member. This process is called "problem-solving in group therapy."

If problems are "solved" through this process, why is it that the same problems are brought up, often by the same people, week after week? What gets solved?

If this is truly group therapy, then why is all the work done by the leader? Isn't this really *individual* therapy in groups?

What do the other members do while the leader is working with the member who has the problem?

When we ask leaders what they think goes on in their groups while they solve one person's problem, we're usually told that the other are "identifying" with that member.

Then why do so many of them appear bored to tears?

We don't believe that a typical group of newly recovering alcoholics represents a good problem-solving forum. That kind of activity is best done on an individual basis, separate from the task-oriented group.

And it seems to us that asking patients to bring up personal problems for examination—just so the leader can eventually say, "What we have here is a failure to communicate"—accomplishes nothing.

There's always a problem facing the group which is directly responsible for 80 to 100 percent of what's wrong with their lives. That problem—alcoholism—is enough to keep *anyone* busy.

9

One on One

O F ALL THE TYPES OF PEOPLE WHO ENTER THERAPY, alcoholics, as a group, may have the worst reputation. We wouldn't even attempt to count the number of clinicians whose experiences with these patients have been so unpleasant or unrewarding that they simply don't accept them for therapy anymore. The reason is simple: for years, alcoholics failed to respond to the model which dominates American mental health care: individual counseling.

For a long while, this puzzled us, because we've found that individual work could be of great value to our clients, especially those who were slow to respond to treatment. Individual counseling could be a real help in getting the alcoholic to focus on problem areas that might lead to relapse, as well as helping in his comparing in process. Though not every alcoholic needed ongoing individual attention, there were quite a few who could benefit in one way or another from a relationship with a counselor. It seemed to us that the sicker the patient, in terms of his degree of denial or tendency towards relapse or resistance to treatment in general, the more effective individual counseling could be.

We suspect now that the reason so many alcoholics were failures in this area had more to do with the way this model was employed than with any irreparable character deficiency on the part of the patient.

We've come to believe that a counselor can make use of individual work with great success. It just won't be with the same techniques employed to treat someone's marital difficulties, depressive illness, or phobia. Alcoholism is very different from these conditions.

Problems in Individual Counseling

Again, it's useful to take a backwards look to see how the alcoholic got his bad rep as an individual counseling patient. This was probably inevitable given the nature of the disease. There were four principal problems which the average therapist wasn't able to understand or to deal with adequately. These four problems, unchecked, interrupted treatment before it started, so to speak.

The first problem involved the alcoholic's much ballyhooed *resistance to treatment,* that profound unwillingness to accept help of any kind, often accompanied by outright hostility towards any potential helper. This, of course, didn't help alcoholics win popularity contests among the helping professions. The second set of problems stemmed from the labyrinth of *defenses* erected around the drinking behavior; alcoholics seemed to work overtime defending the very illness that led to so many of their difficulties. Therapy, then, quickly degenerated into psychological dentistry, with the therapist having to forcibly extract any useful insights against the will of the patient.

Third, the alcoholic was known to *manipulate* others to get what he wanted. This further undermined what trust others put in him; they began to see themselves as victims of his self-serving behavior. As we mentioned previously, counselors went so far as to hang the tag of sociopath on the alcoholic, thus eliminating his chances of rejoining the human race on equal footing.

As a fourth problem, alcoholics were known to be frequently *deceitful*—consciously and intentionally—about their drinking. They lied about it to their therapists as they lied about it to their families and friends. Therapists prefer to believe that *they* know the truth, even if the patient is deceiving everyone else. When it becomes apparent that the professional is as much in the dark as the average family member, he tends to become as mistrustful of the alcoholic as families are.

In combination, these problems made the alcoholic a profoundly unsympathetic character. Even though he might be permitted to view himself as an addictive (or sociopathic or inadequate) personality, on the moral level he remained much more "wrong" than "sick."

And since these defects were so difficult to handle, they tended to overwhelm other aspects of the disease in counseling. In many therapeutic relationships, very little discussion of drinking or alcoholism occurred. The topic, instead, was the patient's emotions, lifestyle, childhood, or personality structure. The counselor would spend the hour focusing on these issues, while the alcoholic would occupy himself with speculations about how he might develop more will power, or who else he might find to blame for his difficulties. Every so often, the disease would rear its ugly head, the alcoholic would get in some new (and more severe) kind of trouble, and counselor and client would be forced to pay attention to it for a while. As soon as the patient seemed to get things back under control, however, both parties returned to their own preoccupations, until the next episode.

We should make it clear that the alcoholic's proclivity for relapse wasn't the key factor in his unpopularity with helpers, who really are quite tolerant of failure. Anyone who has worked in a psychiatric hospital has probably encountered patients who are there for their tenth or twentieth or hundredth visit, or who may actually make their homes in the institution. The alcoholic's big handicap was that he often seemed an unlikable character who was suspected of drinking just to get attention, or to get in out of the cold, or to get even with his spouse, or to get other people to take care of him, or to get three good meals daily at the public expense.

If he was more likable than most—that is, if he was polite to everyone, attended all therapy sessions, didn't show up drunk, seemed to work hard at gaining insights, and came up with good excuses for relapses—he was often allowed to stay in therapy as long as other patients: months, years, even a lifetime.

Unfortunately, being "successful" in therapy in this way had a lot of practical value for the drinking alcoholic. If his spouse threatened to leave, he could get the therapist to intercede in his behalf, warning the spouse that such abandonment could produce depression which would "set therapy back years" or even result in suicide. If drinking endangered his job, the same therapist might be persuaded to go to bat for him in that arena, as well. If a binge produced too much withdrawal discomfort, the alcoholic could get tranquilizers, or even be admitted to the hospital, under the direction of his therapist. His security blanket for his drinking was the same help which was supposed to be remedying it.

The really good manipulators, therefore, were often the "best" patients; rather than resisting treatment, they *used* it to continue drinking.

We should take a close look at those four problems which so interfered with treatment, with an eye towards understanding and avoiding them so the sick alcoholic can be treated.

Resistance

We'll start with the problem anyone encounters first: resistance to treatment. A significant number of alcoholic patients simply don't want to be helped. Several factors contribute to this resistance.

First of all, most people don't like to have, or be diagnosed as having, a chronic illness. There exists a potent denial-of-illness syndrome which has been extensively explored in medical literature, and which affects treatment of all sorts of illnesses besides alcoholism.

This is usually combined with the ignorance about alcoholism that we've discussed throughout this book. Together, these factors lead the patient to active rejection of the diagnosis.

It's also generally true that by the time the alcoholic suspects there's anything wrong with his drinking, he's physically dependent on the drug. He's learned that his body is going to punish him for *not* using alcohol. In order to get well, he's going to have to first get really sick, in the sense of going through an extended withdrawal. If there's a way to postpone or avoid this experience, he'll generally take it. And he often distrusts a doctor or hospital that promises to bring him down slowly with supportive medications—there's no way for him to know he won't be left high and dry.

Another powerful factor in resistance is plain old pride. Despite the increasing acceptance of recovering alcoholics in our society, it's still not exactly a status symbol to be the first on the block to get detoxed. Those around him, entrenched in moral models, still regard his behavior as emphatically wrong. This verdict is especially powerful if delivered by family and friends, many of whom have waited years to say "I told you so" at his first sober moment.

Of course, if the family doesn't choose to approach the illness from a moral standpoint, they have the option of regarding him through other common models—stupid, self-destructive, crazy, or disgusting, among others.

What this means is that we take someone who already denies his illness and then we reinforce that denial with a host of cultural and social misconceptions. We add this to his fear of withdrawal, and throw in his natural reluctance to commit himself to something he fears he might not be able to handle—life without alcohol—and there you have it: a sick person who is resistant to help.

He just doesn't see what is being offered as helpful. It's more of a *threat*.

Defenses

This is precisely where we encounter elaborate defenses. They're all designed to do roughly the same thing: allow the alcoholic to keep drinking, or functioning while drinking, or ignoring the consequences of drinking. The most common is a form of denial: avoiding recognition that a problem exists. Second is usually rationalization: devising reasons which make his behavior more acceptable to himself. A close third involves externalization, through which the behavior may be acknowledged but at the same time blamed on outside forces or events.

These are in no way unique to the alcoholic. All can be found in any problem situation, employed by quite healthy people who are unaware of their use of them. Though we are a reasonable species, in the sense that we have reasons for doing things, we're not really very logical. In fact, many of our most cherished beliefs are really the result of denial, rationalization, and externalization; without knowing it, we shape our thinking to fit our circumstances.

It's even possible for groups of individuals to cooperate in stringing together defense mechanisms which, in their view, justify certain activities for years on end.

Consider the people who live in San Francisco. Experts have been telling them for some time that sooner or later there will occur a stupendous earthquake which may kill as many as twenty or thirty thousand people. It could even happen tomorrow; the necessary geological ingredients already exist.

Do we see a mass exodus from the area? No. Do we see a concerted effort on the part of all the citizens to build earthquake-proof structures? Again, no—their efforts are distinctly less than monumental.

Quite a few San Franciscans simply refuse to believe that such a quake could ever occur. According to the geologists, that attitude represents simple denial. Other San Franciscans believe that the quake's casualties will somehow magically be confined to the ranks of other people, and won't include their own families, friends, neighbors, or themselves. They point to the population of the area—some three million residents—as proof that they could be spared because of the odds. That kind of thinking is a form of rationalization. Some residents claim that they are forced to live in the most vulnerable locations by external forces which outweigh the dangers: convenience to work, financial advantage, and the like. That's externalization.

Some citizens have even managed, despite an elaborate system of checks and balances designed to keep this from happening, to erect a nuclear plant on top of the earthquake fault.

Now *that's* denial. People just don't see it as clearly as they can see the alcoholic's defenses. Most therapists, not being alcoholics themselves, have trouble seeing how their clients have avoided noticing the obvious about their drinking. It's easy: take human self-deception, add lots of alcohol, and stir.

Manipulation

On the other hand, manipulation, for which so many alcoholics were condemned, seems to us to be simply a by-product of dependence. When you're in the position of needing a drug just to feel normal, then anything which threatens your use of this drug will have to be controlled.

If the drug you're addicted to is available only by prescription, then you'll have to learn to manipulate doctors, pharmacists, or hospitals.

If your drug of choice happens to be illegal, as in heroin, then you'll have to become adept at manipulating your black-market suppliers, and even the law and its officers, in some cases, to survive.

If you're a drinking alcoholic, then the primary threats to your drinking come from those closest to you: your family, your supervisor, your physician. They will become the targets of your most manipulative behavior.

But is this manipulation really the problem? We think it's just another result of the *real* problem: drug dependence.

And of course, the ultimate target of this manipulation is the alcoholic himself. As the disease progresses, it becomes necessary to manipulate not only his environment, but *himself,* to continue his activities. He must flatter himself, make excuses for himself, bolster his own ego, push himself when he gets tired, nag himself into doing things he may not want to do . . . a myriad of behaviors all arising from one overriding need: to keep his addiction going.

Deception

It seems to us that even when the alcoholic blatantly lies to someone about the amount, frequency, consequences, or even the very existence of his drinking, the ultimate victim of his deceit is none other than himself. He may believe that he's deceiving you because you "can't take the truth" about his behavior, but in reality he deceives himself because he can't accept it, either. He knows about the large and small lies he tells his spouse and doctor, but is completely unaware of how thoroughly he's fooled himself.

He's done such a good job of self-deception that he may just die of alcoholism before figuring it out.

This is why we don't worry about whether or not our patients are telling us the whole truth. We really don't care. We know that it isn't necessary for an alcoholic to be completely honest with a counselor in order to recover; he just has to be honest enough with *himself* to stop drinking and remain stopped. Usually, this only means that he's acknowledged to some degree his loss of control over alcohol, and that this interferes with his ability to live life the way he wants to. Greater self-honesty comes with time, as long as the addiction isn't resumed.

If an alcoholic wants to lie to us, fine. We don't suffer one way or another from his self-deception; the disease makes sure that ultimately he is the one who pays the price. And since we don't really make a big deal out of rigorous honesty, our patients usually don't bother to deceive us. That leaves us free to concentrate on the real problem, which is how to teach the alcoholic to stop deceiving himself.

A Case Study in Individual Counseling

How should individual counseling be used with an alcoholic?

Simply, to focus on and intensify whatever is being worked on in treatment.

There are two areas in which this kind of focusing is most helpful: facilitating the comparing in process, which results in self-diagnosis, and solving specific problems which might interfere with recovery.

A classic example of the first involves the case of a fifty-four-year-old woman who entered treatment in what counselors often call *complete denial:* not only did she deny the extent and effects of her drinking, she actually denied having done any drinking whatsoever. Her family had coerced her into counseling by offering her no alternative other than commitment to the state hospital.

How did we know this woman was alcoholic? She had alcoholic liver cirrhosis, to the point where she had very recently been near death. Her family had rushed her to the hospital, and she had spent several months recuperating before being transferred to our care.

Group therapy did very little for this woman. Her denial was so strong that other group members were unable to penetrate it, and as soon as they became confrontive, she'd retreat into stony silence. She maintained her story that she had not had anything to drink in over a year, after having "tired of the taste of wine" which she had of course consumed "no more than once a week, with dinner." Her physicians had many times confronted her with the fact that social drinking doesn't normally lead to cirrhosis, but this she dismissed as incompetent medical care. "They don't know what's wrong with my liver," she maintained, "so they try to blame it on me." Her family informed her that they had a number of times found her intoxicated at home in the middle of the day, but this she also rejected: "I was simply tired, not drunk." Since she insisted that she had already quit drinking a number of months ago, this "alcoholism racket" represented to her a ploy by her children to have her declared incompetent so they could take all her money.

Our usual approach in dealing with alcoholic denial is to take whatever symptom the patient *will* acknowledge and confine our discussion to that, rather than trying to forcibly wrest more symptoms from the resistant alcoholic. Once we have that one symptom, we've usually planted a seed of doubt, and can begin to build on that until, at last, the patient begins to question his own version of events. Once that comparing in process begins, we try to back off a bit, allowing the patient, rather than us, to take the initiative in diagnosis. We want the alcoholic to become the active partner because, in the final analysis, his opinion is the one which will mean the difference between success and failure.

Yet in the case of this woman we had no symptoms at all to work with except the cirrhosis. And that, we could see, had already been hammered at without success.

Frankly, we were a bit puzzled at the extent of her denial. Never before had we encountered someone so far gone into alcoholism who seemed so stubbornly unaware of her drinking. It wasn't consistent with cases we had seen previously. Was there something else complicating her denial?

Lacking anything better to do, we began to take the approach that something was very wrong with her awareness itself; so wrong, in fact, that she had managed to forget, difficult as that was to believe, whole weeks and months of drinking.

Of course, we didn't fully believe this. We felt that loss of memory was just a handle by which we could open the door of her denial.

As we began to evaluate the quality of her awareness, however, we began to believe that memory loss had indeed played a crucial role in her denial process.

We conducted practical tests of her short-term memory and discovered that she evidenced real difficulties in this area. She was unable to recall the content of morning group meetings by the early afternoon. She had trouble remembering what she'd had for breakfast each morning. She could remember our names easily enough, but would have difficulty recalling the name of the nurse she'd met that same day. She had difficulty following directions unless they were given right before she performed a task. If there was any appreciable interval between instructions and performance, she frequently forgot them, and sometimes forgot that she was to do the task altogether.

It took us a while to discover that she was trying to disguise these deficits as well. If asked the question about breakfast, for example, she'd reply that she'd had "bacon and eggs and orange juice"; after a few mornings of this, we checked on her, and discovered that she actually ate something different almost daily.

In talking with her family, it also became clear that this patient had experienced alcoholic blackouts at home; she had once even arranged over the phone to have her children visit her, only to be completely surprised when they showed up.

We had little doubt that she had experienced more of these blackouts, but we knew she would deny this. We therefore confined our discussion to areas where we had proof of such occurrences.

Our tests of her memory and awareness disturbed her greatly. She believed we were attempting to trap her into an admission of guilt. Despite her obvious confusion about what it meant to be an alcoholic, we were pleased with her hostility. It meant that she was being compelled to look at things in a new and uncomfortable light. We'd so far managed to avoid most of the "That's not true/Yes, it is" arguments which are cannon fodder to the denying alcoholic, and instead we were beginning to pull her into some degree of acknowledgement that something was wrong with her awareness. And, we implied, if she couldn't trust her own awareness of events, then how could she maintain that she, and no one else, knew what really happened during the year preceding her admission to the hospital with liver cirrhosis?

If her memory were so impaired that even after several months of abstinence she had difficulty recalling the events of that morning, then how bad must it have been *before* she entered the hospital? If when she was at home she regularly experienced alcoholic blackouts without being aware of them, then her story, in part or in its entirety, might very well be fantasy, not fact.

This, we added, would conform with the facts as documented by no less an authority than her own diseased liver.

Eventually, this woman self-diagnosed, though not in exactly the same way as the typical alcoholic. Like an amnesiac, she had to collect evidence about her own behavior over the course of months to fully convince herself that she indeed was the person everyone told her she was.

We taught ourselves a lesson as well. We realized that our emphasis on poor memory and impaired awareness was perhaps more accurate than we'd ever anticipated, and that, indeed, these were more important than an understanding of defense mechanisms in penetrating her defenses. We were again reminded that physiology, rather than psychology, explains much of alcoholic behavior.

Of course, many alcoholics—especially older ones who have no prior history of problems due to drinking—will exhibit extravagant cases of denial. It's this very extravagance which shows the need for individual rather than group counseling, or counseling in conjunction with group work. It's the really sick ones who'll benefit most.

Life-Problems

We also mentioned using individual counseling to solve problems which might interfere with recovery.

A problem, in this sense, is anything which doesn't go away by itself when the alcoholic quits drinking and which could conceivably threaten his ability to give up alcohol.

Suppose, for example, the alcoholic is not only suffering from alcoholism himself, but happens to be married to, or living with, someone who's also a practicing alcoholic. Suppose that for one reason or another, it isn't feasible for him to move out. How does one get sober while living with a drunk?

It isn't easy, but a number of alcoholics have done just that —with a lot of support and guidance along the way. A good counselor can provide a great portion of both ingredients.

What about a newly sober alcoholic who works in a bar? Or one who's an airline flight attendant (read: high-altitude bartender)? Or someone whose livelihood depends on alcohol, such as a liquor salesman or a casino dealer (why are drinks free, if they aren't an integral part of the house's advantage?). These people do get sober; a counselor can help with effective planning and realistic assessments of situations at a time when the alcoholic finds it nearly impossible to be realistic or effective in anything.

There are less direct but equally serious problems which can also make recovery difficult. There are certain alcoholics who customarily allow their emotions to run wild more than the average person does—and therefore continue getting drunk every time they reach a certain fever pitch of excitement. This alcoholic often responds to individual work on his handling of his own emotions. There are also alcoholics who are simply impulsive— that is, they get drunk before they stop to think about its possible consequences.

This impulsiveness, too, can be unlearned with a bit of training and practice.

And, of course, a patient who has a mental illness will require monitoring so that it doesn't prevent his recovering from alcoholism.

Now, all alcoholics have these life-problems to one extent or another. Everybody in the U.S., for example, lives in an environment with drinking alcoholics; our society is a carefully arranged and regulated drinking environment, where alcoholics are allowed to coexist alongside nonalcoholics as long as they stay within certain rules. It's a continual temptation to some alcoholics to attempt to drink within those rules, especially when they come across other people who haven't been diagnosed alcoholic and yet drink even more than they did.

It's also true that most newly recovering alcoholics experience some problems in relationships. In most cases, these can be handled quite adequately through AA. When they can't, a short course of individual counseling will usually do the trick.

Suppose an alcoholic man is going through a divorce. Every time he's called upon to do something in reference to this—file papers, negotiate about property, discuss child support—he's overwhelmed by anxiety attacks which render him largely useless for a week at a time.

Unlike the typical divorcing male, he doesn't have the luxury of anesthetizing himself with a few belts of whiskey, or searching for temporary wife substitutes in bars. He has to come up with alternatives to these time-tested "solutions" to problems.

A counselor can help enormously with this. The recovering alcoholic can be taught how to keep the situation in perspective, to deal with his rebellious emotions, to put life in some semblance of order.

In fact, the modern counselor is very good at exactly this sort of thing. That's how they got into the field in the first place. They're usually sensitive, concerned, insightful, inventive problem-solvers who can assist people in overcoming all sorts of "insurmountable" difficulties.

Unfortunately, many counselors won't do this. Instead of helping the alcoholic solve his problems, they unintentionally help make them worse.

This happens when the counselor chooses to use a nondirective approach.

The Nondirective and Behavioral Approaches

The idea behind nondirectiveness is usually to permit the patient to explore his feelings and attitudes without interference from the therapist. The counselor thus avoids any suggestion of advice-giving; the most a patient can hope for, in this type of therapeutic relationship, is generalized observation or interpretation of something he may have said. As soon as these comments have been made, the nondirective counselor returns to a posture of passive attention.

This is *not* the ideal approach to use in treating alcoholism.

First of all, alcoholics in their first months of sobriety need direction. That isn't to say that they always *want* direction, but nonetheless they do need it. The alcoholic's natural inclination is to return to drinking rather than to stay sober. Left on his own, the typical alcoholic will relapse as surely as the sun rises in the east. Nine chances out of ten, he won't even be able to explain why he relapses — it will seem to him that it just happens.

The way out of this vicious circle does not involve taking a nondirective stance and demanding that the alcoholic flounder around until he figures it out for himself.

We believe that the popularity of nondirectiveness has to do with the fact that so many counselors are trained in this approach; therefore, whether it works or not, they feel comfortable using it. And though it's of some value with purely psychological illnesses, applying it to disorders such as this is simply asking for trouble.

Though it's only a joke, the following illustrates the problem with pure nondirective therapy.

A man went to see a therapist one day, complaining that every time he passed an open window, he felt an overwhelming urge to throw himself out.

"You're saying," the therapist commented, "that you have this powerful urge to throw yourself out of open windows."

"That's right," the man replied. He got up from his

chair and walked over to the open window on the opposite side of the therapist's office. "I'll be passing by a window like this one, and I won't be upset or anything, but I'll still get this desire to toss myself right on out of it."

"You'll be passing by a window just like that one," the therapist echoed, "and even though you're not aware of being upset, you'll get this desire to throw yourself out."

"That's it exactly, Doctor," the man continued, "it'll come over me suddenly, like a wave, and I can hardly resist it, and . . ."

Suddenly, the man seemed to freeze in the middle of his sentence. A look of horror came over his face. Without a word, he hurled himself through the window.

The office was on the thirty-seventh floor. The only sound which could be heard was the man's final cry—"Aaaayyyyyyyy"—followed by the sickening splat as he hit the pavement.

The therapist rose and approached the window where his patient had last stood. He looked out, barely able to see the crumpled form below.

He shook his head sadly. "Aaaayyyyy," he said softly. "Splat!"

Being directive, on the other hand, doesn't mean giving the patient advice about how to get even with his mother-in-law, or taking over responsibility for organizing his life. It means that the counselor has to make sure that the patient begins to treat his illness in the proper fashion, despite any other considerations which might distract him. The counselor's job is to help the alcoholic see the forest—the disease—through the myriad of trees, usually in the form of problems, which disguise it.

If the patient can keep the disease in his sights, so to speak, he can treat it successfully. If he *loses* sight of it, and again begins treating isolated problems which result from it, the chances of relapse are much greater.

There's an AA slogan which accurately reflects this: "Remember your illness!" That's exactly how the counselor can be of most help to troubled alcoholic patients; by teaching them to solve problems without jeopardizing their sobriety.

We also don't recommend purely behavioral approaches, which attempt, in their extreme forms, to set up reward-and-punishment systems which suggest that behavioral disorders can be treated without the cooperation of the patient. Here again is a joke, which we think contains as much truth as it does humor, and illustrates this point exactly.

Once upon a time there was a mother who had two daughters, Charlene and Darlene, ages twelve and thirteen. Seemingly out of nowhere, the two girls developed a most distressing habit: they continually used, as part of everyday conversation, most of the four-letter words known in the English language.

Their mother, needless to say, was very upset. She visited a behavior therapist and explained the problem to him.

"That's an easy one," he said. "You need to punish the offending behavior right when it happens, so that the children know you don't want them doing it. The next time one of the girls uses a four-letter word, punish her swiftly and effectively, and make sure the other child sees you. Then your problems will be over."

The mother returned home and decided to try this approach at the first opportunity.

The next morning, the two girls came downstairs for breakfast.

"What would you like for breakfast this morning, Charlene?" the mother asked her eldest daughter. "How about a nice bowl of Cheerios?"

"Now what the blankety-blank would I want with a blankety-blank bowl of blankety-blank Cheerios?" her daughter replied.

Without hesitating, the mother leaned across the table and smacked her on the side of the head.

Both girls sat there looking stunned. *Now to see if it worked,* their mother thought.

She turned to her younger daughter. "And what," she asked, "would *you* like for breakfast this morning?"

The daughter just stared at her. "I don't know," she replied. "But I sure as blank won't turn down those blankety-blank Cheerios."

Establishing Boundaries

Let's go back, for just a moment, to those difficulties therapists dislike so much and which sabotaged so many of their efforts.

We think we've made it clear by now that the key to ending resistance is education. In fact, our emphasis on improved education of the alcoholic himself is the biggest difference between treatment as it was twenty years ago and as it now exists. Somehow the counselor has to make sure that the patient gets the requisite education as part of treatment. If the counselor can't provide it himself, he can find someone else who will, and he should take advantage of that resource. Trying to treat a patient who knows nothing of his illness is a waste of his time and everyone else's. Every alcoholic's greatest ally in his battle against alcoholism is his own capacity to learn; we have to make sure he gets a chance to take advantage of it.

Since defenses are part of the disease, we have to resign ourselves to their existence, and work around them as best we can. This means that we have to confront them where they most interfere with treatment, and slip around them in areas where the patient will permit no direct approach. Most alcoholics don't penetrate their more subtle defenses until long after they have managed to establish sobriety. We once knew a woman who drank her way through a promising marriage, then quit drinking in the middle of a horrendously expensive and traumatic divorce. When asked how she managed to sober up in an environment of total chaos, she replied: "It was easy. I just denied that I had any problems. After all, it's what I'm good at."

The only way we've ever found to deal with manipulative behavior successfully is by establishing clear behavioral boundaries from the outset of treatment. Rather than relying on our insight to decide when we're being manipulated, we simply let everyone know exactly what we plan to do, and how we plan to do it, and then we stick to those boundaries.

Sometimes, of course, our patients test our adherence to these boundaries. We find that if we maintain them, the patient either stops testing and gets to work, or finds another therapist whom he *can* manipulate. Either way, we solve our problem.

It seems to us that establishing boundaries is also a perfect object lesson in the way this disease works. After it's progressed to a certain point, the alcoholic's choice is reduced to the simplest possible alternative: drink, or don't drink. If you choose to drink, then this or that problem will occur. If you choose not to drink, then that problem will not occur. The alcoholic's task, given the nature of this illness, is to learn to live *within* these boundaries.

That's what recovery is.

In the same fashion, setting boundaries in treatment will save both the counselor and the alcoholic a host of problems.

10

Recovering

The First Stage of Recovery:
Compliance and Change

I N THE FIRST STAGE OF RECOVERY, THE ALCOHOLIC IS
asked to make the most dramatic changes in his behavior, and
he experiences vivid physical changes. In some cases this stage
may last as little as six or nine months; in others it can continue
up to two years. The average length of time spent in the first
stage, we'd guess, is around a year.

Let's examine the nature of these transformations in more
detail. As we do, remember that we're having to generalize quite
a bit, and no alcoholic's recovery experience will be exactly as
we describe it here. But most of the recovering people we've encountered have had experiences which fit within the general
structure of these stages.

Physiology

Think of the alcoholic's body as a factory which is switching over from one primary fuel source to another. The old fuel, of course, was alcohol, and many alcoholics have functioned on alcohol-power for months or years before they enter treatment. While this was going on, other sources of energy were neglected, due to the body's preference for alcohol. Thus, he most likely accumulated quantities of fat in his liver, rather than burning them up for energy.

During this period of running on alcohol, however, he probably developed a number of major and minor vitamin deficiencies which contribute to a state of malnutrition. The alcohol itself is nutritionally empty, so no vitamins came from that source; the presence of alcohol has also interfered with the absorption of vitamins from the food that he did manage to consume. And, since alcohol produces chemicals which suppress appetite centers in the brain, many alcoholics don't eat very much or very well; in addition, increasing withdrawal often results in nausea during eating.

We don't have to go into all of these vitamin and nutrition-related problems, but some of them seem to produce dramatic results in terms of alcoholic behavior. Common deficiencies in thiamine, for example, probably cause one of the most typical ongoing problems which face recovering alcoholics in this stage: *short-term memory loss,* affecting the individual's ability to recall information after an intervening period of distraction. As a result, most alcoholics find themselves constantly forgetting things which they'd arranged or decided on only that morning. To give you an example, we recently asked one of our classes at 4 P.M. if they could, without looking at their notes, recall the title of the lecture given at 9 A.M. that same day. Not a single student—all were less than a month sober—could remember it.

In fact, this turns out to be the most common single complaint among recovering people in the initial stage: "I feel like my brain is a little foggy, and I can't remember things at all."

We also believe that it's a mistake to think that the effects of alcohol withdrawal on the central nervous system are over when the alcoholic leaves detox. They aren't, by a long shot. Our patients often complain of mild withdrawal-like symptoms which seem to come and go during these first few months. Some of these symptoms include *irritability,* transient mild *tremors, insomnia, dizziness,* and even occasional *blurred vision.* Not all alcoholics experience all of these, of course, but most do experience one or two. As far as we can tell, they go away by themselves, and the alcoholic who is worried about any of them can always see a doctor for examination.

It also appears that the sudden absence of alcohol brings to life some old aches and pains which the alcoholic thought had vanished years ago. This is certainly disturbing, but far from fatal, and usually rights itself. The most disturbing of all the apparent transient problems of recovery in this stage, however, is temporary male impotence. However, this too is reversible, and most of the men we've treated report no particular problem after several months.

This also happens to be the period where alcoholics are most likely to experience the well-known "dry drunk"—a period where all the symptoms of withdrawal seem to return despite the fact that the alcoholic is sober. This certainly requires great resourcefulness in avoiding relapse, and very few who aren't in AA are able to survive a dry drunk without turning into a wet drunk.

Fortunately, most alcoholics don't have dry drunks, and may not have to deal with a desire for alcohol stronger than what's called a *craving.* Cravings are probably physically rooted, but can be set off by strong associations with previous drinking—as happens when a recovering alcoholic stops off in a bar to "buy cigarettes."

Emotional augmentation, which grew so important in determining alcoholic behavior during the drinking, continues into this phase. It contributes readily to alcoholic mood fluctuations, and newly sober people still tend to make mountains out of molehills without realizing it. In this sense, the alcoholic is still his own worst enemy, because he tends to create problems for himself by overreacting to everyday situations, thus giving himself plenty of ammunition for a negative, relapse-prone approach to recovery.

"This isn't any better than drinking," you might hear him complain. "I might as well get drunk." Fortunately, if he's followed directions, he's probably telling this to someone at AA, who can give some good advice on how to handle it. If he's complaining to a guy on the next barstool, you can bet he'll be drunk within the hour.

Which moves us into a discussion of the alcoholic's attitude during this stage.

Attitude

Ideally, the alcoholic's attitude is *compliant*. That means that whether or not he understands or appreciates the directions a helper is giving him, he's decided to follow them. That's the key to this stage.

One of the most puzzling things to a typical newcomer to AA is the vagueness of the answers he gets when he asks others how they stay sober. The newcomer is inevitably looking for some kind of trick or device or insight which will make him *want* to stay sober, or lose the desire to drink. What he gets in response to his question is usually a shrug and an answer like, "I don't take the first drink," or "I just take it one day at a time." Which frustrates him, because there must be more to it than that.

Maybe there is, but newly recovering people don't recognize it. The difference, then, between success and failure in quitting is really just heading in the right direction.

Psychologists hate that kind of statement, because they want to know why alcoholics are unable to abstain at this particular juncture when they may have failed innumerable times in the past. What's different about this attempt, they ask? And, like the newcomer, they don't get much of an answer. The alcoholic only knows that he's sober today—he may, in fact, be surprised by that—and the way he did it was by not taking a drink.

A lecturer on alcoholism once started a talk by saying: "I've been sober ten years now, and I owe it all to—not drinking."

Everybody laughed. But it was absolutely true. He certainly didn't make it through the first stages of his recovery because he lost all his desire to drink, or because he learned something wonderful about his upbringing in therapy, or because his life went so smoothly that he didn't even think about alcohol. He made it by not giving in, and by following the directions.

This is why we spend half our time with the counselors we supervise reassuring them that if their patients do what they tell them, it doesn't matter if the patients don't seem very happy, insightful, or comfortable. What they need is compliance. If they can comply, the rest will follow.

You will hear statements like "I don't really feel like I have anything in common with these AA people" from someone who has three drunk-driving tickets, a broken marriage, and four previous detoxes. That's because he's still comparing out in a million different ways, even though he knows he's alcoholic.

This is also the stage where defense mechanisms are still the most active. The alcoholic is almost as likely to rationalize or externalize his behavior now as he was when he was drinking. Therefore, he's likely to talk himself to the point of a relapse without really knowing exactly how. Here the directions become essential; the more decisions he makes without consultation, the more *wrong* decisions he's likely to make.

Lifestyle

The recovering alcoholic has to change his lifestyle—and don't kid yourself, most alcoholics build their lifestyles around drinking—to one built around sobriety. That's hard. He may have to change friends—many of whom are really drinking buddies—relationships, job, or hobbies. He has to change the way he eats. In short, he has to change most of what he does.

What he should avoid are *unnecessary* changes, and these are usually ones he makes because he's erroneously blaming something for his previous drinking. For example, he may have been attributing drinking excesses to the job stress. He enters treatment, learns alcoholism is a disease, and decides to give up drinking. Nonetheless, he insists on changing his job because on some level he still blames it for his troubles. He may quit, be unable to find work, and get drunk in frustration and panic. Now he's drunk because he *doesn't* have a job.

This is also the stage when most alcoholics are having to pay back debts—financial, legal, emotional, interpersonal—accrued while they were drinking. The Twelve Steps of AA have even provided a way for this to be done in an organized fashion, so the alcoholic isn't overwhelmed by the wreckage of his previous life.

Not surprisingly, this is the stage where risk of relapse, though always present in alcoholism, is the greatest. If the alcoholic follows the directions and doesn't quit working at it, he makes it; if he gets distracted by some life-problem, or gets overconfident, or doesn't get involved in some kind of recovery program, he usually doesn't make it. It's about as simple as that.

There's no magic involved, though it may seem that way to someone who's never been able to do it before.

Even if sometimes it's difficult, it's the only thing which will work.

The Second Stage: Involvement

In the second stage, the alcoholic begins to experience the real benefits of recovery on an ongoing basis, rather than only sporadically as in the first stage. He is quite likely to be proud of his achievements over the last year, and is much more willing to discuss his previous alcohol-dominated life in an open fashion, because he isn't as threatened by it, and is probably able to recall more of it than when he originally stopped drinking.

Physiology

Although the really extravagant post-alcohol changes have ceased, our patients report that physical symptoms persist in mild form.

Short-term memory loss, for example, is a frequent complaint well into this stage of recovery, although it's difficult to measure its extent because little research has been done in this area. The improvement in faculties is great enough, however, that an alcoholic who would have had considerable difficulty in academic work several months before is now able to perform adequately.

Weight gain or loss, which is common in the initial months of recovery, is a cause of concern for many alcoholics, particularly women. The second stage usually brings greater stability in weight, and is a much better time to attempt to decrease or increase one's weight than the first stage.

Augmentation of feelings is noticeably less in this phase. That's because the nervous system has settled down a bit. As a result, the alcoholic notices that life seems to be a little easier, and the days go by without so many small crises. He probably sleeps better now than he has in years, and without the aid of sleeping medications.

He doesn't shake when he writes a check, throw up in the morning as he eats a plate of eggs, or get crippling headaches with regularity. He probably doesn't catch every virus that floats through the office, and is healthier, in sum, than he's been in a long time.

Attitude

As a result of this positive experience, the recovering alcoholic is most likely beginning to look around for something new to accomplish. He perhaps has time and energy he doesn't really know what to do with, and wants to put it to productive use. He may think about quitting smoking or caffeine or overeating, or he may want to get more involved in exercise or some other health-related activity.

His defenses, as we commented earlier, have shrunk to closer-to-normal dimensions, which makes him easier to live with and also allows him to gain some insight into his previous behavior. The extent of his drinking history as he relates it, for example, seems to grow before his very eyes; it's common to hear alcoholics talking about their sudden realization that their alcoholism existed not one or two or three years before they quit drinking, but five or ten or twenty.

Of course, there's no guarantee he'll develop a more positive attitude simply because life has improved, and some refuse to. It's easy for them to fall instead into one of the patterns of potential relapse we will discuss in the next chapter.

If we had to boil these changes in attitude down to barest essence, it's this: "Hey, I'm not so bad, after all; now, what do I do next?"

Lifestyle

Generally, for those with new-found energy, the answer is: Get involved.

This may take place through increased participation in AA. We don't mean that the alcoholic necessarily increases the number of meetings he attends, because he often doesn't; the greatest attendance may have been during the initial stage. But he often does increase his *role* in AA, usually through sponsoring a newcomer himself, and beginning to give back some of what he himself received in the way of guidance.

He may decide to return to school, especially to take courses in alcoholism, drug abuse, or psychology. There's been an influx of recovering people into the ranks of counselors over the last decade, and the initial impetus often springs from this desire for greater involvement.

But most significantly, this stage marks an increase in interest in that most problem-laden of all human activities, relationships with other people. As a result, the alcoholic may find himself confronted with a host of new problems which he has never dealt with (sober) before.

Even, for example, at forty or fifty years old. One woman we know expressed it well: "It's tough," she said, "when you have to go through menopause and adolescence at the same time."

Perhaps this is why so many alcoholics develop an interest in therapy at this point; some enroll in training programs, while others buy every self-help paperback which hits the bookshelf and attend every seminar or workshop on communication and relations with the opposite sex. Those who get into therapy, of course, sometimes have to teach their therapists about alcoholism, or the therapist might misguidedly set out to cure the disease, and lead the patient into another relapse.

Nonetheless, this is really a very positive stage for most alcoholics, if they remember their illness, because it represents a chance to do some growing up which they might have missed because of chemical interference. It's just not a particularly peaceful time, for many of them.

The Third Stage: Autonomy

Autonomy doesn't mean independence. Alcoholics don't really ever *leave* AA in this stage. They simply learn to branch out in other directions.

During the second stage, the alcoholic's explorations into new areas probably led to some disquieting realizations about himself, along with understanding that some expectations (even the most cherished ones) may be impossible to fulfill. He will have had to come to terms with this, and as a result his approach to life in general is more realistic.

"Realistic" is a much abused word, but fits the situation. This will be a new view of realism: the alcoholic is much less likely to attempt things he can't do, and thus is much less frequently disappointed in himself and others. He may recognize that concepts such as maturity, personality growth, and adulthood are entirely relative, and that the only thing he can compare himself to is the way he used to be.

Physical changes resulting from the drinking are few during this stage because enough time has passed (usually several years) for the alcoholic to have healed. Attitudinal changes are many, however, and this is the stage which produces the "grateful" alcoholics whose words so amaze the newcomer to AA.

"He's *grateful* he's alcoholic?" the newcomer asks. "Is he crazy?"

No—in fact, he's probably saner than he's ever been—but he no longer finds it hard to go without drinking on a daily basis, and is probably glad he learned some of the lessons he did along the way.

The newcomer thinks alcoholism is a curse. He sees no redeeming value in it whatsoever.

But alcoholism is just a disease, and it seems to us it takes no special act of God for an individual to become alcoholic.

One of us can recall two boys in high school who had diabetes and had to take insulin daily; they were limited in their athletic activities, which we other students thought was incredible, horrible punishment for them to undergo. We thought they would never survive it, and we all pitied them.

That is, until we discovered that they could still beat us in basketball, if they took short rests. Then we started treating them like everyone else.

But one thing was remarkably different about both of them; they were considerably more mature than they had been prior to the diabetes. They seemed to have grown up faster than the rest of us.

That's often what happens in the case of people who successfully treat these chronic illnesses. They get a sense of their own mortality, and all their childhood hopes, dreams, and expectations, along with their adult beliefs, ambitions, and problems, seem much less important.

They're *alive,* aren't they?

They leave depression to the psychiatrists and immortals.

11

Ways
To
Fail

S INCE THE TREATMENT IS RELATIVELY STRAIGHTFOR-
ward, why do so many alcoholics relapse? Why doesn't
every alcoholic achieve lasting sobriety on the first attempt?

Of course, this has been the subject of intense speculation
for generations. Those who believed in the alcoholic personality
used the incidence of relapse to justify their position: the alcoholic's innate flaws of character produced the need for a
chemical crutch to help him cope. Wet Moral advocates criticized
his lack of determination, Dry Moralists insisted the Devil was
behind it, and those in the Impaired model figured he was hopeless in the first place.

Within AA, there are hundreds of favorite explanations for
relapse. To some, it's proof of an inability to be honest with
oneself. To others, relapse means you haven't properly completed one or more of the Twelve Steps, attended enough meetings, hooked up with the right sponsor, or any combination of the
above. When an alcoholic performs these tasks and still relapses,

you'll hear someone say: "Well, alcoholism is cunning, baffling, and powerful."

From what we can see, however, most relapses are not mysterious at all. There appear to be two fundamental paths that an alcoholic can take which will lead him, eventually, to relapse. He can:

• Fail to do the things which will enable him to stay sober, or
• Indulge in counterproductive activities which effectively undermine whatever positive steps he's taking.

There are a number of options to choose from when it comes to precisely *how* he'll relapse, but those options fall into these two general categories.

We think the real problem is that the alcoholic doesn't see his own relapse coming. After he's resumed drinking, of course, that's all the reason he needs to continue; by the time he's gotten sick, or in some kind of serious trouble, he'll be faced with the choice of seeking help or suffering the consequences.

If he's like most relapsers, however, he won't be able to identify what he did wrong, other than the fact that he took the first drink. His insight into his relapse will be as poor as his insight into alcoholism in general.

Thus, relapsers need more education, and that education needs to be geared towards helping them identify the factors involved in their own relapses. A second comparing in process has to occur, wherein the relapser identifies his *relapse pattern* (or patterns) in the same way he previously identified his drinking pattern. He'll need to realize that there are steps he can take to remedy whatever flaws exist in his program for recovery, and that if he's willing to change his behavior a bit, he can avoid further relapses.

We've looked at our own experience with alcoholics and categorized their stories into a number of relapse patterns, which illustrate, we think, the paths that most alcoholics take into relapse. We'll review them individually, and then discuss some suggestions for treating relapsers at the end of this chapter.

Pattern One: Not Enough of the Right Treatment

Even when the alcoholic knows he's an alcoholic, he often chooses to treat his illness in a fashion which almost guarantees failure.

The most common example is the patient who admits himself to the medical-surgical wing of a hospital for withdrawal or alcohol-related illness. As soon as he's over the most acute phase of the shakes, he leaves the hospital, believing that now that the worst is past in terms of physical illness, he can rely on will power to avoid further problems with alcohol.

We knew of one man who had over one hundred admissions to various hospitals for what was essentially alcohol detox, yet who had never once been treated in an alcoholism unit. He was able to convince himself in each instance that somehow this time would be different, and he'd be able to control his drinking after he left the hospital. What he really did was to slap medical bandaids on the worst symptoms of his drinking, and then set out to do still more damage to himself.

Something similar happens to alcoholics who attempt to treat this illness through conventional psychotherapy. As we've discussed previously, alcoholism is regarded in psychotherapy as a symptom of other problems, rather than as a primary disease. Because of this, the patient spends most of his time in therapy discussing his communication problems with his spouse, or whatever, while his drinking continues to worsen. As the drinking progresses, new problems occur which seem to justify still more drinking and which further divert attention from the *nature* of the drinking. A sort of vicious circle develops.

As far as we can tell, most attempts at purely psychological intervention have very little effect on the course of alcoholism. We knew one man, for example, who enrolled in a course of therapy and hypnosis which was supposed to enable him to overcome his periodic drinking binges. He attended sessions twice weekly at a cost of about eighty dollars per visit, and found that though he was able to confine his consumption to two or three drinks nightly during the week, he still got drunk, and stayed drunk, all weekend. He felt this was a sign that he needed more therapy, and was considering adding an appointment on Saturday, when his therapist was called out of town for a month. In his absence, the man discovered that his drinking pattern was exactly the same as it had been when he had regular sessions with the therapist. In other words, the expensive treatment was apparently having no effect on his drinking at all. He was just assuaging his conscience by engaging in a classic half-measure which allowed him to believe he was at least doing *something* about his drinking.

Some alcoholics, of course, are able to recover with no more help than these two approaches, medical and psychotherapeutic, provide; but for every one who makes it, there are ten more who don't.

Pattern Two: No Self-Diagnosis

Sometimes the alcoholic *does* enter treatment which is likely to do some good, but avoids a crucial step: coming to believe that he himself suffers from the illness of alcoholism and therefore must do something about it.

One of our former patients was a research biochemist. In three weeks in the hospital he learned more about this illness than we'd thought possible. He even began correcting some of the physicians on their explanations of liver disease.

Nevertheless, after about six weeks at home, he relapsed. When he landed back in the hospital, he thought quite a bit about what he might have done wrong in terms of his recovery, and came to the conclusion that although he knew alcoholism was a disease, he really hadn't believed that *he* had it.

His drinking, he felt sure, had been in response to environmental stress.

Thus, his learning had been confined to the realm of the purely intellectual; he absorbed information in much the same way that most of us crammed for high-school science tests—which is to say, he planned to forget it as soon as he graduated.

Self-diagnosis of one sort or another seems to be essential for ongoing sobriety. Though most people enter treatment because of a particular crisis in their lives, those crises tend to disappear after a few months of abstinence, and unless the alcoholic has diagnosed himself, his motivation for recovery will disappear also. It isn't important that this comparing in process be done solely in terms of the Disease model. People in AA, for example, often acknowledge only that they're powerless over alcohol, and that their lives have become unmanageable. The important point is that they do acknowledge the presence of alcoholism, however they define it, and therefore begin to approach the problem from the standpoint of an ongoing need for treatment, rather than simply something to be fixed or covered over.

When you hear an alcoholic telling you that his alcoholism was the result of "trying to do too much for others," or "not setting limits on other people's demands," and that he now knows better and won't let that happen again, you're most likely dealing with someone who isn't self-diagnosed. In his estimation, alcoholism remains a response to situational stress, and it will be very hard for him to understand why it's important to treat it when he's *not* under any immediate stress. He'll thus be prone to relapse.

Pattern Three: Experiments with Controlled Drinking

One evening we received a call about an alcoholic who was in an Emergency Room asking for help. When we arrived, we saw it was someone we'd treated two years previously, and then not heard from afterwards. "How have you been doing?" we asked. "Very well," the obviously intoxicated fellow replied, "up until about three weeks ago, when I started drinking again." "Really," we said, "and how long were you abstinent before this relapse—the entire two years since you left the hospital?" "Yes," he answered, then hesitated. "Well . . . do you mean *completely* abstinent?"

That's a pretty standard example of an alcoholic who's been trying to get away with controlled drinking.

First of all, we need to establish the difference between what this relapser thinks he's doing—which he will usually call controlled social drinking—and what he's really doing, which is controlled *alcoholic* drinking.

Controlled social drinking is what people do when they look at the empty glass in their hand and ask themselves if they should have another one. Then, if they've had a couple already, they set the glass back down, saying to themselves that no, they don't really want it.

Controlled *alcoholic* drinking represents an effort of will on the part of an alcoholic to resist:

1. Drinking too much, or
2. Drinking at inappropriate times, or
3. Developing problems as a result of his drinking.

In other words, it's an attempt to avoid the symptoms of loss of control. It's not "normal" drinking by any stretch of the imagination, and it may be social only in the sense that the alcoholic is somewhere within ten feet of another human being. But it's most emphatically *alcoholic* drinking.

This pattern ties in strongly with a fundamental misconception about the nature of the disease. Here, the alcoholic equates alcoholism with the problems it causes, and convinces himself that he can learn to drink *without* problems. This usually starts with the traditional glass of wine with dinner or cold beer on a hot day. Instead of getting in trouble, this alcoholic finds that he's able to stop with one or two, or confine his drinking to a single evening.

He then thinks, "Gee, maybe I'm doing better than I thought I was. Maybe I really *can* drink, now that I've decided not to go overboard. Maybe all those counselors were wrong, and my drinking was just the result of stress, and now that my life is going okay, I won't want to drink so much, and I can stop at one or two."

In other words, he begins to question everything he learned

about the progressive nature of alcoholism and about his inability to drink safely. A week or two later, he has several more drinks and gets away with it again, further convincing himself that something crucial has changed in his life and drinking is no longer dangerous, as long as he keeps an eye on it.

Just when he's most sure of his success at this, he has a few and discovers, to his horror, that he *can't* stop.

Apparently from nowhere, the disease has returned. And soon enough, he's in worse trouble than he ever was.

The alcoholic's capacity to believe that he can restore, through will or insight or magic, his own ability to drink, is legendary. It's as though he's able to forget whatever problems plagued him in the past and focus his attention solely on the belief that maybe, this time, things will be different. Each time he's able to say he got away with drinking, it reinforces the illusion, so that the next time he wants a drink, his defenses are even weaker.

The truth is, the biggest single breakthrough in alcoholism treatment—a breakthrough made by AA, by the way—was simply that helpers stopped going along with the alcoholic's attempts to control his drinking, and started recommending that he stop altogether. That, more than anything else, laid the foundation for the much-improved recovery rates we have today.

It's hard for an alcoholic to quit altogether, but it's still much easier than trying to drink without having problems.

Pattern Four:
Maintaining a Drinking Environment

An alcoholic may stop drinking but continue to spend a lot of time with others who *are* drinking.

This is the pattern of those who agree that alcohol is bad for them and that they ought to abstain from its use, but who insist that their lifestyle must remain tied to drinking. They may, for example, insist on sitting in their old drinking haunts, perhaps on a favorite barstool, sipping Perrier and lime while their mates get progressively drunker. They may claim that these drinkers are their only real friends, and that even if they don't join in the drinking, the bar represents the only interesting social life available to them.

It shouldn't be any surprise that after a few weeks or months of this, these drinkers find that they have a craving for alcohol and, since it's all around them, relapse.

It's also the pattern of the salesman who claims that much of his business depends on his ability to drink with his customers; apparently alcohol is one of America's major sales tools. The relapse rate among salesmen who refuse to take even a few months' break from liquid lunches is high.

Those first ninety days appear to be the most crucial in this respect. Unless the alcoholic can manage to avoid alcohol-oriented situations for at least that long, his chances for relapse increase.

We also advise our alcoholic patients to avoid certain organizations which we won't name but which are usually all male in membership and are sometimes named after animals. These organizations, and others like them, do good works, but also spend a good deal of their time drinking. At one point, we lectured to one of these groups on the nature of alcoholism, and throughout our talk, the members of the audience continued to order and consume drinks. At the end of the speech, we asked the audience a question.

"Now you all represent the leadership of your community," we began, "and all hold jobs, and are successful people. Since it's the middle of the afternoon, we expect that you'll all go back to work as well. Let us ask you: Is there anyone here who's willing to say he's spent the last hour listening to a talk about alcoholism without having anything to drink?" No one raised a hand. "Then how easy would it be," we continued, "for someone who was a recovering alcoholic to sit through this meeting?"

Everyone agreed it would be damned difficult. The whole orientation of the meeting had been towards drinking. Anyone who was abstaining would have stuck out like a sore thumb.

We recommend to our patients that they take a vacation from alcohol-oriented activities. It often saves them a relapse.

Pattern Five: Stress

One of the most popular relapse patterns lays the blame on stress, probably because alcoholism itself is often attributed to it, and also because the term "stress" has become so popular among Americans. It seems as though most present-day illnesses are blamed in part on stress, as once they were blamed on unhappy childhoods.

In relapse, however, the alcoholic who blames his drinking on stress is usually what we call a *problem-accumulator:* someone who seems to collect issues to worry about, rather than solving or, if no solutions are available, ignoring them.

Then, when a sufficient number of problems are accumulated, this alcoholic can point to one and say: "There—that's the straw that broke the camel's back," and proceed to get drunk.

As AA points out, there are two kinds of problems which face the recovering alcoholic: those he can do something about, and those he can't. The task is to figure out which is which, and there is where the problem-accumulator goes astray. He tends to spend all his time on problems he can do absolutely nothing about—while neglecting problems which *do* fall within his sphere of influence. Thus he puts himself into a position where he's constantly subject to frustration, discouragement, depression, and a sense of personal failure or inadequacy. This in turn means that he's always "under stress," and finds sobriety nearly as unhappy as his drinking.

This syndrome is especially common among alcoholics who made a botch of their personal and professional lives while they were drinking, and realize, once sober, exactly how many incorrect decisions they've made in the past. As a result, they become gun-shy, distrusting their intelligence, and are sometimes afraid to do *anything* lest they make an error. This also encourages their problems to mount, since they're not doing anything to prevent them from mounting.

In case you haven't noticed, life tends to keep sending new problems down the pike. If we don't solve the ones we have now, we tend to find we still have them, plus a bunch of new ones, later.

In this syndrome, the alcoholic also fails to let go of problems which really don't exist anymore. He may continue to worry about things which solved themselves months or years ago; things that the passage of time alone was enough to remedy.

If there is a stress-prone alcoholic, we'd say it's one who externalizes a lot, believing that his problems are the result of outside events and forces, rather than of his own choices. He will find himself in a battle against the world—a battle he'll eventually lose, and one that is entirely of his own making. But an alcoholic who believes he has an illness which is influencing him to *choose* to drink will be less stress-prone in sobriety.

Pattern Six: Overconfidence

Ironically, it seems that almost as many relapsers get drunk because they have too *few* problems as those who drink because they have too many.

A few chapters back, we showed you a diagram which we'll reproduce here.

Obviously, what the alcoholic is aware of—the most apparent physical effects and alcohol-related problems—represent only part of the disease. The most enduring and damaging processes, such as the development of tolerance, physical dependence, and most organ changes, occur without his or her awareness.

When the alcoholic stops drinking, 99 percent of these obvious difficulties disappear. He no longer shakes every morning, no longer has extended bouts of alcohol-induced depression, and is able to work and think and communicate again on a normal level with normal people. Sure, it will take a couple of years for him to return to his full level of functioning, but compared to the way he was when drinking, he'll probably seem to be a ball of fire.

Visible and Invisible Changes As Alcoholism Progresses

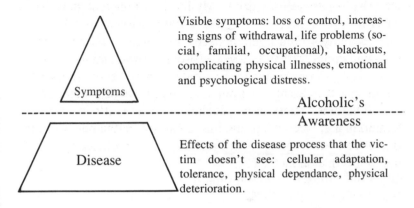

Visible symptoms: loss of control, increasing signs of withdrawal, life problems (social, familial, occupational), blackouts, complicating physical illnesses, emotional and psychological distress.

Alcoholic's
Awareness

Effects of the disease process that the victim doesn't see: cellular adaptation, tolerance, physical dependance, physical deterioration.

Once these overt symptoms have gone, what is left in daily life to convince him that he still has the disease?

In many cases, nothing. Unless he experiences a craving, or many ongoing withdrawal symptoms, there's generally nothing to differentiate him from the nonalcoholic.

Thus, it is very easy for the alcoholic to forget he has a disease.

In fact, we're convinced that if the minute one became alcoholic, the palm of one's left hand turned bright red and never reverted to normal, we would have fewer relapses. There would be a tangible mark to remind the alcoholic that something was different about him, even when he wasn't drinking.

Because this kind of thing doesn't happen, it's easy for the alcoholic who's doing very well in his sobriety to begin letting his recovery program lapse, simply because he thinks he no longer needs it. This is the pattern of the procrastinator ("I'll get to AA over the weekend"), the excuse-maker ("I couldn't get a ride, and besides, I was feeling good anyway, so I didn't really need to go"), and the "program consultant" ("You people do marvelous work, but I think you'd reach a wider audience if you did this.'')

"Why bother?" he says to himself; "I'm doing so well. I don't have a desire for a drink. My life is going great guns. I feel like I'll never want a drink again. I really learned my lesson last time. So why should I get all steamed up about missing a couple of AA meetings? After all, I've been sober almost five months."

Believe it or not, we've seen alcoholics get this attitude with less than a month sober. At that early stage, we call it the Executive Syndrome. An executive is someone who takes the approach that no matter what the problem, he can solve it better than anyone else. He may point to a lifetime of getting his way as evidence of this; nonetheless, he's overconfident from the start about his ability to deal with the disease.

Of course, the Executive Syndrome isn't confined to business executives. We've encountered doctor-executives, longshoreman-executives, retired-army-colonel-executives, and even a few wino-executives. Sometimes it seems as though the disease feeds on this attitude, allowing the alcoholic to think he's going to do just fine once he's on his own, and then pulling the rug out from under him.

Pattern Seven: Physical Illness

Occasionally, patients will have some chronic medical problem which necessitates the use of pain-reducing medication.

Some alcoholics will relapse because they don't take the medication, and some because they do.

The first instance is typified by a patient who suffered from chronic lower-back pain, yet refused any pain-relieving medication because he'd been told to stay away from *all* drugs in the nonmedical alcoholism treatment he entered. Though this kind of abstinence was fine in theory, those who advised him weren't aware that certain kinds of illnesses can turn you into a virtual invalid if you don't take some medication for them. That's what happened to this fellow. He wasn't able to put together any kind of a sober life for himself because of his constant pain, and therefore relapsed every few months. After about a year of this, he was lucky enough to run into a doctor who knew of appropriate medications that provided him with some relief from his pain. His relapses stopped.

The second case is illustrated by a patient who began taking a narcotic for a similar lower-back pain and continued to take it after she stopped drinking. By the end of her sober year, she was taking massive amounts of the narcotic, and frequently found herself as unable to function as she had been while she was drinking. Even after more treatment, she returned to the use of drugs, overdosed, and died.

In both cases, the key to avoiding relapse lay in the nature of the medication used. In the first example, the patient had the mistaken belief that because he was an alcoholic, all medicines were dangerous for him; he used nothing until he stumbled upon something that was safe. In the second instance, the alcoholic gave in to the pain and endangered her recovery by choosing an addictive medication.

What both those relapsers needed was a physician who was familiar with alcoholism. Such a doctor could have prescribed appropriate medicines and other treatments for their physical ailments and monitored their progress for any sign of problems.

Unfortunately, most people have doctors who aren't familiar with this illness; they either "don't believe in it," as one family practitioner told us, or they haven't been taught how to prescribe to an alcoholic. Either way, the patient suffers.

That's why we encourage people to learn as much about their illness as they can, for their own protection, and find a doctor who also knows something about it.

Pain can also be a great *excuse* for relapse. One day we met a fellow on the street who'd been one of our patients a number of years before. He's thirty-two years old, and has suffered so much physically that when you tell someone you've run into him, the first response is always: "You saw Rudy? I thought he was dead." He was carrying a can of beer in his hand and immediately began talking about his recent history. He had been in intensive care units five times since we last saw him, twice for esophageal bleeding, perhaps the most dangerous of alcohol-related conditions. He'd been sober a month, he claimed, but in the last few days had developed a toothache and, since it was a weekend, couldn't get in to see a dentist. Beer, he claimed, was the only pain reliever he had.

There was an emergency dental service about three blocks from where he was standing, but at that point we didn't even bother to tell him. He would just have found another excuse for relapse.

Pattern Eight: Psychiatric Illness

A minority of alcoholic patients have a coexisting psychiatric condition which complicates their recovery. If they attempt to treat alcoholism without treating their psychiatric illness as well, they tend to relapse due to its interference. If, on the other hand, they attempt to treat their alcoholism by treating their psychiatric problems, they relapse because they neglected to deal with the disease directly.

Some of these psychiatric illnesses include bipolar affective disorder (that used to be manic depressive illness), schizophrenia, and depression. All of these conditions, left untreated, can strongly influence the alcoholic towards relapse.

It's also true that all of these illnesses are treatable, usually through a carefully monitored regimen of medication and support. None of the medications commonly used to treat these illnesses are cross-addictive, and can be used safely by the alcoholic under supervision.

Nonetheless, alcoholics are often reluctant to take these medicines. For example, we recently had a patient who badly needed major tranquilizers to help his obvious paranoia and agitation. He resisted using these drugs because he said he didn't want to become a pill head. The irony was that, for once, those around him wanted him to use the drug, and couldn't talk him into it. Their efforts to dissuade him from drinking, however, had been completely unsuccessful despite years of trying.

Some of these twice-afflicted patients complain that it's unfair that they have to be burdened with two illnesses rather than one, but of course, fair and unfair are concepts which nature appears to have trouble understanding. It's really no more unfair than if the alcoholic were burdened with diabetes or emphysema in addition to alcoholism. It just *is,* and must be accepted and dealt with.

Of course, in many cases even symptoms of these psychiatric illnesses are the result of the drinking, and may clear up with abstinence. That's why special care should be taken with a diagnosis based on symptoms that occurred during the course of alcoholic drinking. That way, there will be minimal risk of treating a psychiatric problem which doesn't really need treatment.

Pattern Nine: Unawareness of Normal Recovery Symptoms

Since we've covered recovery symptoms in our chapter on recovery, we'll only say here that in programs where alcoholics are taught about those symptoms, and are given suggestions as to how to handle them, relapses rarely occur.

Where this education has been neglected, however, we see alcoholics frequently relapsing in panic over recurrent episodes of insomnia, or their difficulty with short-term memory, or their own fluctuations of mood and energy, or their vivid dreams about alcohol, or their problems with temporary impotence. These occur most prominently in the first year of abstinence, helping to explain why relapse is more likely during that period than during any subsequent year.

Pattern Ten: Poor Nutrition

There is considerable debate about the effect of poor nutrition in relapses. To some observers, it is the primary reason for alcoholic relapse; to others, it seems incidental in the face of other factors. We would like to withhold our opinion until more data is in, but we do see poor nutrition playing a definite role in *some* cases of relapse. In fact, in those instances it appears to be a deciding factor.

We had a patient at one point who had been sober for more than a year and had followed all of the usual directions given a recovering alcoholic in AA. He went to plenty of meetings, kept his sobriety in a primary position in his life, and made sure that he handled problems as they arose. Nonetheless, he experienced a frequent craving for alcohol. He couldn't point to any cause: he was under no particular stress, felt healthy, was content with his lot. Still, he had a persistent desire for a drink.

Searching for the cause of this craving, we asked him about his diet. It turned out that he customarily ate once a day, at dinner time, and before that meal ate nothing, subsisting while he worked on coffee and cigarettes. Since he lived alone, he ate only fast foods: a hamburger, french fries, and a milkshake. That was his entire diet, all day, every day.

Of course, eating in this fashion will aggravate any residual hypoglycemia which may persist in the alcoholic, and the concomitant heavy use of stimulants like nicotine and caffeine further complicate the picture. When the patient changed his diet to more normal patterns, his craving disappeared.

For anyone who would like more information regarding the role of nutrition in recovery from alcoholism, we recommend *Eating Right to Live Sober,* by Katherine Ketcham and L. Ann Mueller, M.D. (see Suggested Reading in the back of the book).

Pattern Eleven: Treating Alcoholism with Drugs

All right, let's do an experiment. Those of you who aren't doctors, try for a moment to think like a doctor. Those of you who are already doctors, think like yourselves. Here's the problem: a good percentage of your patients, whether you're a psychiatrist, G.P., internist, or whatever, seem to be alcoholic. They drink excessively, can't seem to stop themselves, make everybody around them unhappy, get outrageously sick and obstreperous, and call you for help, invariably in the middle of the night.

You, in turn, find them hospital beds, detoxify them, and

care for their ailments. In a few days they feel pretty good, and in a few weeks they feel just fine.

Whereupon a significant percentage go out and repeat the whole experience. Maybe once, twice, thirty times, even more.

So you ask yourself: what is the problem here? It obviously isn't that hard to get the alcoholic *off* alcohol; it's just a matter of a week or so. The problem is that they resume drinking, and put themselves through the whole thing all over again.

Why, for God's sake?

You decide to go to the horse's mouth and *ask*.

The alcoholic considers the question carefully. Why, he asks himself, did I get drunk again? And he proceeds to tell you the same things he will tell himself: it was because of the pressure, stress, other people, anxiety, and the rest of the things to which alcoholics traditionally attribute drinking.

You, being the doctor, will hear this and think, Well, I certainly can do something about stress, tension, anxiety, and pressure. I can prescribe drugs! Then, being no longer anxious, this fellow will have no more need of alcohol, and therefore will stop calling me at all hours of the night, thus saving not only his marriage, but mine!

(A physician friend of ours once told us that the impetus behind all medical research was the quest for a way to eliminate the midnight phone call.)

And so you will prescribe one or two of the usual remedies with the intention to banish alcoholism by ending the alcoholic's need to drink.

When you've done this, you'll have created the most enduring of modern approaches to alcoholism: the Substitution model. You will be substituting one drug for another. In the belief that the new drug will replace alcohol without leading to the same problems.

The first substitute that we can remember learning of was morphine, in Kentucky in the nineteenth century. There, the doctors believed that addicting an alcoholic to morphine, which happened to be cheap and available, was at least easier on his family than having to bail him out of jail after alcohol-induced bar fights. Well-supplied morphine addicts tend to sit at home and contemplate their navels, rather than wandering about in an alcoholic blackout and getting into trouble.

After morphine came the barbiturates. These drugs became so popular that they were prescribed for almost every nervous disorder, including alcoholism. As a result, we hit a new high in the incidence of alcohol-plus-barbiturate overdose. Alcoholics soon restored alcohol to its prominent position in their lives, yet continued to take the barbiturates to facilitate withdrawal.

We kept introducing new, "safe" medications in our efforts to find a way to treat alcoholism with sedatives, and proceeded through meprobamate, methaqualone, and the benzodiazepines. By the 1950s and '60s it was nearly impossible to receive treatment for alcoholism at many clinics *without* being put on a maintenance dose of some sedative. If you told the examining physician that you didn't want the drug, he'd try to convince you to take it anyway. He invariably believed that alcoholism was best treated by the substitution of another drug.

Needless to say, most of these patients relapsed. Many would remain abstinent for weeks or months while taking the medications, and this would help convince the treatment staff that the medication was essential. But what most failed to notice was that very few patients obtained any *lasting* sobriety using medications, and if they didn't relapse with alcohol, a significant percentage developed major addictive problems with the prescribed drugs.

So-called recovering alcoholic patients began showing up in treatment centers with histories of abstinence from alcohol for months or even years, but taking phenomenal doses of tranquilizers in a maintenance fashion, and suffering the withdrawal symptoms they'd had when drinking. To give an extreme example, we had one patient who weighed only ninety-five pounds but consumed approximately one hundred sedative tablets a week. She had been sober, her doctor informed us, for ten months.

It seems to us that what these alcoholics were really doing

during their periods of abstinence was a form of controlled drinking, using tranquilizers instead of liquor. In the early and middle stages of alcoholism (described in the box at the end of the book), many alcoholics are capable of exercising this degree of control. What they do with pills is not very different from what they do with alcohol in their efforts to regain the ability to drink without problems. And obviously, it can be done—for a while.

Substitution of other drugs isn't only a favorite approach of physicians; it's popular among newly recovering alcoholics as well. One of the first questions we're asked by new patients is: What can I take instead of alcohol when I'm nervous or upset? Young alcoholics tend to favor the idea that they can still use marijuana, while older ones want to rely on minor tranquilizers. "I'll only use it when I need it," is the common promise. However, when you need it changes as your body adapts to the presence of the drug. Sitting in the hospital, you may believe you'd only use such a drug when a relative died, or some other catastrophe occurred. When you're back home, a sleepless night or little argument with one of the kids can send you scurrying to the medicine cabinet.

What *does* substitute for alcohol? To be blunt, nothing substitutes for it exactly. Alcohol is one of those things that an alcoholic can never replace with another substance on an exchange basis. Then he'd be addicted to whatever had replaced it. *Life* replaces alcohol in recovery—which means a variety of experiences exist where drinking (and recuperating from drinking) once held sway.

As we've said before, there isn't any easy way out of it: the alcoholic simply has to *change*. As this change takes place, the need for a substitute of one kind or another will dissipate, as the need for alcohol itself diminishes. Sedative drugs have no role in this recovery process.

Pattern Twelve: The Family Feud

Even after quitting drinking, many alcoholics live in homes which might more accurately be described as war zones.

The tactics of combat will vary—one family might favor the sudden skirmish, while another prefers the traditional cold war with occasional sniper attacks—but the result is the same: an environment dominated by hostility and conflict.

In other words, the worst possible milieu in which to change any type of long-standing behavior pattern. With so much chaos in the air, who has time to reflect on one's *own* needs and activities?

Families such as these are always marked by provoking behavior. A classic example appeared in Chapter 6, where we discussed the relationship between Buddy and his long-suffering sister. If you recall the steps she took to drive him back to drink, you'll understand how likely relapse is when such a situation exists.

What motivates these feuds? A variety of factors. But first and foremost, the issue of conflict is usually not what is happening now but, rather, who is responsible for what went on *before* the alcoholic stopped drinking. Families in this situation are dealing with issues like:

- If he/she can stop drinking now, why didn't he or she stop years ago, instead of putting us through all this torture?
- Don't give me this "disease" stuff—that just gives alcoholics an excuse for weaseling out of responsibility for their selfishness.
- Well, now that he/she/ is dry, it's my turn to get out some of the resentments *I've* had for all these years.
- Just because he/she is dry, does that mean the rest of us are supposed to act like none of this ever really happened? What about the lying, cheating, stealing, neglect, and all that? We're just supposed to forget it?
- As far as we're concerned, this alcoholic has one hell of a lot to prove before being accepted back into this family. And we're not letting anyone forget it for a minute.

What's obvious to any therapist, and even to the casual observer, is that despite the legitimacy of the family's attitude, given their previous experience, the result of their approach is likely to be exactly the opposite of the result they claim they want—a sober alcoholic in the family.

The result they *will* get? Either relapse, divorce, or, worst of all, a permanent state of impenetrable hostility between the now recovering alcoholic and those who supposedly love him.

It isn't possible to treat this relapse pattern without treating the whole family, for obvious reasons. But we would caution against the common therapeutic assumption that the best way to treat these problems is by treating the whole family *together*.

With families as sick as some of these, it's best to begin by addressing the members separately, developing treatment plans for them nearly as comprehensive and individualized as for the alcoholic. Counseling must be supplemented with insistence on Al-Anon involvement. The family may resist this, in much the same way as the alcoholic fights AA, but it could mean the difference between success and failure.

And we also caution against directing efforts towards the type of emotional catharsis that many therapists mistake for attitudinal change. The real goal should be an increase in the family's understanding of the disease process, and the development of a willingness on their part to live *outside* the long shadow of the past. This is very different from what cathartic therapies produce. As one clinician advised us: "People can 'cathart' all afternoon in a therapy group, and then frequently go out and make the same mistake all over again."

Using the Relapse Evaluation Profile

The Relapse Evaluation Profile was developed so that helpers can assist in spotting problem areas for alcoholics who have tried to recover and have relapsed. The goal is to develop a recovery plan that the relapser has been actively involved in creating. Following are some pointers for the helper.

• Give the profile to the relapser with directions to complete it to the best of his ability. Be sure he understands the words. If he's unable to read well enough to complete it, you may have to go over it together verbally. If he's truly illiterate, it many be helpful to have him speak his responses into a tape recorder, so he can play them back to himself.

- Most relapsers are weak in two, three, or four areas. Some are weak in nearly all areas. If this is the case, it's important to determine priorities; which areas need attention first?
- Devise treatment goals with the relapser, based on the weak areas in his or her program as determined by the profile.
- In each goal, there should be one objective designed to have the relapser state how he or she is going to respond if this problem should arise again.
- After using the treatment goals, the relapser can summarize what he has learned in a prevention plan which details how he plans to avoid future relapse. Unacceptable would be anything based exclusively on will power or insufficient AA involvement, and this should be pointed out to the relapser prior to formulation of the plan.
- Note that the cause of relapse in several situations may have been the use of drugs, prescribed or nonprescribed. If that is the case, make sure the alcoholic realizes the problems of cross addiction and that other alternatives can be found.
- In composing the prevention plan, the relapser is making recommendations normally made by a counselor at the time the person is discharged from the counselor's care. The recovering alcoholic, along with a helper, is in effect taking the counselor's role.

Relapse Evaluation Profile

1. Did you follow through on recommendations made to you during your treatment or recovery program?
2. Do you believe that alcoholism is a chronic, progressive disease, and that you have it?
3. After you left treatment, did you change your lifestyle so it was conducive to sobriety, or did you allow it to remain conducive to drinking?

4. After your treatment, did you sometimes experiment with drinking?

5. Did you use any mood-altering drugs after treatment? If so, which ones? What was your purpose in using them?

6. Did you find you were unable to solve problems as they arose, or did they seem to accumulate? Did you find that you were dwelling on problems you couldn't really do anything about?

7. Did you maintain your recovery program as you had begun it, or did you allow it to lapse? Did you reduce your involvement with AA? Did sobriety lose its primary position in your daily life?

8. Did you suffer from any serious physical illness? Did it interfere with your recovery? Did you take steps to treat it properly? Did you take medications for it? If so, what medicines?

9. Do you suffer from any coexisting mental illness? Did this interfere with your recovery?

10. Were you bothered by any of the following symptoms during abstinence: frequent insomnia, dizzy spells, fluctuations in mood and energy level, depression, or sexual problems? If so, which ones? Did you take any steps to remedy them?

11. Have you been maintaining a proper diet? Did you experience a persistent craving for alcohol or any other drug?

12. Do you believe that your family (if you have one) supports your efforts to recover? Do you believe it in any way interferes with your recovery?

13. Are there any other factors in your lifestyle or other behavior which you feel contribute to relapse rather than to recovery? If so, what are they?

12

Sobriety Works

O VER THE PAST TWELVE YEARS OF WORKING WITH
alcoholics on a daily basis, we have come to the conclusion
that the one great stumbling block in the path of effective treatment is a simple misunderstanding about the nature of this disease.

It's clear to us that alcoholics suffer from the stigma attached to alcoholism.

Imagine a society in which most people firmly believed that
cancer resulted from moral weakness on the part of the victim.
How many cancer patients would volunteer for early treatment?

Or think of a nation where every diabetic was referred to a
psychoanalyst for an expensive investigation into the supposed
childhood roots of his disease. Each would know in advance that
such "treatment" would not restore his ability to eat candy bars
whenever he wanted. What percentage, do you think, would seek
out such help?

And picture a world in which every heart patient refused
medication, insisting on his or her inalienable right to control

blood pressure through sheer will power. Wouldn't the incidence of heart attacks skyrocket?

Yet this is exactly the problem that confronts every counselor who works with alcoholism. And because of it, effective treatment often takes a back seat while alcoholic, family, and physician experiment with such irrelevancies as stress reduction, will power, and psychoanalysis.

This is alcoholism's equivalent of the garden path. By the time the alcoholic and family have exhausted these alternatives to success, the disease process is inevitably well advanced. Years are wasted, as much through ignorance as through the action of the disease itself.

In this climate, it makes us uneasy to hear so many people blithely discussing "prevention" of alcoholism. We suspect that many such attempts, however earnest, are based on misconceptions. As a result, they may contribute more to the problem than to the solution.

Education Regarding Alcoholism

We once encountered a school system's drug-prevention program aimed at deterring kids from alcoholism and drug problems by instituting a series of value-clarification classes. Students who learned to understand their own values supposedly would be better able to cope with stress, and thus wouldn't need to turn to chemical aids.

This program was, in fact, hailed as a showpiece of intelligent planning. But as far as we're concerned, it flew in the face of most of what we know about how alcoholism works.

We have nothing against value clarification—we used to teach it ourselves, in fact—but could someone explain how having clear values retards the onset of a disease? And are we to assume that the difference between alcoholic and nonalcoholic is largely a matter of moral and ethical standards?

We were under the impression that we had left that view behind us.

We figure that programs like this should produce a generation whose alcoholics have very clear values, but still drink.

Obviously, any successful effort towards prevention should place special emphasis on recognition of symptoms, not only in ourselves, but in those around us.

Once people come to understand that such symptoms don't indicate weakness of will, temporary situational stress, or deep underlying personality disorders, they will be less reluctant to treat them.

Women, for example, have learned that a lump in the breast can mean cancer. Most of them, despite being scared of what they may find out, will have it examined. They did not understand this fifty years ago. What made the difference? Simple education.

But broad education isn't enough. Morris Hill, who introduced us to the concept of treating alcoholism as a disease, has pointed out that certain people are more likely to develop alcoholism than others. They represent the high-risk population, and any educational effort should target them for special attention.

Think about the rate of alcoholism among Native Americans and Eskimos. Obviously, knowledge about alcoholism is more likely to benefit a Navajo than a Jewish student in Boston.

Adolescents and senior citizens, two groups in positions of apparent vulnerability to alcoholism, need intensive education. And the really high-risk population, if studies are to be believed, are those who have a history of alcoholism in their immediate family.

Though most children of alcoholics do not themselves develop the disease, their chances of becoming alcoholic are about four times greater than someone from an alcoholism-free background.

Those odds, we think, are not because of any particular pattern of parenting. They're the result of an inherited defect in resistance to the disease, which initiates the addictive process. All the individual has to do to become alcoholic is to drink alcohol beyond the limits of his or her resistance.

Such susceptibility is a fact of life in many illnesses. Recent studies suggest, for example, that people of Latin ancestry have a rate of diabetes as much as five times that of other Caucasians. It will doubtless require a massive education effort within the Latin community to encourage early diagnosis and treatment.

And it's the same type of education, we believe, which is needed to replace the misinformation which currently dominates alcoholism education.

Is Treatment Necessary?

Now it's time to take a look at the really important question that everyone asks, sooner or later, about this disease. And that is: How necessary is treatment in the recovery of the typical alcoholic? Would he or she get sober without it?

In other words, if all the treatment centers in North America closed up shop tomorrow, would exactly the same number of alcoholics, sick and tired of being sick and tired, find their way into Alcoholics Anonymous, and therefore into sobriety?

After all, we acknowledge that it's AA which continues to do the bulk of the work. Most of the sober alcoholics in this country are sober in, and because of, AA. An alcoholic who learns everything there is to know about the disease but refuses to go to AA has, we believe, a poor prognosis.

So once again: Is treatment other than AA really necessary?

To answer that, we have to take a look at how AA works.

To the best of its ability, AA tries to keep statistics. Since it's by nature a flexible organization with an amorphous, shifting membership, these statistics would never serve as the basis for scientific research. Nonetheless, they serve as valuable guidelines for understanding the strengths and weaknesses of the organization.

According to AA, about half the people who enter the program—that is, attend meetings regularly for the purpose of getting help for their drinking—are successful. They give up alcohol without further relapse, and maintain their abstinence within AA. Many of their psychosocial problems, we must assume, clear up when they stop drinking.

Another 25 percent who attend AA, we're told, seem to need to experiment with drinking again. These people are often referred to as the "research division" of AA—those who are still trying to find a way to drink without problems. Eventually, these alcoholics give up, re-enter AA, stop drinking, and remain sober.

A final 25 percent, it's implied, drop out of AA, resume drinking, and don't return. We are left to infer that these alcoholics continue to suffer from their disease, or, in some cases, find other methods of giving up alcohol such as religion, or therapy.

But one thing is clear: the bulk of relapses, both for those alcoholics who return to AA and for those who drop out forever, occurs during the first months of abstinence.

It's those first twelve months, in fact, which represent the crucial period of adjustment, and the difference between success and failure. As each successive year of sobriety passes, the likelihood of relapse, though always present, becomes less and less.

Alcoholics get better the longer they remain abstinent. Even if, three years after his last drink, he's not exactly the picture of serenity, the alcoholic is demonstrably better able to cope with life than when drinking.

So sobriety works. The key to success, as we see it, lies primarily in assisting the patient through that difficult first year. Anyone who can facilitate his involvement in AA, and help to ease the transition from drinking to abstinence, will do him a great favor.

In the early stages, professional treatment can be of unparalleled importance. Skillful counseling and accurate information prepare the alcoholic better than anything we can imagine for the rigors of life without his favorite poison. AA's very lack of structure, which makes it so successful as an organization, renders it ineffective as an educational tool. That's where treatment is far superior; a knowledgeable professional providing clear information is worth a lot of meetings.

Treatment can make the difference between someone who would normally drop out of AA, never to return, and someone who becomes a valuable participant. It can help an alcoholic who might otherwise devote himself to some painful ''research'' to accept the necessity for abstinence.

And in some cases, treatment simply reaches people who would otherwise never make it to an AA meeting. The very old and the very young, for example. Treatment has learned how to reach out and grab alcoholics, which AA will never be able to do efficiently.

As a result, more and more alcoholics are getting sober, and more are entering AA, and alcoholism is slowly but surely losing its reputation as an untreatable illness. And that, we believe, is exactly the direction in which we should continue to go.

This is how we justify working in this field. For all its difficulties, the struggle to restore to the alcoholic his membership in the human race is making clear progress.

In our classes, we see more good counselors than we once did. Among physicians, we see more understanding than we once saw. Among our patients and their families, we perceive a greater willingness to accept and treat alcoholism for what it is.

We don't have to worry about ourselves suffering from burnout, because we have learned not to take responsibility for the success or failure of our patients. After all, who gets sober? We give all the credit to the alcoholics themselves. We just give a few simple suggestions.

And we don't bother getting upset if we run into someone in one of our lectures who continues to insist that alcoholics suffer from personality disorders which compel them to drink. And if they think every alcoholic needs a long course of psychoanalysis to recover, then who are we to begrudge them the opportunity? There will always be plenty of candidates for a chance to talk about childhood.

But we think alcoholics have a right to know that they don't necessarily *have* to undergo such treatment, if they don't choose to. There are other answers.

Once upon a time, in a land close to the western ocean, there lived a therapist who had learned something about alcoholism.

This wasn't uncommon; in this day and age, *every* therapist knew something about alcoholism.

One day, an alcoholic came to seek advice on how to get his wife to stop nagging and criticizing him. According to him, her complaints centered mainly on his occasional stress-related episodes of problem drinking, which were really the result of other people's failure to understand his true emotional needs.

After further discussion, the therapist looked the patient squarely in the eye and said, without hesitation:

"Mr. Green, you have a lot of the symptoms of alcoholism. No matter how much you may believe your wife is at fault, there's a good chance that unless you quit drinking and seek some type of treatment for alcoholism, you are simply going to experience worse problems than you currently have. This would be true even if you were to divorce your wife and marry the woman of your dreams tomorrow. So I'm not going to take your money if you won't permit me to treat what I think is really wrong with you."

Stunned, the patient thought for a moment and then replied, "Good Lord, I had no idea I could be alcoholic. But my father was, and I know that's a factor... I'm still not sure I'm alcoholic, but no way am I going to take a chance on that. I know what happens to an alcoholic who keeps drinking. I'll quit, and do whatever you tell me, and then see if what you say makes sense. I guess if my problems with my wife clear up, that means it really was the alcohol, huh?"

One year later, the therapist attended the alcoholic's anniversary of sobriety. When it was the alcoholic's turn to speak, he told his story briefly, and added one comment:

"You know, I'm just really glad that a year ago I ran into someone who told me what was wrong with me, in a way that I could understand. And I'm glad that I'd already learned what alcoholism could do from the experience of others, instead of having to learn my lesson over my own dead body."

Sound far-fetched? Not to us. We think that all such a

change in attitude requires is accurate information, a little effort, and a willingness to listen to a new approach.

We all need to remember one thing, however, to guard against a return to old attitudes, old approaches, and old failures.

And that is: *Don't help.*

The Stages of Alcoholism

Early "Adaptive" Stage

This is when the liver and central nervous system adapt to alcohol, affecting the way alcohol is metabolized (taken into the system). Destruction of cell membranes at this stage is linked to later convulsions, hallucinations, DTs, and heart damage.

1. Physical tolerance begins; alcohol is metabolized more efficiently, and tissue changes allow the alcoholic to drink without becoming intoxicated.
2. Ability to function deteriorates quickly when the alcoholic stops drinking, improves as the B.A.L. rises.
3. Early withdrawal symptoms appear: anxiety, tremors, agitation, weakness, insomnia, loss of appetite, impaired memory, etc.

Middle Stage: Physical Dependence

1. Withdrawal is difficult. In *acute* withdrawal, which lasts up to a few days, activity is disrupted because of fluctuating hormones and enzymes, blood-vessel constriction, and a drop of blood-glucose level. The alcoholic will suffer hangovers, nausea, vomiting, DTs, and related psychological effects such as guilt, self-loathing, and despair.

Protracted withdrawal can last months or even years. Major causes: malnutrition; hypoglycemia; dysfunction of the nervous system; atrophy of the cortex (affecting reason, memory, and control of the senses and motion); and depletion of amines in the brain (contributing to depression, anxiety, tension, and irritability). Nutritional therapy can help here.

2. A craving for alcohol takes over, and the victim no longer has the psychological strength to overcome the physiological need.
3. Loss of control now causes the alcoholic to drink more than intended, more often than intended.

Late "Deteriorative" Stage

This stage lasts indefinitely, depending on treatment. The victim has a lessened tolerance for alcohol and suffers increasingly severe withdrawal symptoms, including convulsions and hallucinations.

Physical problems include heart failure, liver diseases, pancreatitis, malnutrition, ulcers, gastritis, respiratory-tract diseases (tuberculosis, bronchitis, pneumonia), and increased risk of cancer of the head, neck, esophagus, lungs, and liver.

Adapted from James R. Milam and Katherine Ketcham, *Under the Influence:* Seattle, Madrona Publishers, 1981.

Treatment Plan for the Recovering Alcoholic Insufficiently Involved in AA

NAME:		PROBLEM: A history of insufficient AA involvement, resulting in relapse.		GOAL: Increased AA involvement.
LEARNING OBJECTIVES	RESOURCES	FIRST PROJECT	SECOND PROJECT	
1. To learn about sponsorship, and find a sponsor.	AA pamphlet "Questions and Answers on Sponsorship"	Read pamphlet, write briefly on how sponsorship can promote sobriety.	Find two temporary sponsors and arrange to meet them at meetings.	
2. To select an AA home group and take on responsibilities within the group.	Directory of local AA meetings	Select meetings close to your home and attend for several weeks consecutively. Then, select one as your home group.	Volunteer for an office or other responsibility in your home group.	
3. To begin working on the Twelve Step Program.	Books: *Twelve Steps and Twelve Traditions* and *The Twelve Steps Revisited* (see Suggested Reading).	Read the books and discuss with other members of your group the best methods of working the first three steps of AA.	Begin working the steps during your daily life. Keep a Step Journal in which you chronicle your experiences on a weekly basis.	
Date begun	Signature of person seeking help	Helper's or counselor's signature	Date completed	

254

NAME:		PROBLEM: A history of sedative use in addition to alcohol — could promote relapse.		GOAL: Increase knowledge of dangers of sedative use in recovery; explore alternatives.
LEARNING OBJECTIVES	RESOURCES	FIRST PROJECT	SECOND PROJECT	
1. To identify which sedatives have been used in the past.	List of sedative-hypnotic drugs (see page 109).	Review list, checking any drugs you have used. Make note of symptoms for which a drug was prescribed, who prescribed it, and approximate dates of use	Discuss what you have learned with three other group members who have used sedatives. Compare their experiences with yours.	
2. To learn how sedative use may precipitate relapse in recovering alcoholics.	Read about multiple-drug use in Chapter 5.	Read the chapter, write out definitions of cross-addiction and cross-tolerance. Give two examples of how sedatives promote relapse.	Teach definition of cross-addiction to two other group members.	
3. To develop a plan to avoid future reliance on sedatives.	Read appropriate sections in Chapter 11.	Write a plan describing options for treating discomfort without sedative drugs.	Review your plan with the group; ask for feedback from members and from your physician.	
Date begun	Signature of recovering alcoholic	Helper's or counselor's signature		Date completed

NOTE: Dates for starting and ending each project help to establish a time frame and deadline for the activity.

Suggested Reading

These books provide a solid background in alcoholism and its treatment. Obviously, we have had to leave out a number of useful works for the sake of brevity.

Alcoholism

Under the Influence: A Guide to the Myths and Realities of Alcoholism. James R. Milam and Katherine Ketcham, Seattle, Madrona Publishers, 1981.

The best description of alcoholism as a chronic, hereditary, physiological disease—bar none. Milam's model forms the basis for our approach.

Guidance for the Alcoholic

The Twelve Steps Revisited. Ronald J. Rogers, C. Scott McMillin, & Morris Hill, Seattle, Madrona Publishers, 1988.

A re-examination of AA's Twelve Steps, which are the basis of AA's program. The steps are looked at in the context of today's understanding of alcoholism as a chronic physical disease.

Help for the Family

Getting Them Sober (Parts 1 and 2). Toby Rice Drews, Plainfield, NJ, Bridge Publishing, 1980.

Simple, Al-Anon-influenced advice for family members faced with the task of living with an alcoholic, whether drinking or sober.

Intervention

I'll Quit Tomorrow. Vernon Johnson, New York, Harper & Row, 1980.

The first real description of the process of structured intervention with alcoholics. Some of the book is outdated but it is still of interest to families and friends as well as professionals.

Intervention: How to Help Someone Who Doesn't Want Help. Vernon Johnson, Minneapolis, Johnson Institute, 1986.

A practical guide to the process of intervention. More detailed that *I'll Quit Tomorrow,* this book includes examples of family confrontation.

Publications of Alcoholics Anonymous
(New York, AA World Services)

Alcoholics Anonymous (often known as "The Big Book"). Bill W., 1955.

AA's bible. Early AA members came from all walks of life, and their stories of addiction and recovery form the backbone of this book, illustrating AA's strength: the ability to discover and make use of *common experience* as the basis for recovery.

Twelve Steps and Twelve Traditions. Bill W., 1953.

An explanation of the Twelve Steps that includes suggestions for working the AA program.

Living Sober. 1975.

An unimposing little book that nonetheless is a helpful guide to the first weeks and months without alcohol.

Recovery

Eating Right to Live Sober. L. Ann Mueller, M.D., and Katherine Ketcham, Seattle, Madrona Publishers, 1983.

A guide to nutrition and diet specifically for those recovering from alcoholism.

Recovering: How to Get and Stay Sober. L. Ann Mueller, M.D., and Katherine Ketcham, New York, Bantam, 1987.

General information about the treatment and recovery process, with a good description of alcoholic behavior, soundly based on Milam's Chronic Disease model.

Ronald L. Rogers and Chandler Scott McMillin are both directors of addiction treatment centers in Maryland (Baltimore Recovery Center and Addiction Treatment Center, respectively). Together they have written *The Twelve Steps Revisited* and *Freeing Someone You Love From Alcohol and Other Drugs*.